# BECOMING HUMAN

The Upper Palaeolithic era of Europe has left an abundance of evidence for symbolic activities, such as direct representations of animals and other features of the natural world, personal adornments, and elaborate burials, as well as other vestiges that are more abstract and cryptic. These behaviours are also exhibited by populations throughout the world, from the prehistoric period through to the present day. How can we interpret these activities? What do they tell us about the beliefs and priorities of the people who carried them out? How do these behaviours relate to ideologies, cosmology, and understanding of the world? What can they tell us about the emergence of ritual and religious thought? And how do the activities of humans in prehistoric Europe compare with those of their predecessors there and elsewhere?

In this volume, fifteen internationally renowned scholars contribute essays that explore the relationship between symbolism, spirituality, and humanity in the prehistoric societies of Europe and traditional societies elsewhere. The volume is richly illustrated with fifty halftones and twenty-four colour plates.

**Colin Renfrew** is Emeritus Disney Professor and Senior Fellow of the McDonald Institute for Archaeological Research at Cambridge University. He is the author and editor of many publications, including *Archaeology: Theories, Methods and Practice*, with Paul Bahn, which is one of the standard textbooks on the subject.

**Iain Morley** is a Research Fellow of Darwin College and Fellow of the McDonald Institute for Archaeological Research at Cambridge University. The author of numerous articles in academic journals and books, he is also coeditor, with Colin Renfrew, of *Image and Imagination: A Global Prehistory of Figurative Representation*.

# BECOMING HUMAN: INNOVATION IN PREHISTORIC MATERIAL AND SPIRITUAL CULTURE

*Edited by*

## COLIN RENFREW
*McDonald Institute for Archaeological Research,
Cambridge University*

## IAIN MORLEY
*McDonald Institute for Archaeological Research,
Cambridge University*

CAMBRIDGE
UNIVERSITY PRESS

CAMBRIDGE UNIVERSITY PRESS

Cambridge, New York, Melbourne, Madrid, Cape Town, Singapore, São Paulo, Delhi

Cambridge University Press
32 Avenue of the Americas, New York, NY 10013-2473, USA

www.cambridge.org
Information on this title: www.cambridge.org/9780521734660

First published 2009

Printed in the United States of America

*A catalog record for this publication is available from the British Library.*

*Library of Congress Cataloging in Publication data*
Becoming human: innovation in prehistoric material and spiritual culture/[edited by]
Colin Renfrew, Iain Morley.
    p.   cm.
  Includes bibliographical references and index.
  ISBN 978-0-521-87654-4 (hardback) – ISBN 978-0-521-73466-0 (pbk.)
  1. Religion, Prehistoric.  2. Anthropology of religion.  3. Material culture –
  Europe.  4. Paleolithic period – Europe.  5. Europe – Antiquities.  I. Renfrew, Colin,
  1937–  II. Morley, Iain, 1975–  III. Title
  GN799.R4B43 2009
  306.0936–dc22      2008020473

ISBN 978-0-521-87654-4 hardback
ISBN 978-0-521-73466-0 paperback

# Contents

v

# List of Figures and Plates

## Figures

### Plates

*Colour plates follow page xvi*

## Picture Acknowledgements

Thanks are given to the following photographers, authors, or institutions who hold copyright to the photographs used in the figures and plates:

Natural History Museum, London: Figure 6.1, Figure 6.3, Figure 6.5;

Jean Vertut and Paul Bahn: Figure 6.2, Figure 6.6, Figure 6.8, Figure 6.9, Figure 6.10;

Pedro A. Saura Ramos: Plate XIII;

Jean Clottes: Plate XIV, Plate XV, Plate XVII;

State Museum, Windhoek, Namibia: Plate XVI;

Paul Bahn: Plate XVIII;

Norbert Aujoulat, Plate XIX;

Klaus Schmidt: Plate XX, Plate XXI;

Erella Hovers: Plate XXII 1–3 (photograph by Gabi Laron);

L. S. Dubin: Plate XXII a, b, c, e, g;

Roger de la Harpe: Plate XXIII d, f;

M.-L. Beffa and L. Delaby: Plate XXIII h (© Publications Scientifiques du Muséum national d'Histoire naturelle, Paris).

# Contributors

**Colin Renfrew** is Emeritus Disney Professor and Senior Fellow of the McDonald Institute for Archaeological Research at Cambridge University. He is the author and editor of many publications, including *Archaeology: Theories, Methods and Practice*, with Paul Bahn, which is one of the standard textbooks on the subject.

**Iain Morley** is a Research Fellow of Darwin College and Fellow of the McDonald Institute for Archaeological Research at Cambridge University. The author of numerous articles in academic journals and books, he is also coeditor, with Colin Renfrew, of *Image and Imagination: A Global Prehistory of Figurative Representation*.

**Jean Clottes,** Conservateur Général du Patrimoine, is President of the International Federation of Rock Art Organizations and former Scientific Adviser for prehistoric art to the French Ministry of Culture. He is also the editor of *INORA* (*International Newsletter on Rock Art*). He is coauthor, with Jean Courtin and Luc Vanrell, of *Cosquer redécouvert* (2005).

**Margaret W. Conkey** is Professor of Anthropology and Director of the Archaeological Research Facility at the University of California, Berkeley. She has published extensively on the interpretation of the visual culture and "arts" of Paleolithic Europe, including the coedited volume, with Olga Soffer et al., *Beyond Art: Pleistocene Image and Symbol* (1997).

**Francesco d'Errico** is a CNRS Director of Research at the Institut de Préhistoire et de Géologie du Quaternaire, University of Bordeaux 1, and Research Professor in the Department of Anthropology at the George Washington University in Washington, DC. He is the author of two monographs and more than 150 journal articles, including "*Nassarius kraussianus* shell beads from Blombos Cave: Evidence for Symbolic Behaviour in the Middle Stone Age" (2005), with Christopher Henshilwood, Marian Vanhaeren, and Karen van Niekerk.

**Merlin Donald** is Professor Emeritus at Queen's University, Ontario, and Adjunct Professor of Cognitive Science at Case Western Reserve University. He is the author of many scientific papers and two books, *Origins of the Modern Mind: Three Stages in the Evolution of Cultural Cognition* (1991) and *A Mind So Rare: The Evolution of Human Consciousness* (2001).

**Christopher Henshilwood** is Research Professor and holds a South African Research Chair in the Origins of Modern Human Behaviour at the Institute for Human Evolution, University of Witwatersrand, Johannesburg, South Africa. He is Professor of African prehistory at the Institute for Archaeology, History, Culture, and Religion at the University of Bergen, Norway. He is the author of many academic articles including, with Curtis W. Marean, the article in *Current Anthropology*, "The Origin of Modern Human Behavior: A Review and Critique of Models and Test Implications" (2003).

**David Lewis-Williams** is Professor Emeritus at the University of Witwatersrand, Johannesburg. He was founder and formerly director of the Rock Art Research Institute and is the author of *The Mind in the Cave: Consciousness and the Origins of Art* (2004).

**Henry de Lumley** is director of the Institut de Paléontologie Humaine in Paris, France. He has organized many large archaeology excavations in the southeast of France, and has published numerous journal articles and monographs, including *La grand histoire des premiers Hommes Européens* (2007).

**Paul Mellars** is Professor of Prehistory and Human Evolution at the University of Cambridge. He is the author of many academic papers and has authored and edited many books, including *The Neanderthal Legacy: An Archaeological Perspective from Western Europe* (1996).

**Steven Mithen** is Professor of Early Prehistory and Head of the School of Human and Environmental Sciences at the University of Reading. He is the author of *The Singing Neanderthals: The Origins of Music, Language, Mind and Body* (2005).

**Jane M. Renfrew** is a Fellow and De Brye College Lecturer in Archaeology at Lucy Cavendish College, University of Cambridge. She is the author of *Palaeoethnobotany: The Prehistoric Food Plants of the Near East and Europe* (1973).

**Paul S. C. Taçon** is Professor of Anthropology and Archaeology in the School of Arts, Griffith University, Queensland. He is coeditor, with Christopher Chippindale, of *The Archaeology of Rock-Art* (1999) and the author of more than 135 academic and popular papers on prehistoric art, body art, material culture, colour, cultural evolution, identity, and contemporary indigenous issues.

**J. Wentzel van Huyssteen** is Princeton Theological Seminary's James I. McCord Professor of Theology and Science. He teaches courses on the role of worldviews in theological reflection, theology and the problem of rationality, theology and cosmology, and theology and evolution. His lecture series at the University of Edinburgh was published as *Alone in the World? Human Uniqueness in Science and Theology* (2006).

**Keith Ward** is an Emeritus Student of Christ Church, Oxford, where he was formerly Regius Professor of Divinity. He has also been Professor of Moral Theology at London University; Professor of the History of Religion at London; and Professor of Divinity at Gresham College, London. He was Dean of Trinity Hall, Cambridge, where he is now an Honorary Fellow. He is also a Fellow of the British Academy. He is the author of *The Big Questions in Science and Religion* (2008).

**Plate I.** Rose coloured handaxe (*Excalibur*) from Sima de los Huesos. Atapuerca Sierra, Castille Leon Province, Spain.

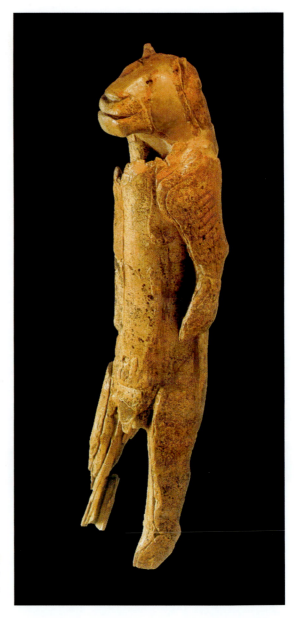

**Plate II.** Statue of a man with lion's head from Hohlenstein-Stadel, Vogelherd, Baden-Würtemberg, Germany. Aurignacian culture. 32,000 ya.

**Plate III.** Scene from Lascaux shaft. Prostrate man with bird's head and erection, and disembowelled bison. Early Magdalenian. About 16,000 yrs B C.

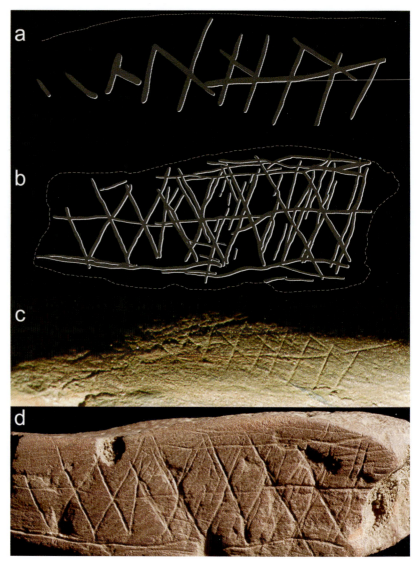

**Plate IV.** Engraved ochre from Blombos Cave, 75 Kya levels. A,C – SAM-AA8937; B,D – SAM-AA 8938. (Credit: Christopher Henshilwood)

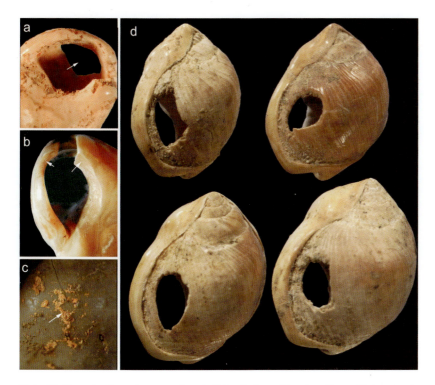

Plate V. *Nassarius kraussianus* marine shell beads from Blombos Cave, 75 kya levels: (a) perforated hole opposite aperture; (b) use wear facets on aperture; (c) ochre traces on bead; (d) beads with apertures showing wear traces. (Credit: Christopher Henshilwood)

**Plate VI.** A small therianthrope holding spears appears to be chasing a Dynamic Figure that holds boomerangs and a spear, Kakadu National Park, Northern Territory, Australia, at least ten thousand years old. (Photo: P.S.C. Taçon)

**Plate VII.** A seated kangaroo-headed being with legs crossed holds a spear with hand and foot in a typical Aboriginal way. It lies in a remote part of Kakadu National Park, Northern Territory, Australia, and is at least ten thousand years old. (Photo: P.S.C. Taçon)

**Plate VIII.** A rare depiction of the "Eagle Ancestor" was discovered in a remote part of Wollemi National Park, New South Wales, Australia, in 1998. It was originally made in charcoal over fifteen thousand years ago but has been remarked with white pipe clay. Stencils of a boomerang and a hafted stone axe were placed over the wings to signify its supernatural nature. (Photo: P.S.C. Taçon)

**Plate IX.** This typical early depiction of a Rainbow Serpent, Australia's most elaborate animal-animal composite being was discovered in Kakadu National Park, Northern Territory, Australia, in 1985. It is between four thousand and six thousand years old. (Photo: P.S.C. Taçon)

**Plate X.** Rainbow Serpents are often associated with flying foxes (fruit bats) in oral history and rock-art. This one a few thousand years old has thirteen on a strand that extends from its neck, making it highly significant and unusual for Aboriginal people. (Photo: P.S.C. Taçon)

**Plate XI.** Double-headed creatures are rare worldwide but do crop up among cultures widely dispersed in time and space. This double-headed thylacine from Kakadu National Park, Northern Territory, Australia, is unique to the region. The thylacine became extinct at least five thousand years ago, but the depiction is in a much older style. (Photo: P.S.C. Taçon)

**Plate XII.** This thylacine, from a site in Arnhem Land, Northern Territory, Australia, wears a woven bag in a way similar to humans. It is part of a large composition of Dynamic Figures that is at least ten thousand years old. (Photo: P.S.C. Taçon)

**Plate XIII.** Painted bison on the ceiling at Altamira Cave, Spain. The first example of Franco-Cantabrian cave art to be recognised (in 1879), ca. 15,000 BP. (Photo by Jean Vertut. From Bahn, P. & J. Vertut, 1997, *Journey Through the Ice Age*, p. 105)

**Plate XIV.** Painted horse, Le Portel Cave, France, ca. 12,000 BP. A strikingly 'naturalistic' outline, typical of Franco-Cantabrian cave art, but not seen elsewhere until the Holocene period. (Photo courtesy of Jean Clottes, from Clottes, J. & J. Courtin, 1996. *The Cave Beneath the Sea: Paleolithic Images at Cosquer* p. 163)

**Plate XV.** Rhinoceroses, Grotte Chauvet, France, c. 30,000 BP, and so among the earliest known cave art. (Photo by Jean Clottes)

**Plate XVI.** Feline painted on a stone slab, Apollo 11 Cave, Namibia, ca 25,000 BP. This is one of the few known examples of painted figurative decoration found outside Europe prior to ca. 12,000 BP. (Photo courtesy of Paul Bahn and the State Museum, Windhoek, Namibia, from Bahn, P. & J. Vertut, 1997, *Journey Through the Ice Age*, p. 31)

**Plate XVII.** Hand stencils, Gargas, France. A typical product of the cave art of Upper Palaeolithic France and Spain, but not seen elsewhere until the Holocene period. (Photo courtesy of Jean Clottes. From Clottes, J. & J. Courtin, 1996, *The Cave Beneath the Sea: Paleolithic Images at Cosquer*, p. 67)

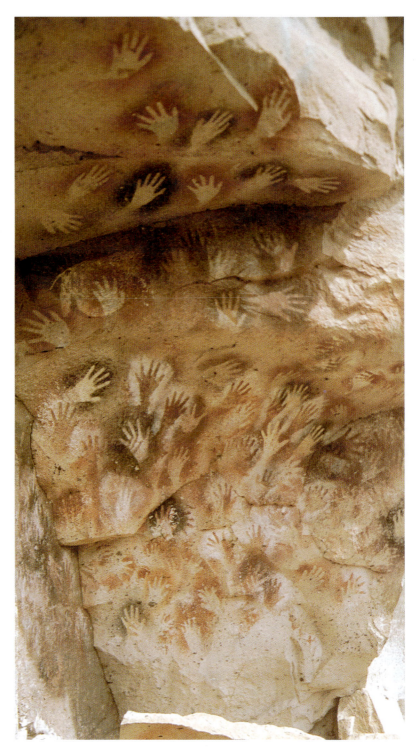

**Plate XVIII.** Hand stencils, Los Taldon, Argentina, ca. 11,000 BP. Although remarkably similar to the Upper Palaeolithic hand stencils of France and Spain, these are dated to the early Holocene period. (Photo by Paul Bahn)

**Plate XIX.** Palimpsest of painting and engraving, Lascaux, France, ca. 17,000 BP. (Photo courtesy of Nobert Aujoulat, from Clottes, J. & J. Courtin, 1996. *The Cave Beneath the Sea: Paleolithic Images at Cosquer*, p. 181)

**Plate XX.** The world's first built sanctuary? Monolith at Göbekli Tepe, Turkey, ca. 11,000 BP, and so in the early Holocene period. With many thanks to Klaus Schmidt for the image. (Photo courtesy of Klaus Schmidt)

**Plate XXI.** Monolith at Göbekli Tepe, Turkey, ca. 11,000 BP. From this time onwards, figurative iconography is seen in many parts of the world. With many thanks to Klaus Schmidt for the image. (Photo courtesy of Klaus Schmidt)

**Plate XXII.** Modified pigments and ochred stone artefacts from the Mousterian levels of Qafzeh, Israel (1–3), the Middle Stone Age levels of Klasies River (4) and Blombos Cave (5), South Africa, the Mousterian levels of Pech-de-l'Azé I, France (6, 7), and the Middle Stone Age levels of Sodmein cave, Egypt (8) (after Hovers et al. 2003, photograph by Gabi Laron [1–3], Wurz 2000 [4], Henshilwood et al. 2001 [5], Van Peer & Vermeersch 2000) Scale bars = 1cm.

**Plate XXIII.** a: shaman's box from Alaska, b: Tlingit shaman's necklace, c: Haida shaman's curing necklace, d, f: objects used by Zulu diviners, e: pair of swans in flight made of ivory (Dorset culture), g: male and female ivory shaman figures from the Bering Sea area, h: shaman's costume from Eastern Siberia. (a–c, e, g modified after Dubin, 1999; d, f modified after Derwent et al. 2000, h: after Beffa & Delaby 1999, © Publications Scientifiques du Muséum national d'Histoire naturelle, Paris)

**Plate XXIV.** Some of the small beads and other deposits recently made at Arrow Rock, in Montana (USA). (Photo: J. Clottes)

## Foreword

Sir John Templeton believed that in their quest to comprehend foundational realities, scientists, philosophers, and theologians have much to learn about and from one another. For a decade now, the Humble Approach Initiative, a program of the John Templeton Foundation, has held symposia with a changing international cast of the most creative scholars from many disciplines who come together to pursue big, difficult, and invariably riveting questions. Some that have long engaged me, as student and teacher, stem from the fact that religious ideas often seem to develop in interaction with material culture. Looking at Palaeolithic art and recognizing that it is unlikely that there is only one meaning to thirty-five thousand years of image making, it is intriguing, nevertheless, to speculate whether these magnificent Ice Age representations of animal forms, rare human figures, and mysterious signs on cave walls may be expressions of religious feelings and notions – and, indeed, may actually shape subsequent emotions and concepts by serving as "tools" for future ritual practice. In light of a rich history of interpretation of these masterpieces – for example, theories that they signal a passage from the work world to the play world in a new era of free time and abundance; suggest totemism; reflect magical practices undertaken to bring about such desired ends as a plentiful hunt, fertility, and the destruction of enemies; or express concepts related to the structure and organization of the living world – what evidence, if any, exists that innovations in material cultures may be related to developments in religious ideas and behaviour? Can we infer anything from early prehistoric images about a possible link between spiritual development and human cultural creations? Is the deep cave filled with engravings and paintings a precursor of the shrine and temple? What was the artist thinking as he or she drew? What accounts for the appearance of icons in some early prehistoric societies and not in others? Can studies of early cognition provide clues to the roots of spirituality in the underground chambers of the world? Does the content of mobiliary and parietal art, their archaeological contexts, and ethnological comparisons support a shamanic or other religious interpretation of subterranean picture making? Could the material expressions of the first biologically modern humans affect as well as reflect emerging systems of belief? Or are the productive, functional, and symbolic categories of Palaeolithic art makers forever beyond our grasp? Even as experts laboured to control the spread of fungi and bacteria in one world-renowned cave, France's celebrated Lascaux in the southernmost part of the Dordogne, the Périgord Noir, thirteen scientists and theologians met nearby in the village of Les Eyzies, the "capital of prehistory", to explore conjectured relationships between innovations in material and spiritual cultures, in the spring of 2004. One brought from a Middle Stone Age site in South Africa a few tiny perforated shells, dating back seventy-five thousand years, which may have been worn as beads and, if so, indicated symbolic thinking; all brought perspectives that caused their colleagues to look again at old questions in new light. Their conversation, which led to this book, fulfilled its sponsors' hopes that such symposia discussions will not only act as a corrective to parochialism but will also encourage discovery and accelerate its pace.

Mary Ann Meyers
Senior Fellow
John Templeton Foundation

## Introduction: Becoming human: changing perspectives on the emergence of human values

*Colin Renfrew*

This book is significant as one of the first wide-ranging surveys which embodies, reflects and develops the consensus that has emerged at the beginning of the twenty-first century about the emergence of humankind. Perceptions have shifted very substantially. The so-called human revolution, referring to the emergence of our species *Homo sapiens*, and with it the shift to modern and complex behaviours (Mellars and Stringer 1989), is no longer seen as something which happened in Europe, or possibly in Western Asia, something like forty thousand years ago. Instead we realise, with the wealth of new anthropological data available in Africa, that our species emerged there something like 200,000 or 150,000 years ago. Molecular genetic evidence confirms and amplifies the emerging picture (Forster 2004), indicating that our species, *Homo sapiens*, emerged in Africa, and first dispersed from there to Arabia and so to the rest of the world around sixty thousand years ago. The important new discoveries from the Middle Stone Age of Africa, including the crucial evidence from the Blombos Cave discussed here (Henshilwood, this volume), reveal that those new behaviours associated with the human revolution were already developing in Africa (McBrearty and Brooks 2000), where they are well documented some seventy thousand years ago.

The Symposium from which this volume arose took place, appropriately, in the Dordogne region of France, at Les Eyzies, in the very area where some of the key first discoveries were made during the nineteenth century relating to the early achievements of our species. It was by then realised that the 'stone age' earlier proposed by the Scandinavian antiquaries could be divided into the Neolithic (the new stone age, the time of the early farmers) and the Palaeolithic, the much longer preceding period when humans pursued a hunter-gatherer way of life. The

Neolithic period succeeded the climatic improvements which came with the end of the Ice Age, the Pleistocene period, some ten thousand years ago. And it soon became clear that remains of our own species, *Homo sapiens*, were found there no earlier than the Upper Palaeolithic, whose beginning can now be set by radiocarbon dating, some forty thousand years ago. By 1860, human remains had been identified, near Les Eyzies, in the rock shelter of Aurignac. In 1879 came the momentous realisation that the animals painted on the ceiling of the cave at Altamira in north Spain should be dated to the Upper Palaeolithic period – the recognition of Palaeolithic cave art. Very soon comparable discoveries were made in the Dordogne, many of them close to Les Eyzies, as indeed is the painted cave at Lascaux (although this was not discovered until 1940). As discussed later, the painted caves are found mainly in south France and north Spain, and this Franco-Cantabrian cave art is a notable feature of the European Upper Palaeolithic. So, too, are the carvings, on bone and ivory, found in the caves, rock shelters and open sites from the same period and area, although their distribution is a wider one.

If we are looking at the early development of human culture, these finds have a very special significance. For while humans had been tool makers for hundreds of thousands of years, as Henry de Lumley reminds us in his Prologue, those very early hominids clearly did not have the ability or, we infer, the mental capacities associated with our own species, *Homo sapiens*. It is only with our own species that we find the range of new behaviours seen here in the Franco-Cantabrian Upper Palaeolithic, reflected in new tool kits (with a blade technology replacing the earlier flakes), with greater variety in stone tools, with the use of bone, antler and ivory, and crucially with the first personal adornments (beads mainly) and the first representational art (Mellars 1991).

A key aim of the Symposium, which was funded by the John Templeton Foundation, was to consider the early emergence of the various qualities which we may consider particularly human. The use of a complex language is one of these, but its appearance is notoriously difficult to assess on the basis of material culture alone. Other human qualities are more accessible, not least through the remarkable range of artefacts which appear in the Franco-Cantabrian Upper Palaeolithic. To reconstruct the activities which took place in the painted caves, and to make inferences as to their meaning is, however, no easy task. But if we are interested in the origins of ritual, of religion and of human spirituality, then they are of crucial relevance.

In his Prologue, de Lumley reviews briefly some of the earlier behaviours – tool manufacture, the use of fire, and deliberate burial of the dead – which are seen already before the Upper Palaeolithic and prior to the appearance in Europe of *Homo sapiens*. These are indeed activities which are special to the genus *Homo*, seen already in such earlier hominids as *Homo erectus*, and which are not seen among other genera of the animal kingdom. But the Upper Palaeolithic period brings something more, and it is with that 'something more', with these early intimations of what we may call spirituality, that our Symposium was particularly concerned.

This is what gave the meeting – and, I believe, this volume – its very special character of controlled speculation. We were able to bring together some of the leading specialists in the archaeology of the Palaeolithic period, and to invite them to consider the problems of postulating the new aspects of human experience and behaviour which may be inferred from these abundant, suggestive and yet sometimes enigmatic finds. We managed, I hope, to avoid some of the technicalities of the archaeological specialist, aided by the scrutiny and the commentary of two distinguished theologians, Keith Ward and Wentzel Van Huyssteen, with whom we were able to consider and debate such notions as 'religion' and 'spirituality' at a very general level.

Another important feature was the worldwide scope of our subject matter, and of the discussions of it. For while the wealth of Franco-Cantabrian evidence was inescapably close to us, situated as we were in its heartland in Les Eyzies, we were anxious to take a global view. The significant new evidence from South Africa was brought to us by Christopher Henshilwood, one of its leading researchers, as well as by Francesco d'Errico, who has worked extensively on the beads and adornments not only from Blombos but also from the European Upper Palaeolithic. The crucially important case of Australian rock art, and of the Australian Palaeolithic, was introduced to our discussions by Paul Taçon, one of its leading exponents. And Henry de Lumley, Jean Clottes, Paul Mellars and Margaret Conkey were able to bring their unrivalled knowledge of the French Palaeolithic to bear on our discussions.

The creative explosion, to use the term introduced by John Pfeiffer (1982), seen so clearly in the Franco-Cantabrian cave art of the Upper Palaeolithic, certainly presents the modern observer with a challenge. At what point in the archaeological record can we document the emergence of ritual, and of what we might regard as religious behaviour?

At this point, however, we have to consider more carefully the hominid population already present in Europe, and in the Dordogne, when these first representatives of our own species arrived some forty thousand years ago. Here we turn to 'Neanderthal Man', to use an older terminology, to the Neanderthals. That remarkable species *Homo neanderthalensis*, which preceded our own species in Europe, with its accompanying Mousterian material culture, can no longer be seen to represent a universal stage in human evolution, the immediate predecessor of our own species. Rather, the Neanderthals were evolving in Europe and Western Asia at just the same time that our species was appearing in Africa. But the overlap period, the contact period in Europe, when the incoming *sapiens* humans lived alongside their Neanderthal predecessors for some thousands of years (how long is in dispute), becomes one of absorbing interest. For some of the behavioural traits seen in Europe during the Aurignacian period, with the arrival of *Homo sapiens*, seem to be anticipated by the earlier Neanderthals. Deliberate human burial is a good example, which seems to be well documented among Neanderthals even before our own species arrived. And other features developed in both groups at the same time. Did the Neanderthals learn them from the sapient incomers? Or were these features an indigenous development? These questions are of interest in their own right. But they become even more so when considered within the context of emerging spirituality, and of the development of what we have come to regard as specifically human values.

As we shall see, there are indeed forms of behaviour seen in the Upper Palaeolithic period which seem to mark new kinds of self-awareness, implying the development of new value systems, which we have always regarded as unique to our own species. If we hoped to find evidence in the archaeological record for the first appearance of the human soul, this would be the place for it. Evidence of ritual documents what we may consider as the first concrete indication of religious belief. The remarkable representations of animals and of humans, which for convenience we call 'art', become so abundant that we are obliged to see them as reflections of a new awareness of what it is to be human, and what it is like to be aware as humans of our place in a wider world. But if some of these first awakenings developed also among the Neanderthals, how many of them did so autonomously and independently? If they did, surely we may think and speak also in terms of Neanderthal spirituality, just as we may of sapient spirituality at this early time? At first that seems reasonable and perhaps unsurprising. But on reflection it would represent a radical new departure: it would challenge our assumption that the human species to which we today all belong is unique, standing apart in our experience of self-consciousness, in our perception of the nature and inevitability of death (and perhaps of the hereafter), and in the unique qualities of the new kinds of social relationships which can develop when we are fully human.

## Neanderthal reflections

One of the most interesting features of the meeting in Les Eyzies from which this book developed, was indeed the very thoughtful consideration given to the cognitive archaeology of the Neanderthals. It was recognised moreover that there is a need to distinguish carefully between two phases of Neanderthal experience. The first is the long period, associated in Europe with the Middle Palaeolithic and with Mousterian culture, when the Neanderthals were the only hominids around. The same was broadly true for those areas of western Asia in which Neanderthal remains are found. The second phase comes after the first arrival in Europe (and in Western Asia) of our own species, *Homo sapiens*, around forty thousand years ago, following the out-of-Africa dispersal some fifteen thousand or twenty thousand years earlier. For a few thousand years the two populations must have lived side by side. There is speculation, indeed controversy, as to whether they interbred. Current DNA studies have sometimes concluded that the DNA of the Neanderthals did not make a significant contribution to that of the modern human gene pool, although that view has been contradicted. These are matters which DNA studies can be expected to clarify over the next decade or so.

A strong focus of current interest is the development of the so-called Châtelperronian culture, which shows continuing Mousterian features, yet with innovations which resemble those of the Aurignacian culture. This is generally held to have been brought in with the new sapient population. It is a focus of intense debate whether such innovations should be regarded as the result of acculturation – that is to say the direct result of contacts between the two populations – or whether they may represent independent innovations produced by the Neanderthal population themselves which would have taken place even if *Homo sapiens* had not been present.

The evidence of originality and innovation in Neanderthal communities is reviewed here by Jane Renfrew. Her position is supported to some extent by David Lewis-Williams (this volume) in his consideration of early spirituality, and of the degree to which we may associate this with the Neanderthals. The position taken by Francesco d'Errico is rather different. In his perspective, most of the significant innovations seen in Europe are to be associated with the incoming sapient population.

In a few years we may be in a position to understand more clearly the significance of the highly interesting 'overlap' period between the Neanderthals (before their extinction) and the new *sapiens* population. It is difficult to speculate about what might have been the Neanderthal contribution, about what they might have contributed had not their trajectory of development been modified and ultimately terminated by the new *sapiens* incomers. But here we touch on a further controversy: to what extent was the extinction of the Neanderthals brought about by the competitive influence of the new *sapiens* population? Or were they a doomed species who might not, in any case, have survived the climatic severities of the Late Glacial Maximum and then of the climatic warming which followed?

## The human contribution

The nature of the 'creative explosion', and particularly its location, was considered in the paper by Colin Renfrew. During the Upper Palaeolithic period, cave painting seems to have been restricted to France and Spain, with a few outliers in Italy. The most notable exception is that of Aboriginal painting, discussed with authority in the paper by Paul Taçon. There are of course other instances, discussed briefly in the paper by Renfrew, but most rock art is first seen after the Pleistocene, in the Holocene period. The possible reasons for this precocious flowering of cave art in France and Spain are systematically considered in the paper by Paul Mellars.

Palaeolithic sculpture, mainly in the form of the small 'Venus' figurines, extends during the Gravettian period east from France and Spain through Germany to the Czech Republic to the Ukraine and indeed as far east as Siberia. Again there are comparable finds from Italy. But the remarkable thing is that such small human representations are in general not a feature of the Upper Palaeolithic period in any other part of the world. In the Pacific, terracotta sculptures on this scale are indeed seen in the Jomon or Proto-Jomon culture of Japan from early dates, before 10,000 BC. And there may be other early finds in the Pacific. But this interesting circumstance does not undermine the validity of the general observation that such small sculptures of figurines are not more widely seen until the development of the Holocene period, some of them accompanying early farming. Again, representation in the Upper Palaeolithic is a very localised phenomenon.

The important point is developed in the paper by Meg Conkey, that these various representations which are often designated as 'art' may have a wider significance. In some cases it may have been the very action and process of making such representations which was significant, rather than the end products themselves. This approach is strengthened by the detailed study by Jean Clottes of a strange practice, presumably of symbolic significance, yet which cannot be assimilated under the rubric of 'art' – or at least not of representational art. The paper by Iain Morley dealing with the place of music and the production of sound in early ritual again supports the view that the focus upon visual 'art', interpreted in a modern sense, gives too narrow a perspective in the consideration of the rich symbolic behaviours and rituals which were developing during the Upper Palaeolithic period.

## Human values and spirituality as universals

In the course of the meeting there was much discussion about the inferences about belief which might reasonably be formulated on the basis of the representations or 'art' found in the Franco-Cantabrian Upper Palaeolithic, but also in other Palaeolithic contexts, notably in Australia. The paper by Paul Taçon recognises that representation or 'art' may have antecedents going back much earlier than the Upper Palaeolithic, a point which bears on the discussion of Neanderthal self-awareness and spirituality.

The crucial question as to the extent to which the figurations and representations seen in the Upper Palaeolithic are the product of rituals which might be considered to be 'religious', and hence to document the inception of religion, is considered in different ways in the papers by Merlin Donald and by Steven Mithen, as indeed in that of David Lewis-Williams. Both Donald and Mithen lay emphasis on the significance of involving the material world in the ritual and cognitive process by the activity of actually making things and doing things. One of the pervasive themes of the symposium and of this book is that spirituality and materiality cannot be separated. The roots of religion are to be found in ritual practice. And ritual practice, as documented by the material record goes back before the Franco-Cantabrian 'explosion', back indeed before the Blombos engravings, to repetitive activities undertaken very much earlier and documented in the material record, which we may infer were meaningful to their practitioners, and which may be regarded as ritual.

The volume concludes with reflections, by Wentzel Van Huyssteen and by Keith Ward, on these themes. These are scholars well versed in the varieties of experience to be found in the history of religious thought. One interesting conclusion which arises from this scrutiny of the archaeological record of the palaeolithic period is that the development of symbolic practices, and thus perhaps of spirituality, has been a some-what gradual one. To be sure there are moments of intense innovation, such as is seen in France and Spain with the 'creative explosion' of Franco-Cantabrian cave painting. But these developments had their analogues, although in a quieter way, in Australia, in Africa, and perhaps more widely. More significantly, they are no longer seen as representing a sudden and amazing first step, an initial burst in human expression and spirituality. Already, more than thirty thousand years earlier, the human revolution was already taking place in Africa. Anatomically modern humans emerged there, and many of the behaviours which have been associated with modernity (in the archaeological sense) can also be recognised there.

As this volume clearly shows, the process of becoming human has been a slow and gradual one. Early indications of self-awareness and what may be termed spirituality are seen first in Africa, and may be discerned in Australia as well as in Europe. That remarkable creative explosion, which soon brought about the decoration of the Grotte Chauvet, and later of Lascaux and of Altamira can now be recognised as a local episode which did not have its counterpart in Asia or in the Americas. It should not be generalised as representing a stage in human cognitive and spiritual development. But at the same time the richness of the evidence found there, in the Upper Palaeolithic of France and Spain, offers fertile ground for speculation upon the relationship between the production of symbolic material culture, the practice of ritual, and the roots of spirituality.

## Acknowledgements

We are very grateful to the John Templeton Foundation for initiating and supporting the Les Eyzies meeting. In this enterprise, it was represented by Mary Ann Meyers, who undertook all aspects of the practical organisation of the meeting, although at her invitation Colin Renfrew articulated its programme. Charles Harper and Paul Wason, both of the Templeton Foundation, attended the sessions and participated fully in the discussions. Iain Morley was not able to be present at the Symposium, but he has contributed a paper and has coedited the present volume.

We would also like to express our gratitude to the Templeton Publishing Subsidy Program for the grant allowing the inclusion of the colour plates in this volume, and to the contributors for their patience over the course of a lengthy editing process.

**REFERENCES**

Forster P., 2004. Ice ages and the mitochondrial DNA chronology of human dispersals: a review, *Philosophical Transactions of the Royal Society of London, Series B* **359**, 255–64.

McBrearty S. & Brooks A. S., 2000. The revolution that wasn't: a new interpretation of the origin of modern human behaviour, *Journal of Human Evolution* **39**, 453–563.

Mellars P., 1991. Cognitive changes and the emergence of modern humans in Europe, *Cambridge Archaeological Journal* **1**, 63–76.

Mellars P. & Stringer C. (eds.), 1989. *The Human Revolution*. Edinburgh, Edinburgh University Press.

Pfeiffer J., 1982. *The Creative Explosion: An Inquiry into the Origins of Art and Religion*. New York, Harper and Row.

2

# The emergence of symbolic thought: The principal steps of hominisation leading towards greater complexity

*Henry de Lumley*

Symbolic thought represents one of the essential dimensions of human cognition, transcending the material world and integrating cogitation within a universe richer than that of the senses, and combining concepts, that is to say abstract notions, into a system of complex relations. The advent of *Homo sapiens*, whose brain shows developed frontal lobes, areas of which were involved in functions essential for symbolic thought, coincides with the appearance of evidence for a high level of symbolic activity. Humans later invented the first jewellery, as well as decorative and parietal art.

But well before the appearance of Modern Humans, the first elements of symbolic thought gradually developed in human cognition, in parallel with the emergence of consciousness.

Accompanying the development of cranial capacity and of cerebral complexity, the major steps in hominid technological and cultural evolution, crossed significant thresholds, and were marked by the progressive emergence of symbolic thought, in the processes of the acquisition and treatment of data. The tool serves not only to dominate the exterior world but also to understand it. The transmission of knowledge and skills indicates the appearance of the human communication system: the development of language structured from social experience.

## The first tools and the emergence of conceptual thought

The earliest stone-tools, found at Kada Gona in north-eastern Ethiopia, date to 2.5 Mya (see Figures 2.1–2.4). These tools may be taken to indicate the presence of conceptual thought and the ability for early humans to conceive of a model. But it is clear that the only preoccupation

**2.1.** Chopper on a trachyte pebble. Gona EG 10, Hadar, Ethiopia, 2.55 Mya.

of their makers during the production of these tools was to obtain a sharp instrument with which to disarticulate large herbivore carcasses or to cut up meat.

## The first handaxes and the emergence of a sense of harmony

The earliest current evidence for handaxes comes from West Turkana, Kenya, dated to 1.65 Mya. Similar finds have been made at Konso, again in Ethiopia, dating to 1.5 Mya (see Figure 2.5). These tools show both lateral and bifacial symmetry, thus demonstrating early human acquisition of the notion of symmetry. Soon after this, the Acheulean culture produced perfectly symmetrical and very regular tools (see Figure 2.6), sometimes with the choice of rocks of a pleasing colour for their

**2.2.** Rhyolite flake. Gona EG 10, Hadar, Ethiopia, 2.55 Mya.

**2.3.** Chopper on a quartz pebble. Fejej FJ-1, South Omo, Ethiopia, 1.96 Mya.

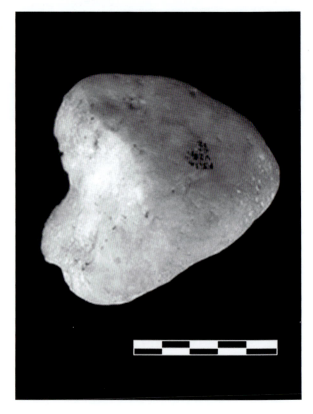

**2.4.** Quartz flake. Fejej FJ-1, South Omo, Ethiopia, 1.96 Mya.

**2.5.** Basalt handaxe. Afar region. Ethiopia, 1.4 Mya.

**2.6.** Quartz handaxe. Caune de l'Arago, Tautavel, France, 500,000 ya.

fabrication (see Figures 2.7 and 2.8). Symmetry and colour do not affect the functional effectiveness of a tool. This means that humans were looking for beauty and that they developed an appreciation for a job well done. Hominisation thus passed a new threshold in the path towards greater complexity: the emergence of the sense of harmony.

### Ritual cannibalism and the earliest treatment of corpses

Excavations at the Caune de l'Arago cave site in Tautavel, Pyrénées-Orientales, in France, have brought to light more than one hundred fossil hominid remains dating to around 450,000 years ago. Among these human remains are elements of several skulls and jaws, some femur fragments, fibulae, tibiae, humeri, radii, and a hip bone. Yet, not a single rib is present, not one vertebra, only one metatarsal and one phalange from the hand. The relative proportions of the bodies' different bones therefore do not correspond to a normal representation for complete skeletons.

However, in the case of the remains of large herbivores such as mouflons, fallow deer, red deer, reindeer, bisons, or horse, all hunted for

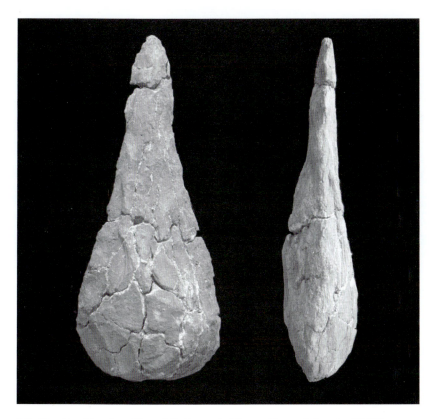

**2.7.** Hornblend handaxe (*Durandal*). Caune de l'Arago, Tautavel, France, 500,000 ya.

**2.8.** Handaxe from Nadaouiyeh, El Kowm, Syria. Level 9, 400,000 ya.

subsistence purposes, the vertebrae, ribs, carpals and tarsals, metapodials, and phalanges are more numerous than crania and mandibles. They indicate the use and dispersion of whole skeletons.

It would appear therefore that the treatment of human bodies was not the same as that of large herbivores killed during organized hunting expeditions. It is evident that the meat on human bones was also removed and the bones broken, which we may observe from spiral fractures, impact points and cut marks undertaken on fresh bone. It seems, however, that this activity was not carried out with the same purpose as for the animal bones.

There was a deliberate selection among the human bones treated, with a preference for the crania and the mandibles, as well as the most meaty parts of the body (thighs, legs, arms, etc.). It is possible that the skinning and butchery of the human crania might be an indication of practices of ritual cannibalism some 450,000 years ago.

### The domestication of fire and the birth of regional cultural identities

Around four hundred thousand years ago, with the appearance of the first hearths (Terra Amata, in Nice, Menez Dregan in Brittany, and Verteszöllos in Hungary) (see Figures 2.9 and 2.10), a more organised

**2.9.** Hearth at Menez Dregan I, Finistère, France, 400,000 ya.

**2.10.** Hearth at Terra Amata, Nice, France, 400,000 ya.

social life began to develop around the fire. Fire was a formidable driving force for hominisation. Its light extended daytime and shortened the night; it allowed humans to penetrate deep into caves. Fire provided warmth, prolonged summertime and shortened winters. Fire allowed humans to occupy the cooler temperate areas of the planet. It enabled humans to cook food and, as a result, to reduce parasitosis. It helped to improve tool making by providing heat to harden the points of spears. But fire was mainly a factor inspiring conviviality. Group spirit was surely kindled around the hearth. This was the birth of the first myths. It is at this point that the first regional traditions emerged: the first cultural identities, showing styles and *designs* in the manufacture of some tools.

## The burial in the sink-hole at the Sima de los Huesos: the application of symbolic thought

Some three hundred thousand years ago, *Homo heidelbergensis* at the Sima de los Huesos, in the Atapuerca Sierra, Castille Leon province in Spain, showed the first incontestable signs of symbolic thought. In this 15m deep sink-hole, located today 400m from the entrance of Cueva Mayor, an immense cave of the Sierra of Atapuerca, Eudald Carbonell i Roura, Juan-Luis Arsuaga, and José-Maria Bermudez de Castro

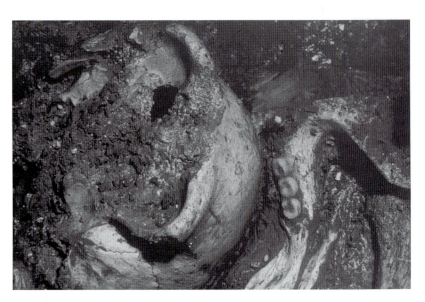

**2.11.** Accumulation of human remains at the bottom of the sink-hole, at Sima de los Huesos. Atapuerca Sierra, Castille Leon Province, Spain, 300,000 ya.

discovered more than thirty-five hundred human bones, generally unbroken, belonging to thirty-two individuals (see Figure 2.11).

The proportions by relative age of the individuals represented reflect those of a population with a natural death ratio: a high percentage of children's deaths between seven and ten years old, female deaths at around fifteen years old, that is to say, at the age of their first childbirth, adult deaths between eighteen and twenty three years old and a small percentage of deaths at more than thirty years old (see Figure 2.12). The long bones are not broken, suggesting that the individuals had been thrown into the sink-hole in a state of rigor-mortis. It seems obvious that *Homo heidelbergensis* ritually threw thirty-two of their dead into this sink-hole, into the world of the dead, into an invisible world.

No large herbivore bones were found at the site, but among a number of handaxes, there is one that is particularly magnificent, discovered amongst the heap of human bones (see Plate I). It was made from a naturally pink-coloured block of quartzite, brought from a source about thirty kilometres from the site. It was perfectly regular and symmetrical and remarkably well-made, and the freshness of its cutting edges gives the impression that the piece had never been used. It was evidently a funerary gift.

We are in the presence of the oldest sepulchral deposit known, and the first expression of ritual thought.

## The first burials and the birth of metaphysical anguish

It was, however, a little less than one hundred thousand years ago that the first real burials appeared, in a Mousterian cultural context in the Near East where early modern humans are also found (see Figure 2.13). In Europe and in central Asia the first burials are of Neanderthals, a culmination in the evolution of the pre-Neanderthals.

In these cases an oval or rectangular pit was dug in which to lay the deceased person. Usually these were individual graves, as at La Chappelle-aux-Saints in Corrèze, Régourdou, in the Dordogne, or at Spy, in Belgium, at Amud and at Tabun, in Israel. Sometimes there is in effect a cemetery, as at La Ferrassie in the Dordogne where seven graves were discovered (see Figure 2.14), or at Qafzeh, near Nazareth in Israel, where more than thirty individuals were buried.

In the graves, funerary gifts for the voyage into the after-life were often made: reindeer body or bison leg at La Chappelle-aux-Saints, deer antlers at Qafzeh. The graves may have been filled with field flowers at Shanidar IV in Iraqi Kurdistan, as suggested by the frequencies of

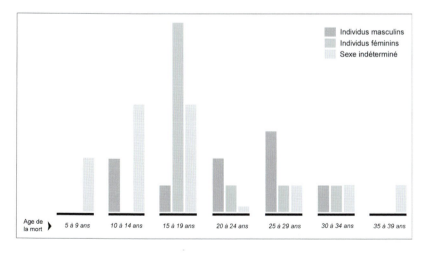

**2.12.** Individual mortality according to age and sex at Sima de los Huesos. Atapuerca Sierra, Castille Leon Province, Spain.

**2.13.** Child's grave at the Qafzeh cave, Nazareth, Israel, 95,000 ya.

pollen discovered in the grave. At Teshik Tash in Central Asia, five pairs of ibex antlers surrounded the burial of a ten year old child. Sometimes a paving stone (at La Ferrassie and Shanidar I) was placed above the pit.

In the cave at La Chappelle-aux-Saints, a toothless old man of about fifty, a venerable age for that period, was placed in a rectangular pit (see Figure 2.15). He lay on his back, up against one corner of the pit, supported by a few stones, with his right arm bent, bringing the hand towards the head, and his left arm straight. His legs were bent into a forced position against his torso.

In the large rock shelter at La Ferrassie, seven burials were discovered. One contained the complete skeleton of a man lying on his back, his head turned towards the left and his legs bent towards the right. In a second grave, a woman was buried facing him. Nearby, five other pits contained the skeletons of children and newborn babies.

In the Qafzeh cave, there was a careful burial of a nine year old child, dating to ninety-five thousand years ago (see Figure 2.14). The arms of the child, in the Paleo-Christian praying position, held a deer antler; its legs are bent and turned to the side. Let us remember that, among Indo-Europeans, the deer is a symbol of fertility, of eternal youth and, even of resurrection, since although the antlers are lost in Autumn, they grow back in the Spring, like the leaves of plants. Perhaps this idea of symbolic rebirth had begun already in Mousterian cultures, some one hundred thousand years ago.

Burial was at this time sporadic – the practice was in fact not yet in general use among the Neanderthals – and it bears witness to the fact that humans, in protecting their dead and bringing them offerings, question the meaning of their existence, and their place in the history of life. They seem to deny death, as each one of us indeed does. They desire to follow the path towards their ultimate goal: life after death. In other words, burial may be said to constitute evidence for the birth of metaphysical anguish and for the emergence of religious thought.

**2.14.** Neanderthal burial at La Ferrassie, Dordogne, France, 40,000 ya.

**2.15.** Neanderthal burial at La Chapelle-aux-Saints, Corrèze, France, 40,000 ya.

### Jewellery, sculpture and cave art: the explosion of symbolic thought

Finally, truly modern *Homo sapiens* appeared on the scene, with their high, straight foreheads and their well-developed frontal lobes. They developed associative thought, permitting the emergence of a high level of symbolic thought. At this point sapient humans made the first use of jewellery, using shells, fossils and pierced teeth to make necklaces and bracelets, or to sew them onto headdresses or clothing.

Sculpture and parietal art now make their appearance. We find decorative art for the first time, and with it the creation of sculpture, that is to say, of representation on stone, ivory, bone, or clay. These now actually reproduce animals in three dimensions, such as the statuette of a mammoth from Hohlenstein-Stadel in the Vogelherd Bad-Würtemberg.

Sometimes even imaginary figures are found, such as humans with lion's heads from Hohlenstein-Stadel (see Plate II) and from Hohle Fels, near Ulm (see Figure 2.16). These are dated to more than thirty-two thousand years ago and attributed to the Aurignacian culture. Later, about twenty-eight thousand years ago, in the Gravettian culture, female figures were made, with corpulent forms apparently symbolizing fecundity (see also Renfrew, this volume). Figurative parietal art was also created.

**2.16.** Statue of a man with lion's head from Hohle Fels, Ulm, Germany. Aurignacian culture, 32,000 ya.

Through engraving or painting, humans reproduced on a flat surface in two dimensions what existed in the natural world in three dimensions; this may be said to constitute the invention of the image.

Jewellery, decorative art, and parietal art all bear witness to the newly acquired conceptual capacities of humankind and, of course, to the development of symbolic thought, further elaborated in relation to mythic stories and religious thought (see Plate III). Control of the symbol, a complex cognitive process characteristic of modern humans, was finally achieved. The explosion of symbolic thought, arising from the growing complexity of the brain, seems to be a feature specific to modern humans.

### The first ideograms: humans transmit a message through space and time

From the end of the fourth millennium before Christ, between the Tigris and Euphrates rivers, Sumerian pictographic writing appears (3,300 BC), and in the Nile Valley, Egyptian hieroglyphs are first seen (3,500 BC). On the rocks of the sacred Bego Mountain in Tende, in the Alpes-Maritimes (3,300 BC), people were already carving ideograms (see Figures 2.17

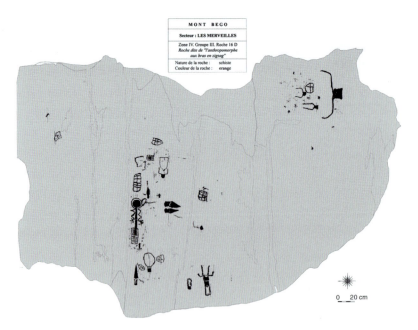

**2.17.** Carved stone known as "The Sorcerer" (Z VII. G. R3(4), opposite), Merveilles Valley, Mount Bego, Tende, France. About 3,000 yrs BC.

MONT BEGO

Secteur : LES MERVEILLES

Zone VIII. Groupe II. Roche 3(4). Face e
*Dalle dite du "Sorcier"*

| Nature de la roche : | schiste |
| Couleur de la roche : | orange |

0        20 cm

**2.18.** Carved stone known as "Anthropomorphic figure with zigzag arms" and "acephalic horned praying figure" (Z IV G III. R16D). The divine primordial couple, Merveilles Valley, Mount Bego, Tende, France. About 3,000 yrs BC.

and 2.18). Through the association of signs, they were able to combine ideas which may have transmitted their myths, their religious thoughts, their knowledge, and their concepts of the world: a message sent down through space and time.

Among the Great Apes, we may say that the emotional or motivational brain uses continuous relationships in order to establish simple ties such as stimulus-response; among humans, cognitive activity relies on more complex relationships in the form of propositions which presuppose the knowledge of a goal and the verification of results. Should we not consider the invention of manufactured tools, embedded in an operational schema in fulfilment of an intention, as the first definition of what it means to become human?

At the same time, should we not conclude that this progressive enrichment of cognitive processes, with the emergence of symbolic thought and its explosion among modern humans, is a proof that humans may be said to be in a state of perpetual becoming?

# AFRICAN ORIGINS,
# EUROPEAN BEGINNINGS,
# AND WORLD PREHISTORY

3

# The origins of symbolism, spirituality, and shamans: exploring Middle Stone Age material culture in South Africa

*Christopher Henshilwood*

## Introduction

The rapid and widespread appearance of 'symbolically mediated' material culture characterizes the Upper Palaeolithic associated with *Homo sapiens* after c. 40 kya. Among others, cave art, personal ornaments, and tools with elaborate engraved designs are typically portrayed as central to understanding the origins of our symbolic abilities (Mellars 1973, 1989; Mithen 1996; Gamble 1999). At the core of this 'symbolic explosion' was the development of fully syntactic language that provided the means for "semantically unbounded discourse" (Rappaport 1999). Archaeological relics from the period provide evidence for individuality, innovation, and a rapidly evolving social complexity (Gabora 2001). While the interpretation of these 'symbolic' finds may be polysemic (Conkey 1996), it has long been argued, too, that the first inklings of what is euphemistically referred to by archaeologists as 'spirituality', 'ritual' or 'shamanism' (Insoll 2004: 154) can be teased out from a plethora of symbolic material culture (e.g. Haddon 1934; Childe 1958; Gamble 1999; Gabora 2001; for a review, see Insoll 2004). Representational wall paintings of animals in deep cave recesses, abstract geometric patterns and elaborate grave goods suggest that the exosomatic evolution of *H. sapiens*, at least in Europe, included 'spiritual' values, 'shamanistic' practices and belief in an afterlife (Clottes & Lewis-Williams 1998). Although beyond the scope of this paper, a similar line of reasoning is suggested for Neanderthal modernity emerging at about this time or just earlier (for a review, see d'Errico et al. 2003).

In the absence of written records or ethnographic analogy, interpretation of these ancient finds is open to error: "unfortunately the external symbols themselves never contain enough information to allow us to rediscover the detailed thought-habits of an ancient culture *a posteriori*. Symbolic artefacts, even of the more elaborate kind, rarely encode the conventions governing their use" (Donald 1998: 184).

Despite these sentiments a common assumption is that the origins of symbolism and religion are closely linked (e.g. Lewis-Williams & Dowson 1990; Clottes & Lewis-Williams 1998; see a review in Insoll 2004). Essential perhaps to the early development of religious beliefs and practices was a society mediated by symbolism. Without symbolism there could arguably be no link to supernatural agency, a key feature, some believe, of most religious concepts (Boyer 2003; Lewis-Williams & Pearce 2004). Once symbolism was in place, innovative material culture, including 'religious' icons, flourished in Europe and continued to do so in subsequent generations. As Lock (2000) points out "the process of elaborating the symbolic support for, and amplification of, cognitive abilities, is embedded in a nexus of influences that feed forward and back to each other". The crafted physical settings of cave art (see Lewis-Williams & Dowson 1990; Clottes & Lewis-Williams 1998), for example, may have functioned symbolically in multiple dimensions, one perhaps being a conduit for 'spirituality' or 'religious notions', another perhaps being the means of entry into another world. Associated with the adoption of a 'spiritual' culture is a social behaviour that is increasingly complex and probably mediated by these emerging belief systems.

Interpretations of the archaeological evidence from the African Middle Stone Age (MSA) suggested, until recently, that modern human behaviour developed late on the continent and probably not before about 45 kya (Klein 2000). With some exceptions (see McBrearty & Brooks 2000) evidence for symbolically driven material culture seemed absent from the MSA and initially patchy in the Later Stone Age (LSA) – a few beads at c. 40 kya and some mobiliary art at c. 27 kya. In their review Lindly and Clark (1990: 233) conclude that "neither archaic *H. sapiens* nor morphologically modern humans demonstrate symbolic behavior prior to the Upper Palaeolithic".

An obvious question is if anatomically modern *H. sapiens* had evolved in Africa by at least 160 kya (White et al. 2003), and probably before 200 kya (Ingmann et al. 2000) then were the same features that define behavioral modernity in Europe (Mellars 1973; Gamble 1996) present in Africa before 50 kya? Did anatomically modern *Homo sapiens* who left

Africa between 70 and 40 kya have the capacity for symbolism and was their behaviour symbolically driven? *If* the earliest evidence of religious practice does lie in Africa, then when modern humans left the continent to spread across Eurasia the capacity for spirituality, for 'religious', for 'shamanistic' experience must already have been in place. They must have been behaviourally modern when they left. Does the available evidence support this scenario or could the earliest evidence for religion and symbolism in Africa fit only into a post 50 kya timeframe?

## The Archaeology of Religion

Different methodological tools are required for examining the origins of religion, whether religious behaviour has ecological determinants, the development of religious institutions and whether religion is adaptive (Sosis & Alcorta 2003). In this paper the physical evidence for early religious practice is highlighted. Seeking the 'origins of spirituality' in prehistory is fraught with the same kinds of problems that confront archaeologists seeking material evidence for the origins of language. No direct evidence for language exists and similarly evidence for religion. Recovered material culture arguably provides the only means of recovering such data.

A starting point in this search is the suggestion by Boyer (2003) that religion cannot function without symbolism. Evidence that early members of our species, *H. ergaster* or *H. heidelbergensis* or even early *H. sapiens*, were functioning symbolically is scarce. Even if they were capable of symbolic behaviour, as has been argued for the production of handaxes, then the symbol systems they were using were minimally elaborated (Lock 2000). Psychologists generally agree that we have several different kinds of 'intelligence' or types of cognitive abilities that are associated with specialised situations: social sense, naïve physics, numerosity, and so on. Cognitive fluidity occurs, Mithen (1996: 143) argues, when the separate domains of thought (natural history intelligence, technical intelligence, social and linguistic intelligence) are integrated – his description is a 'super-chapel' of the mind, in an analogy in which a number of the specialist small 'chapels' dedicated to specific functions are amalgamated. Sperber's (1994) "module of meta-representation", a place where we represent facts about representation itself, is likened by Mithen (1996) to this 'super-chapel'. Early hominids, Mithen (1996) argues, had not linked these intelligences and were thus incapable of cognitively fluid communication. Belief in noncorporeal beings (the supernatural) is the most commonly offered definition for religion in anthropology, although the distinction between the supernatural associated with ritual practices and paranormal beliefs that are not ritualised is often ignored (Sosis & Alcorta 2004: 265). Only when religious ideas are translated into material artefacts, Mithen (1996) suggests, can religion become possible. These material artefacts take on the role of 'anchors', in some ways similar to that of a rosary, that enable early modern humans to recall, understand and transmit these ideas.

If we assume then that hominids prior to *H. sapiens* in Europe were not cognitively modern (see Mithen 1996), then we should not expect to find physical evidence of symbolic artefacts, ritual or other material culture associated with the paranormal in sites that predate the Upper Palaeolithic, or in the Middle Stone Age in Africa – *but* we should find this evidence in sites occupied by behaviourally modern *H. sapiens*. The argument is somewhat circular but begs the question – how do we recognise material culture associated with the paranormal and how do we distinguish artefacts that may have functioned in a symbolic but non-religious mode from those that were integral to a belief system or perhaps even ritualised? Also is the separation likely to be distinct? According to Mithen (1996: 165) there is no evidence that material symbols existed beyond the start of the Upper Palaeolithic, and he maintains that without them shared ideas about supernatural beings could not exist. It is at this point, about 30 kya that ritual, symbolic culture and emerging cognitive fluidity intersected – what Mithen describes as a "spandrel of religion". This assertion, if correct, may make the task of the archaeologist seeking these material beginnings of religion somewhat easier, or at least constrains the period within which such 'sacred' or 'ritual' objects are likely to first appear.

A brief review of what religion is, or might have been, may also contribute some ideas to the above questions but anthropology has no widely accepted, universal definition of the concept 'religion' (Lambeck 2002). Insoll (2004: 155) describes it as an "an awe-inspiring creature . . . irreducible and complex". "What sort of science is it", Durkheim asks of religion, "whose principal discovery is that the subject of which it treats does not exist?" (Jones 1986). He rejected animism as a basis for religion on the grounds that such a doctrine implies that religious symbols are products of the vague, ill-conceived hallucinations of our dream-experience. To him this was untenable as was naturism whereby religion ultimately rests upon a real experience, that of the principal phenomena of nature and which is sufficient to directly arouse religious ideas in the mind (Jones 1986; Insoll 2004). In *The Elementary Forms* published in 1912 Durkheim opted instead for totemism (Sosis & Alcorta 2004). Totemism is not a religion of emblems or animals or men at all, but rather of an anonymous, impersonal 'force', immanent in the world and diffused among its various material objects. He stressed that God is nothing more than society apotheosized (Haddon 1934; Jones 1986). Interestingly, this argument was bound to his conception of the role of symbols in society. Symbols can stand as expressions of social sentiment but also serve to create the sentiments themselves. Collective symbols are attributed solely, he thought, to the mutual reactions of individual minds, one upon the other and representations would rapidly diminish or disappear in the absence of these collective symbols. Society "in all its aspects and in every period of its history, is made possible only by a vast symbolism" (Jones 1986; Insoll 2004). To confirm his theories for the origins of religion Durkheim turned to ethnography and the Arunta in Australia. In this, he failed as first he ignored counterbeliefs of nearby groups and second, his developed argument contained a *petitio principii* (Jones 1986). Durkheim, with minor changes effectively presumed the conclusion, which was at question in the first place.

Durkheim's search for the 'essence of religion' among the Arunta contains a stark warning for archaeologists seeking to associate 'religious intent' with ancient material culture. "What one finds among the Arunta are the beliefs and practices of the Arunta, and even to call these 'religious' is to impose the conventions of one's own culture and historical period" (Geertz 1973: 22). Carrying the theme further to the archaeology of religion, Insoll (2004: 153) emphasizes the importance of examining the context of recovered material culture in both its individual and communal forms before we can begin to reconstruct relevant past meaning.

The 'essence of religion' is obviously multifacetted and extraordinarily complex and is perhaps the reason that humans are the only species that engage in religious behaviour (e.g. Mithen 1999). It is also the contradictory nature of religion that is one of its critical and complex features (e.g. Rappaport 1999; Wilson 2002; Boyer 2003). Factors that favoured religious practice in our evolutionary history may help shed some light on how the material culture of religion may manifest in the archaeological record. What is also puzzling is how religious behaviour is apparently so pervasive throughout human populations after about 30 kya (Mithen 1996:149).

A comprehensive review of the history of religion-orientated research is elegantly presented by Insoll (2004). Three approaches that may be useful for archaeologists contemplating the material evidence for religion are briefly considered here: one that religion is adaptive, two, that its origins lie in a biological capacity for hypnosis (*shamanism*) and, three that it is a byproduct of brain function. Individual actions are generally not effective in the exploitation of resources and to maximise the benefits humans groups coalesce. These adaptive units that form do so because they have moral systems and the group's behaviour is regulated through religious imagery and symbolism (Wilson 2002). Cultural selection, an ongoing process, adaptively selects for those religious practices most beneficial to the group and may reject or modify those that are delete-rious. The latter may not necessarily be the case as maladaptive traits are known also to survive among some groups (Mithen 1996). Groups function as adaptive units through their ability to relate to supernatural agents. The essence of Wilson's argument is that unifying systems enable humans to form adaptive groups and that religion is one example of this. He emphasises that group selection does occur, that intergroup solidarity is promoted by religion and that the genetic isolation of religious groups could lead to fitness differences (see also Boyer 2004). His viewpoint is not in agreement with an emerging consensus that is rooted in evolutionary psychology (see, e.g., Mithen 1996; Boyer 2001, 2003; Rappaport 1999). Both the possibility and importance of group selection are highlighted by Wilson who is opposed to the individual or gene-level selection model (Boyer 2004: 431). But perhaps the major problem with the adaptive approach for archaeologists seeking the origins of religion in prehistory is that Wilson's approach considers religions that are institu-tionalised and whose beliefs and dogma are controlled and managed by doctrinal specialists – in essence the religions of complex state society.

Nevertheless, if religion in early hunter-gatherer societies was adaptive would it leave material traces and if so what? One could argue that reciprocity formed an essential part of inter- and intragroup cohesion to maintain amicable social relations. One part of this may have been exchange and reciprocity – in essence 'gift giving'. Imbued with value due to rarity or fine craftsmanship gift items may acquire intrinsic symbolic/spiritual meaning. The recovery of such items may be one indicator of symbolically mediated behaviour, without which spirituality can arguably not function.

An innate biological function that underlies hypnotic capacity is argued by McClenon (2001) as the origin of religious beliefs and healing practices. In 1870, Lubbock proposed a not dissimilar idea except that he ranked shamanism low on an evolutionary scale of religion and just above totemism, then fetishism and atheism (Insoll 2004: 43). A hypnotic capacity that produces an altered state of consciousness enhanced survival, reproduction and aided with recovery from disease. Manifestations during a hypnotic state include creative visions, perceptions of spirits and out of body experiences. It is the association of these anomalous experiences during hypnosis and ritual that form the foundations for shamanism and religion (McLenon 2001). Supporting this argument Lewis Williams & Pearce (2004: 36) contend that a neurological foundation lies at the base of a diverse, worldwide spirituality – "spirituality is a construct, but one with a material, neurological function".

The contribution of individuals in the evolution of cultural complexity is a topic addressed by a number of researchers (e.g. Gabora 1997; Richerson & Boyd 1998; Pearce 2002; Alvard 2003). Individual innovation may have played a key role in the origins of religion (also see Gabora 2001) as hypnotic experience enhanced access to the unconscious mind. The most distinctive characteristic of human cultural evolution is described as the 'ratchet effect', by Tomasello (1999) as it allows for the ideas and inventions of an individual to build on the ideas and inventions of others. Modifications to an artefact or a social practice made by one individual or a group of individuals may spread within the group, and then stay in place until some future individual or individuals make further modifications. Which memes spread and which die is determined by the dynamics of the entire society of individuals which hosts these ideas and inventions (Gabora 1997: 5). Creativity is a collective affair that derives from within the group's cognitive system and the concept of individual creativity should not however obscure that fact.

Most agree that the birth of a creative idea can only lie with an individual. A group of individuals may discuss the pros and cons of a new concept and each individual within the group may contribute ideas but the final idea that is accepted by the group would have been generated by one individual, even if it came about through group input. Gabora's (2000: 3) concept of an 'inkling', describes well the concept of individual creativity:

> An inkling, then, is a collapse on an association or relationship amongst memories or concepts that, although their distribution regions overlap, were stored there at different times, and have never before been simultaneously perturbed, and evoked in the same collapse. Although it is a reconstructed blend, something never actually experienced, it can still be said to have been evoked from memory. It is like getting a 'bite' on many fishing rods at once, and when you reel them in you get a fish that is a mixture of the characteristics of the various fish that bit.

Richerson & Boyd (1998: 14) suggest that the complexities of subsistence systems, artistic productions, languages, and the like would have prohibited one individual from inventing them. The same reasoning can equally be applied to formative conceptions of spirituality. It was most likely the incremental, marginal modifications of many innovators, arguably with some change being contributed or created through altered states of consciousness that over many generations contributed to the complexity of religious practice and behavioural modernity.

Altered states of consciousness and hypnosis interrupt the normal cycle of transmitters producing a dreamlike state of mind, anomalous experiences and assist with physical recuperation. McClenon (2001) proposes that biology provides the basis for religion, physiologically and genetically. Spirits, an after life, haunting, possession and out of body experiences are universal features of shamanistic healing and point to a neurological foundation for religious experience and spiritual healing. An almost universal belief in a tiered cosmos with spiritual realms above and below the level in which they live is produced by the human nervous system and can be verified by altered states of consciousness (Lewis-Williams & Pearce 2004: 35). Hallucinating shamans or seers that retell of this phenomenon are thought to have access to unseen realms beyond the ordinary. A powerful tool is created for understanding the origins of human cultural complexity, and archaeological materials, by linking shamanic and other religious experiences and beliefs with contemporary hypnotic phenomena. Can material culture be a proxy for that which cannot be seen in the past, for that which existed primarily within the human brain? How are we to interpret these fragmentary remains? Unraveling the origins and meaning of abstract imagery, representational paintings, personal ornaments and other symbolic material culture may be aided by reference to shamanistic practice but caution is advised. We just cannot be certain that the neurological systems of *H. sapiens* 70 kya were the same as ours, or that the recovered material we now label as nonfunctional, symbolic, religious, and so on was generated within the same frame of reference (Insoll 2004: 32).

Some evolutionary psychologists consider the origins of religion and religious thought to be 'natural', a by-product of brain function (e.g. Kirkpatrick 1999; Mithen 1996, 1999; Pinker 1997; Boyer 1994, 2001, 2003, 2004). Religious ideas develop as a result of cognitive capacities within the human brain that developed originally to handle non-religious information (Boyer 2001). Religion is therefore not an intrinsic part of the cognitive capacities of modern humans, as is the case for language acquisition. Boyer (2001) argues that all normal humans acquire a natural language and that this acquisition is an adaptation. Not so for music or religion, he says, and the evidence is that although most humans can recognize music and religious concepts, the extent to which they may enjoy music or adhere to religious concepts may be profoundly different. Not all humans are naturally religious, in fact many are not. Evidence that some genes code for religion and that religion is therefore a function of natural selection has not been proven – despite the fact that Hamer (2004) deduced from a questionnaire that sampled about one thousand people that there was a correlation between the presence of a particular gene and his interpretation of the meaning of 'spirituality'.

Boyer's (2000: 11) criticism of most 'origin of religion theories' is that they are functionalist and untestable. Accounts of religious systems are often ethnocentric and focus on cognitive and emotional aspects of religion that cannot be generalized for human society. Others seek to account for our mortality, justify social orders, and seek life's meaning. Adherents to the 'by-product' view maintain it is empirically justifiable and more prudent to consider religion as the offshoot of an evolutionary cognitive system that developed through natural selection (Boyer & Ramble 2001), although some argue this approach is essentialist (Insoll 2004: 93). Evidence for this approach is that religious ideas do not fall within a separate realm of cognitive functioning. Boyer (2001) provides three reasons why religion is 'natural' and not the result of a 'sleep of reason'.

First, religion defies many of our most basic instinctual perceptions and hence are relevant (e.g. we all grow old and die but spirits do not); second, the survival of religious concepts confirms many of our intuitive principles; third, the systems that create similar norms, like moral intuition, or emotions, like a fear of contaminants, are the same ones that drive religious ideas and emotions. To sustain religious thoughts, such as ancestor spirits, an afterlife or ghosts means tweaking ordinary cognition. Intuitive physics tells us that unsupported objects fall, that humans cannot fly unaided, and so on, yet we adhere to many religious notions that defy our own logic (see Boyer 2000:197). The reason, Boyer (2001) argues, is not because humans suspend ordinary cognitive processes but rather because the context in which these cognitive resources are used is different to that for which they were designed.

A potentially useful insight for archaeologists is the view that there are not many ways of tweaking intuitive ontology (Boyer 2000: 198). This suggests that supernatural concepts produced within the human mind may be constrained to include only person, animal, plant, artefact, natural object. Violations of these basic categories are produced by 'breach' or by 'transfer'. Breaching is a contradiction of intuitive expectations, for example, an animal that disappears and thus breaches intuitive physics (see Boyer 2000: 197). Transfer is when intuitive knowledge of one category is extended to another category, for example a rock that flies. The resultant list of templates is thus relatively small and compatible, according to Boyer (2001: 199) with the anthropological record. Most religious concepts, the evidence suggests, are based on one of these 'templates'. While the possible physical evidence for religious practice may still be considered wide this concept may aid archaeologists at least in narrowing down likely evidence for 'religious' material culture. Interestingly, artefacts are included in this list. Alterations of artefacts are likely to be by breach of physical expectations, by transfer of biological expectations and by transfer of psychological expectation. Of course, these alterations are most likely conceptual and may not be visible on recovered material. Nevertheless it does suggest that at least some artefacts, apart from paintings or carvings may have been imbued with religious significance. The challenge of how this might be recognized on a bone or stone tool made fifty thousand years ago remains.

Religion and its origins is a neglected area of archaeological method and theory. The few approaches to religion that were touched on above provide some insights into the problems faced by archaeologists in constructing an archaeology of religion. Whether religion evolved as a by-product of the brain, because it was adaptive, or due to the physiological ability of humans to go into trance, will continue to stimulate debate. Sosis and Alcorta (2003: 272) suggest that a basic point that has been missed is that traits are adaptive with respect to a particular set of selective pressures. Whether religious traits contribute directly to reproductive success, as has been suggested for selection within ecological contexts, has yet to be demonstrated. The selective pressures within various ecological contexts may also lead to religious behaviour adapting. The maladaptive traits that are suggested as being costly in religion (see Mithen 1996) may not be so; in fact, the contrary may be true in that costliness may be a critical adaptive feature of religious behaviour (Sosis & Alcorta 2003: 272). It is appropriate that archaeologists keep an open mind and adopt a critical, multidisciplinary approach. The stones won't speak but perhaps some aspects of the material culture of ancient religions will be revealed if the door is kept open.

## Modern Humans in Africa

> If the 'Out of Africa' hypothesis is correct . . . it is in Africa that we shall find clues that point to the earliest manifestations of 'spirituality' – if only we can spot them. The problem is that we do not know what they may look like. (Lewis-Williams & Dowson 2004: 5)

If human cognitive abilities underwent a major transition about 45 kya, is there physiological evidence of this? While nothing palaeoneurological can be said with confidence about possible changes with the emergence of anatomically modern *H. sapiens* (Holloway 1996) it seems certain that hominid brains evolved through the same selection processes as other body parts (Gabora, 2001). Biological evolution selected for genes that promoted a capacity for symbolism thus the foundations for symbolic culture must be grounded in biology.

New genetic and fossil evidence suggests that humans were anatomically near modern in Africa by 160 kya (e.g. Ingman et al. 2000; Cavalli-Sforza 2000; White et al. 2003). Key questions are whether anatomical and behavioural modernity developed in tandem, and what criteria archaeologists should use to identify modern behavior. Correlating anatomical with behavioural modernity is problematic as, unlike fossils, the evidence for behaviour is not easily extractable from the archaeological record. It is probable that post–c. 160 kya the only hominid in Africa was anatomically modern *H. sapiens*, and behavior changes during this period are restricted to one species of hominid.

A review of the African evidence by McBrearty & Brooks (2000) indicates a variable mosaic pattern of cognitive advances associated with anatomically modern humans (AMH) can be detected in the MSA. A number of other authors also make the point that the development of 'modern' behaviour is likely to have been a vast and complex series of events that developed in a mosaic way, and that the likely scale and repertoire of 'modern' behavior in the Middle to Late Pleistocene is enormous (cf. Chase & Dibble 1990; Foley & Lahr 1997; Gibson 1996; Renfrew 1996; Deacon 1998; McBrearty & Brooks 2000; Henshilwood & Marean 2003). For example, at 160 kya, AMH's in Ethiopia show evidence for deliberate treatment of the dead associated with modern type behaviour yet their lithic technology remains a mix of Acheulean and MSA (Clark et al. 2003). At Katanda in West Africa sophisticated bone harpoons are manufactured at c. 90 kya (Yellen et al. 1995; Brooks et al. 1995). During the transition from Mode 2 to Mode 3 (Foley & Lahr, 2003) there is directional change but the development of inter-assemblage variation is mainly the result of local style developing. The Still Bay dated at c. 75 kya (Henshilwood et al. 2002; Jacobs et al. 2003a, 2003b) is specifically regarded by Foley and Lahr (2003: 121) as one example. In southern Africa, Wurz et al. (2003) demonstrate distinct technological changes in lithic style between the MSA I period (c. 110–115 kya) and the MSA II (c. 94 –85 kya). They identify these MSA substages as separate 'techno-traditions' and argue for volatility rather than stasis at the MSA I/II interface that can be extended to other parts of Africa. Cognitively modern behaviour, they contend, is associated with these observed changes in technological conventions at the Klasies MSA site.

What defines modern or nonhuman behaviour? A typically classic marker of nonmodern human behaviour is a lack of innovation in material culture. For instance, some archaeologists take the relative technological stasis of the Middle Stone Age between about c. 250–240 kya as an argument against behavioural modernity. It seems there is no clear agreement as to what constitutes 'modern' or 'fully modern' (cf. Chase & Dibble 1990; Gibson 1996; Renfrew 1996; Foley & Lahr 1997; Deacon 1998; McBrearty & Brooks 2000; Henshilwood & Marean

2003). One definition is that fully modern behavior is mediated by socially constructed patterns of symbolic thinking, actions and communication that allow for material and information exchange and cultural continuity between and across generations and contemporaneous communities (Henshilwood & Marean 2003). The key factor here is the use of symbolism to mediate behaviour rather than just having the capacity for symbolic thought. Donald's (1991) three-stage model provides a useful framework. In the third stage he suggests that the ability to store and apply symbols externally allows material culture to intervene directly on social behavior. The transition to symbolically literate societies, according to Donald (1991, 1998) is a defining factor for behavioral modernity.

Critical innovative elements for defining modern behaviour include, among others, advanced subsistence practices especially fishing, shaped bone tools, rapid change in tool kits, art and personal ornaments, and deliberate burial with grave goods. This is an approach based on a comparison of the material culture of Neanderthals with that of Cro-magnons at c. 35 kya in Europe (see Mellars 1973). Alternative approaches to recognising modern behaviour in the archaeological record have been proposed (e.g. McBrearty & Brooks 2000; Henshilwood & Marean 2003). Principal among these is the recognition of material culture that carries an implicit symbolic message. Agreement on the best approach is lacking and for many the European 'list'-based approach holds sway.

## Blombos Cave – early evidence for symbolism

Over the past twelve years, Blombos Cave (BBC), situated near Still Bay in the southern Cape, South Africa, has yielded a well preserved sample of faunal and cultural material in MSA levels. The MSA phases are separated from the < 2 kya LSA levels by a blanketing aeolian dune sand 5–50 cm thick dated at c. 70 kya by optically stimulated luminescence (OSL) (Henshilwood et al. 2002; Jacobs et al. 2003). Careful examination of sediments and anthropogenically derived deposits within individual levels over the past few years have allowed us to subdivide the MSA levels into three major phases: (i) a Still Bay, or M1 phase dated at c. 75 kya by OSL and thermoluminescence, (ii) a middle M2 phase, perhaps early Still Bay, provisionally dated by OSL at c. 78–82 kya, (iii) a lower M3 phase that is provisionally dated at > 125 kya. Subsistence behaviour in the upper two phases is similar to that found in the LSA levels and includes the ability to hunt large bovids, collect shellfish, and catch large marine fish. Artefacts unusual in a Middle Stone Age context have been recovered. These include engraved ochre and bone, marine shell beads, and finely made bifacial points in M1, and shaped bone tools in M1 and M2. The likely symbolic significance of these finds suggests levels of cognitively modern behaviour not previously associated with Middle Stone Age people. Two of these finds are described here: the engraved ochres and the shell beads.

### ENGRAVED OCHRES

More than eight thousand pieces of ochre, many bearing signs of utilisation, have been recovered from the MSA layers at BBC. Nine pieces are potentially engraved and under study. Two unequivocally engraved pieces were recovered in situ from the M1 phase (Henshilwood 2002) (see Plate IV). Both specimens were located in a matrix of undisturbed and well consolidated ash and sand. On one piece, SAM-AA 8937 both the flat surfaces and one edge are modified by scraping and grinding. The edge has two ground facets and the larger of these bears a cross-hatched engraved design. The engraving on the second piece, SAM-AA 8938 consists of a row of cross-hatching, bounded top and bottom by parallel lines, and divided through the middle by a third parallel line which divides the lozenge shapes into triangles. Choice of raw material, situation and preparation of the engraved surface, engraving technique, and final design are similar for both pieces indicating a deliberate sequence of choices and intent. Arguably the engraved BBC ochres are the most complex and best formed of claimed early representations (Noble & Davidson 1996; d'Errico & Villa 1997; Bahn 1998; Lewis-Williams & Pearce 2004). They are not isolated occurrences or the result of idiosyncratic behaviour, as suggested for many early 'palaeo-art' objects. They would certainly not be out of place in a UP context. The transmission and sharing of the symbolic meaning of these pieces must arguably have depended on syntactical language.

### MARINE SHELL BEADS

Thirty-nine marine shell beads were recovered from the M1 phase and two from the M2 phase (Henshilwood et al. 2004; d'Errico et al. 2005). The beads were made by piercing *N. kraussianus* 'tick' shells and then stringing them, probably for use as personal ornaments (see Plate V).

Tick shells occur only in estuaries and were probably brought to the site from rivers located 20 km west and east of the cave. All the tick shells found in the MSA levels are adult, contra-indicating a random collection and rather a deliberate selection for size. Non-human taphonomic processes are known to produce pseudo personal ornaments that appear morphologically similar to human-modified and used beads. Unlike a natural collection all the recovered MSA shells are perforated dorsally, and 88 per cent have unique medium size perforations located near the lip (d'Errico et al. 2005). These perforations are anthropogenic and deliberate. Microscopic analysis of the MSA tick shells reveals a distinct use-wear consisting of facets which flatten the outer lip or create a concave surface on the lip close to the anterior canal. A similar concave facet is often seen opposite to the first one, on the parietal wall of the aperture. Use-wear patterns on the tick shells are consistent with friction from rubbing against thread, clothes or other beads and are the principal factor that defines the MSA shells as beads. Microscopic residues of ochre detected inside the MSA shells may also result from such friction or deliberate colouring of the beads. Beads were found in groups of two to seventeen, clustering in the same or neighbouring 50 x 50 cm quadrates. Within a group, beads display a similar size, shade, use-wear pattern and type of perforation. Each cluster may represent beads coming from the same beadwork item, lost or disposed during a single event (d'Errico et al. 2005).

A new dimension is added to the modern human behaviour debates by the excavation of the MSA beads from accurately dated and stratigraphically secure horizons at Blombos Cave; that beads are regarded as symbolic is undisputed (Henshilwood et al. 2004). The symbolic meaning of these beads must have been shared and transmitted through syntactical language, as is suggested for the engraved ochre pieces. The recovery of shell beads provides material evidence that by 75 kya human communication was mediated by symbolism, an unambiguous marker of modern human behavior.

## Discussion

Neural reorganisation within the human brain over millennia, rather than as a punctuated event, may have led to periods of rapid innovation or stasis depending on selective criteria that favoured or disfavoured innovation. The introduction of innovative ideas such as a new subsistence practice, remodelling of space within a living site or the shaping of a bone point may act as crucial archaeological markers for the recognition of 'modern'-type behaviour in sites such as BBC. However, detecting evidence for symbolically mediated behaviour is distinctly more subtle. An essential attribute of cognitively modern societies is their capacity to create symbolic systems and to reflect these visibly in their material culture. The combined presence of shell beads and engraved ochres in the same MSA phase provides absolute evidence that the behaviour of the makers and users of these artefacts was mediated by symbolism. Perhaps, the Blombos evidence also tells us that at this point modern humans were cognitively fluid and already possessed a generalized type of intelligence, as suggested by Mithen (1996).

Does the BBC MSA provide any indicators for supernatural imagination, a behaviour closely linked to religious notions? We have no evidence for two of the categories that may be typical indicators of religion (Boyer 1994); first, spirits after death and second the performance of rituals aimed at spiritual manipulation of the natural world. A third category, the 'divine' ability of individuals who have a different 'essence' to others within a group (Boyer 1994) and are able to communicate with supernatural agencies is open to interpretation. Innovative behaviour, such as the engraving of abstract images on ochre, may be the result of the inspirational 'essence' of one individual, perhaps a 'shaman', and be generated by 'religious' thoughts typically activated when people deal with emotions like death, disease or birth (Boyer 2003). Similarly, the Blombos beads may also represent a 'religiously' derived symbol that mediates and is mediated by group behaviour. Both categories of material culture are symbolic and innovative, and plausibly were linked to religious agency.

The 'identity' imparted by the engravings and beads probably formed part of a collective set of characteristics by which these and other symbolic items were recognizable within a cognition system that operated in imaginary and real dimensions that were inseparable. Symbols change through time because of remodeling the original concepts. Meanings can also change and the origins of the concept can be lost. This may have been the case for the BBC engravings and beads as succeeding MSA phases in the region do not, as far as we know, contain similar artefacts. Individuals play a major role in this process, either stimulating changes in the meanings of symbolic representations or experimenting with novel material expression of the same concepts. Some change may be driven by individuals' intuitive 'religious' thoughts, salient personal experiences or interpretation of doctrine. As Boyer (2003: 119) points out, religious thoughts are not a dramatic departure from, but a predictable by-product of, ordinary cognitive function. Religious concepts likely derive from the same notions experienced in dreams, fantasy and legends. The same functionally distinct neural resources that are activated by concepts such as social exchange, moral intuition and representations of animacy are also activated by religious concepts but some tweaking is likely that allows notions of supernatural agency to be intuitively plausible (Boyer 2003).

The Blombos evidence and new finds at other African sites is debunking the myth that Africans were behaviourally non-modern until about the time of the Palaeolithic cultural revolution. Although evidence of a 'symbolic explosion' in the African MSA is lacking it can be argued that by at least 75 kya the social intelligence of humans had been invaded by non-social ideas to create what Sperber (1994) describes as the "superchapel of the mind". Once the human mind had advanced to this point, peoples' cognitive domains could expand into spiritual dimensions not previously explored. The origins of religion may not have been a dramatic phenomenon, or even had particularly auspicious beginnings. It may have started in a cave somewhere in Africa, perhaps a cave like Blombos, at least seventy-five thousand years ago, probably earlier. Whether religion was inevitable or not is debatable, but it seems certain that only when human cognition allowed for the interpretation of one's own mental state that belief in supernatural agents became possible.

## REFERENCES

Alvard, M. S., 2003. The adaptive nature of culture. *Evolutionary Anthropology* **12**, 136–49.

Bahn, P. G., 1998. *Prehistoric Art*. Cambridge: Cambridge University Press.

Bahn, P. & J. Vertut, 1997. *Journey through the Ice Age*. London: Weidenfeld & Nicolson.

Boyer, P., 1994. *The Naturalness of Religious Ideas: A Cognitive Theory of Religion*. Berkeley: University of California Press.

Boyer, P., 2000. Functional origins of religious concepts: ontological and strategic selection in evolved minds. *Journal of the Royal Anthropological Institute* **6**, 195–214.

Boyer, P., 2001. *Religion Explained: Evolutionary Origins of Religious Thought.* New York: Basic Books.

Boyer, P., 2003. Religious thought and behaviour as by-products of brain function. *Trends in Cognitive Science* **3**, 119–4.

Boyer, P., 2004. Religion, evolution and cognition. *Current Anthropology* **43**, 430–3.

Boyer, P., & C. Ramble, 2001. Cognitive templates for religious concepts: cross cultural evidence for recall of counter-intuitive representations. *Cognitive Science* **25**, 535–64.

Brooks, A. S., D.M. Helgren, J. S. Cramer, A. Franklin, W. Hornyak, J. M. Keating., R. G. Klein, W. J. Rink, H. Schwarcz, J. N. Leith Smith, K. Stewart, N. E. Todd, J. Verniers, & J. E. Yellen, 1995. Dating and context of three Middle Stone Age sites with bone points in the Upper Semliki Valley, Zaire. *Science* **268**, 548–553.

Cavalli-Sforza, L. L., 2000. *Genes, Peoples and Languages.* New York: North Point Press.

Chase, P. G. & H. L. Dibble, 1990. On the emergence of modern humans. *Current Anthropology* **31**, 58–9.

Childe, V. G., 1958. *The Prehistory of European Society.* London: Penguin Books.

Clark, J. D., J. Beyene, G. Woldegabriel, W. K. Hart, P. R. Renne, H. Gilbert, A. Defleur, G. Suwa, S. Katoh, K. R. Ludwig, J. Boisserie, B. Asfaw & T. D. White, 2003. Stratigraphic, chronological and behavioural contexts of Pleistocene Homo sapiens from Middle Awash, Ethiopia. *Nature* **423**, 747–52.

Conkey, M., 1996. A history of the interpretation of European 'Palaeolithic art': magic, mythogram, and metaphors for modernity, in *Handbook of Human Symbolic Evolution*, eds. A. Lock & C.R, Peters. Oxford: Clarendon Press.

d'Errico, F. & P. Villa, 1997. Holes and grooves: the contribution of microscopy and taphonomy to the problem of art origins. *Journal of Human Evolution* **33**, 1–31.

d'Errico F., C. Henshilwood, G. Lawson, M. Vanhaeren, A.-M. Tillier, M. Soressi, F. Bresson, B. Maureille, A. Nowell, J. Lakarra, L. Backwell & M. Julien, 2003. Archaeological evidence for the emergence of language, symbolism and music – an alternative multidisciplinary perspective, *Journal of World Prehistory* **17**, 1–70.

d'Errico, F., C. Henshilwood, M. Vanhaeren & K. van Niekerk, 2005. *Nassarius kraussianus* shell beads from Blombos Cave: evidence for symbolic behaviour in the Middle Stone Age. *Journal of Human Evolution* **48**, 3–24.

Deacon, H. J., 1998. Modern human emergence: an African archaeological perspective. *The Archaeology Of Modern Human Origins: Dual Congress Proceedings, Colloquium 17.* Sun City: South Africa.

Donald, M., 1991. *Origins of the Modern Mind.* Cambridge (MA): Harvard University Press.

Donald, M., 1998. Hominid enculturation and cognitive evolution. In *Cognition and Material Culture: the Archaeology of Symbolic Storage*, eds. C. Renfrew & C. Scarre. Cambridge: McDonald Institute Monographs.

Durkheim, E., 1912. *The Elementary Forms of Religious Life*. New York: Free Press.

Foley, R. & M. M. Lahr, 1997. Mode 3 technologies and the evolution of modern humans. *Cambridge Archaeological Journal* 7, 3–36.

Foley, R. & M. M. Lahr, 2003. On stony ground: lithic technology, human evolution and the emergence of culture. *Evolutionary Anthropology* **12**, 109–22.

Gabora, L., 1997. The origin and evolution of culture and creativity. *Journal of Memetics – Evolutionary Models of Information Transmission*, **1**.

Gabora, L., 2001. *Cognitive Mechanisms Underlying the Origin and Evolution of Culture*. Ph.D. thesis. Center Leo Apostel For Interdisciplinary Studies, Vrije Universiteit Brussels, Brussels, Belgium.

Gamble, C., 1999. *The Palaeolithic Societies of Europe*. Cambridge: Cambridge University Press.

Gibson, K., 1996. The biocultural human brain, in *Modelling The Early Human Mind*, eds. P. Mellars & K. Gibson. Cambridge: McDonald Institute Monographs, 33–46.

Haddon, A. C., 1934. *History of Anthropology*. London: Watts & Co.

Hamer, D., 2004. *The God Gene: How Faith Is Hard-Wired Into Our Genes*. London: Doubleday.

Henshilwood, C. S. & C. W. Marean, 2003. The origin of modern human behaviour: a review and critique of models and test implications. *Current Anthropology* **44** (5): 627–51.

Henshilwood, C. S., F. d'Errico, R. Yates, Z. Jacobs, C. Tribolo, G. A. T. Duller, N. Mercier, J. C. Sealy, H. Valladas, I. Watts, & A. G. Wintle, 2002. Emergence of modern human behaviour: Middle Stone Age engravings from South Africa. *Science* **295**, 1278–80.

Henshilwood, C. S., F. d'Errico, M. Vanhaeren, K. Van Niekerk, & Z. Jacobs, 2004. Middle Stone Age shell beads from South Africa. *Science* **304**, 404.

Holloway, R. 1996. Evolution of the human brain, in *Handbook of Human Symbolic Evolution*, eds. A. Lock & C.R., Peters. Oxford: Clarendon Press.

Ingman, M., H. Kaessmann, S. Pääbo & U. Gyllensten, 2000. Mitochondrial genome variation and the origin of modern humans. *Nature* **408**, 708–13.

Insoll, T., 2004. *Archaeology, Ritual, Religion*. London: Routledge.

Jacobs, Z., A. G. Wintle, & G. A. T. Duller, 2003. Optical dating of dune sand from Blombos Cave, South Africa: I – multiple grain data. *Journal of Human Evolution* **44**, 599–612.

Jones, R. A., 1986. *Emile Durkheim: An Introduction to Four Major Works*. Beverly Hills (CA): Sage.

Kirkpatrick, L., 1999. Toward an evolutionary psychology of religion and personality. *Journal of Personality* **67**, 921–51.

Klein, R. G., 2000. Archaeology and the evolution of human behavior. *Evolutionary Anthropology* **9**, 17–36.

Lambek, M., 2002. *A Reader in the Anthropology of Religion.* Malden (MA): Blackwell.

Lewis-Williams, J. D., & T. A. Dowson, 1990. On Palaeolithic art and the neuropsychological model. *Current Anthropology* **31**, 407–8.

Lewis-Williams, J. D., & J. Clottes, 1998. *The shamans of prehistory: trance magic and the painted caves.* New York: Abrams

Lewis-Williams, J. D., & D. Pearce, 2004. *San spirituality: roots, expressions and social consequences.* Cape Town: Double Story.

Lindly, J. M. & G. A. Clark, 1990. Symbolism and modern human origins. *Current Anthropology* **31**, 233–61.

Lock, A. J., 2000. Phylogenetic time and symbol creation: where do ZOPEDS come from? *Culture and Psychology* **6**, 105–29.

McBrearty, S., & A. S. Brooks, 2000. The revolution that wasn't: a new interpretation of the origin of modern human behaviour. *Journal of Human Evolution* **38**, 453–563.

McClenon, J., 2001. *Wondrous Healing: Shamanism, Human Evolution, and the Origin of Religion.* DeKalb (IL): University of Northern Illinois Press.

Mellars, P., 1989. Major issues in the emergence of modern humans. *Current Anthropology* **30**, 349–85.

Mellars, P. A., 1973. The character of the Middle-Upper Palaeolithic transition in South-West France, in *The Explanation of Cultural Change*, ed. C. Renfrew. London: Duckworth, 255–76.

Mithen, S., 1996. *The Prehistory of the Mind.* London: Thames and Hudson.

Mithen, S., 1999. Symbolism and the supernatural, in *The Evolution of Culture*, eds. R. Dunbar, C. Knight & C. Power. Edinburgh: Edinburgh University Press, 147–69.

Noble, W., & I. Davidson, 1996. *Human Evolution, Language and Mind: A Psychological and Archaeological Enquiry.* Cambridge: Cambridge University Press.

Pinker S., 1997. *How The Mind Works.* New York: Norton.

Rappaport, R. A., 1999. *Ritual and Religion in the Making of Humanity.* Cambridge: Cambridge University Press.

Renfrew, C., 1996. The sapient behaviour paradox, in *Modelling the Early Human Mind*, eds. P. Mellars & K. Gibson. Cambridge: McDonald Institute Monographs, 11–14.

Richerson, P., & R. Boyd, 1998. The Pleistocene and the origins of human culture: built for speed. Paper Presented at *The 5$^{th}$ Biannual Symposium on the Science of Behaviour: Behaviour, Evolution and Culture.* February 23, 1998. University of Guadalajara, Mexico.

Sosis, R., & C. Alcorta, 2003. Signaling, solidarity, and the sacred: the evolution of religious behavior. *Evolutionary Anthropology* **12**, 264–74.

Sperber, D., 1994. The modularity of thought and the epidemiology of representation, in *Mapping the Mind: Domain Specificity in Cognition & Culture*, eds. L.A. Hirschfeld & S.A. Gelman. Cambridge: Cambridge University Press, 39–67.

Tomasello, M., 1999. *The Cultural Origins of Human Cognition*. Cambridge (MA): Harvard University Press.

White, T. D., B. Asfaw, D. Degusta, H. Gilbert, G. D. Richards, G. Suwa, & F. Clark Howell, 2003. Pleistocene Homo Sapiens from Middle Awash, Ethiopia. *Nature* **423**, 742–47.

Wilson, D. S., 2002. *Darwin's Cathedral: Evolution, Religion, and the Nature of Society*. Chicago: The University of Chicago Press.

Wurz, S., N. J. Le Roux, S. Gardner, & H. J. Deacon, 2003. Discriminating between the end products of the Earlier Middle Stone Age sub-stages at Klasies River using biplot methodology. *Journal of Archaeological Science* **30**, 1107–26.

Yellen, J. E., A. S. Brooks, E. Cornelissen, M. J. Mehlman, & K. Stewart, 1995. A Middle Stone Age worked bone industry from Katanda, Upper Semliki Valley, Zaire. *Science* **268**, 553–6.

4

# Neanderthal symbolic behaviour?

*Jane M. Renfrew*

Ever since the first remains of Neanderthals were discovered in 1856 in the Feldhofer cave in the Neander valley in Germany, they have suffered from a bad press. This was partly due to a reluctance to accept that modern humans might be descended from more primitive ancestors, after all these fossils were found some three years before Darwin published his *Origin of Species*, and partly due to the reconstruction by Marcellin Boule, from the French National Museum of Natural History, of the man from La Chapelle-aux-Saints, one of a series of fossil remains of Neanderthals found in the Dordogne region in the early years of last century. Boule misconstructed the skeleton so as to make the Neanderthal appear like a shuffling, hunch-backed ape. He described the Neanderthals as having a clumsy, muscular body and a heavy jawed skull which indicated a purely vegetative or bestial kind of mind. This he contrasted with the more elegant, Upper Palaeolithic Cro-Magnons' larger foreheads and the evidence for their material skills and artistic and religious preoccupations – indications of abstract thought. This attitude towards the Neanderthals has stuck firmly in the literature.

More finds and recent studies have given a much fuller picture of the Neanderthals (e.g. Mellars 1995; Stringer & Gamble 1993). It is now probably time to re-examine the evidence in a less prejudiced way in order to get a more accurate picture of the Neanderthals' contribution to the origins of symbolic behaviour. The evidence for their abilities for abstract thought, beyond the practicalities of everyday survival, may be summarised under three headings: human relationships, relationships with cave bears and evidence for artistic endeavour.

## Human relationships

Caring for severely disabled members of the community must be one of the indicators of respect for the individual and for human life. It is clear that Neanderthals fed and looked after severely handicapped members of their communities who were too disabled to contribute to the food quest. For example, the Shanidar 1 individual found in a cave in the Zagros Mts in Iraq had suffered from a withered right arm and shoulder probably from birth, his right ankle showed extensive arthritic degeneration, and he had received a severe blow to the left side of his face which was not fatal but would certainly have blinded his left eye. Without the support of his group he could not have survived to the age of forty (Klein 1989: 333). Another skeleton, La Quina 5, from SW France, also had a withered arm (Klein 1989: 334). The "old" man of La Chapelle-aux-Saints, aged 40–45, was also severely disabled. He had suffered from severe osteoarthritis in his mandible, spine, hip and foot, and had also lost most of his teeth (Klein 1989: 333). Other Neanderthal skeletons show injuries to their limbs: for example the original Neanderthal skeleton, and one from Krapina, Croatia, both had damaged ulnae which deformed their forearms; La Ferrassie 1 had a damaged femur, and the Shanidar 3 skeleton had arthritis in his ankle and foot (Klein 1989: 334) which must have made them both lame.

There is evidence for another interesting aspect of Neanderthal attitudes to life: study of two of the skulls found in the Shanidar cave, Shanidar 1 and 5, show signs that their heads had been bound and artificially distorted, probably with a flexible band worn for six to twelve months when they were very young, which made their heads flat in front and rounded behind. This Trinkhaus describes as showing "a sense of personal aesthetic" (Trinkhaus 1982: 198).

Another aspect of respect for the individual can be seen in the treatment of the dead. The Neanderthals were the earliest people in the archaeological record to have deliberately buried their dead. Some colleagues have questioned this (e.g. Gargett 1989: 157f: Stringer & Gamble 1993: 158), but in Western Europe the burials at La Chapelle aux Saints, La Ferrassie and Le Moustier can only be satisfactorily explained as being deliberate burials in pits (Mellars 1995: 375f). Some sites have produced a number of burials: at La Ferrassie there were at least seven, at Shanidar nine. The burials consist of largely intact flexed skeletons. At La Ferrassie the rock shelter seems to have served as a cemetery: it contained pits with skeletons of a man, woman (buried head to head), two children about five years old and two infants. There were also a number of hollows and mounds which did not contain any human bones. Burial no. 6 (of a child) was separated from the others and the fill of the pit was topped by a large triangular stone decorated on the underside with artificial cupmarks. The skull of the child lay at a distance from the rest of the skeleton (Constable 1973: 98). A similar burial to this was found in the Mezmaiskaya Cave, northern Caucasus, where twenty-four cranial fragments from a Neanderthal child aged one to two years were found in a pit covered by a limestone block (Pettitt 2002: 16).

The Shanidar finds consist of seven more or less complete adults deposited in the cave over a period of fifteen thousand years (Shanidar 1 and 5 from c. 45,000–50,000 years BP: Shanidar 4, 6–9 dating to 60,000 BP or earlier) together with the incomplete remains of two others (Shanidar 8 and 9) who were probably not deliberately buried.

A number of Middle Palaeolithic burials have been excavated in the Near East, especially in the Tabun, Skhūl and Kebara caves on Mount Carmel, near Haifa and at Qafzeh near Nazareth. They are interesting and enigmatic since the populations represented are of mixed morphologies although they are all associated with Mousterian tool industries. Dating techniques have shown that the more modern-looking skeletons from Skhūl and Qafzeh are in fact much older (at c. 100,000 BP) than the more typical Neanderthals from Tabun and Kebara (at c. 70,000 BP). The burial of a child, Qafzeh 11, was accompanied by the skull and antlers of a large deer (Stringer & Gamble 1993: 98). At the Skhūl cave the burial Skhūl 5 lay on his back with his head bent down on his chest and his legs tightly flexed and in his arms he was holding the jawbone of a large wild boar (Stringer & Gamble 1993: 97). These two special burials have been treated as Neanderthal in the literature but it is not now clear whether this is appropriate anymore (for a concise discussion of the position see Stringer and Gamble 1993: 104). At the very back of the Shanidar cave in Iraq Ralph Solecki found the grave of a Neanderthal, Shanidar 4, with a badly crushed skull. Subsequent examination of soil samples from the grave showed that the body had been laid on bedding of woody horsetail. The presence of clusters of pollen and parts of flowers including grape hyacinths, bachelor's buttons and hollyhocks suggested that flowers may have been put on the grave: it is too far inside the cave for the pollen to have blown in accidentally (Pfeiffer 1985: 153), although the fact that two of the members of the excavation team wore flowers in their sashes whilst excavating (Johanson & Edgar 2006) has prevented interpretations from being clear-cut.

Two flexed burials, of an adult male and an infant, were found in an artificially widened natural hollow in the floor in the lower layer at Kiik Koba in the Crimea. At Teshik Tash in Uzbekistan the grave of an eight- to ten-year-old boy was discovered surrounded by six pairs of Siberian mountain goat horn cores still attached to their frontlet bones (Stringer & Gamble 1993: 158) It seems that these pairs of horns had been driven into the ground around the body possibly for some sort of symbolic protection. Deliberate burials and funerals imply the belief that some essential quality of human existence – spirit or soul- cannot be destroyed and lives on in some form after death.

Much has been made of the fact that the Neanderthal burials have been found only in caves. It has even been suggested that carnivores at this time had changed their behaviour patterns away from using caves and rock shelters, and thus left the corpses undisturbed. Stringer and Gamble describe it as "corpse disposal" rather than burials (Stringer & Gamble 1993: 160).

Apart from deliberate burials there are indications of other treatments of the dead. At the Grotta Guittari, Monte Circeo, an upturned skull was found with a greatly enlarged foramen magnum, surrounded by a setting of stones (Constable 1973: 106). This individual had been killed by a blow to the head. Another example of the enlargement of the foramen magnum comes from a female skull found at Ehringsdorf, Germany (Constable 1973: 105). She, too, had met a violent death by repeated clubbing on the forehead. The enlargement of the foramen magnum is not a new Neanderthal phenomenon: the female skull from Steinheim, dated to the Mindel/Riss Interglacial about 250,000 years ago and probably belonging to Archaic *Homo sapiens* (*Homo heidelbergensis*), also showed signs of the forcible enlargement of the skull base, after the removal of the skull from the rest of the body. There is no evidence in this case that it was done by hyaenas or other non-human agency (Adam in Delson 1985: 275–6). It has been argued that the enlargement of the foramen magnum might as well have been done by hyenas as humans to extract the brain (Bahn in Jones et al. 1994: 330). It is interesting to note, however, that the extraction of the brain through an enlarged foramen magnum is exactly the technique used by contemporary head-hunters in New Guinea, who then cook it and eat it (Constable 1973 106).

Cut marks on the long bones of some of the mutilated remains of 20 Neanderthals found at Krapina, Croatia, indicate that they had been defleshed after death: the fact that some of the bones had been split and crushed and others showed signs of burning have suggested that they might have been cooked (Bahn op. cit. 330; Constable 1973: 104). Recent finds from the excavations at Moula-Guercy, Ardèche (level XV), by Alban Defleur, of six Neanderthals: two adults, two teenagers and two children, about one hundred thousand years old, show clear evidence of cannibalism (Defleur 1999). Careful study of tool marks and fractures of their bones reveal that the cheek muscles of children were filleted out, tendons were sliced and skulls were cracked open to remove the brains. Other cut marks show that thigh muscles were removed and in at least one case the tongue had been cut out. All the skulls and limb bones were broken apart and only the bones of hands and feet remained intact. None of the bones show any signs of having been gnawed by wild animals nor are there any signs of charring, suggesting that the meat was eaten either raw or cooked off the bone. Cut marks on Neanderthal bones from Engis, Belgium; Marillac and Combe Grenal, France may also represent to defleshing (Pettitt 2002: 12).

Contemporary peoples who eat their fellow humans rarely do so out of sheer hunger, but for ritualistic reasons: either to derive strength from the departed or to prevent their ghosts from haunting them.

In one or two cases Neanderthal skulls have been found without the rest of their skeletons – for example, the child's skull from the Rock of Gibraltar, and the woman's skull from Ehringsdorf – and this has led some authors into thinking that the Neanderthals may have had some sort of skull cult whilst others have suggested that they may have become detached from the rest of their skeletons by natural causes such as the activities of hyenas (Constable 1973: 105). It is clear that the Neanderthals' treatment of their dead was varied, complex and multidimensional.

## Relationships with cave bears

Perhaps the most controversial aspect of possible symbolic behaviour of the Neanderthals is in their reported treatment of cave bear skulls and occasional long bones. The reputed collection and storage of these bones in box-like constructions of stone has been doubted most notably by the Swiss palaeontologist F. E. Koby who claimed that natural roof-falls could have led to the apparent formation of these structures which happened to enclose cave bear skulls that were lying on the cave floor quite naturally. Nonetheless it is worth revisiting the evidence which comes chiefly from three sites: the Věternica cave, Croatia, the Régourdou cave in France and the cave at Drachenloch in the Swiss Alps. In the Věternica cave a stone recess contained a bear skull and femur in a middle Palaeolithic layer. The recess was then blocked off with large stones set one above another (Jelinek 1989: 47). At Régourdou two stone boxlike constructions had been made in the cave, capped by large stones-one weighing nearly a ton (Jelinek 1989: 47). Here a rectangular pit contained the bones, mainly skulls, of more than twenty cave bears, the other contained a complete cave bear skeleton (except for the skull) (Pfeiffer 1985: 150). Another pit contained a Neanderthal burial with a cave bear humerus bone. The Drachenloch cave, at a height of eight thousand feet in the Swiss Alps, to the south of Lake Constance, was excavated by Emile Bächler between 1917 and 1923. The front part of the cave was occupied by Neanderthals, and a hearth between the second and third sections of the chamber has yielded a carbon 14 date of more than 50,000 B.P. Further back in the cave Bächler found a cubical stone chest, something over a metre square, containing seven bear skulls with their muzzles facing the cave entrance, topped by a capstone. At the back of the cave six bear skulls were found set in niches along the walls, some with limb bones, not necessarily from the same bear. One of the skulls of a three year old bear had a femur of a younger bear thrust through its zygomatic arch, which could not have happened naturally, and it rested on long bones from two other animals (Coles & Higgs 1969: 256–7; Constable 1973: 108–9). It is a great misfortune that Bächler did not record his finds more systematically or give clear plans and sections of the stone chest in which the cave bear skulls were found. Another interesting find from Bruniquel in France where Mark Berkowitz reported a structure made from broken stalactites and stalagmites several hundred metres inside the cave, which contained a burnt bear bone dated to 47,600 BP (Berkowitz 1996: 22). There are a number of other sites in Switzerland, France and Germany where cave bear skulls and bones and Mousterian tools have been found together. In the Petershöhle near Velden, Central Franconia, Germany, for example, Dr Hormann found bears' skulls carefully deposited in holes and niches in the cave wall. In one instance, five bear skulls, two femurs and a humerus were found in a recess some four feet above the cave floor: it is difficult to see how they could have got there by natural means.

These stone built chests and niches in cave walls filled with cave bear bones were not merely hunting trophies. A related find suggestive of hunting magic comes from the Basua Cave (Cave of Witches), near Genoa, Italy. Here, some fifteen hundred feet from the entrance, Neanderthal hunters threw clay pellets at a stalagmite with a vaguely animal shape. The fact that they went so far into the cave suggests that this was more than just target practice or some sort of children's hunting game (Constable 1973: 108).

No doubt Neanderthals and cave bears were in competition for the shelter of caves at the onset of the last glaciation. Cave bears were ferocious creatures, larger than grizzly bears, and an unlikely choice for food when easier prey was available, but possibly prized for their skins to make warm clothing.

These special repositories of bones may well represent some form of bear ritual as is practised today in some northern areas from North American Indians to the Lapps to the Ainu of northern Japan. In some places bears are regarded as mythical first men, and in others as intermediaries between man and the spirits of the land (Ainu bear sacrifice is well described in Coon 1972: 340–4). The cave bear became extinct during the Würm glaciation.

A related find – but not of a cave bear – was made by Ralph Solecki in 1970 at Nahr Ibrahim near Beirut, Lebanon. Here he found the dismembered skeleton of a fallow deer, *Dama mesopotamica*, laid out on a bed of stones and sprinkled with red ochre (Campbell & Loy 1996; 440f). It is interesting that the bears depicted in Upper Palaeolithic cave art appear to be brown bears rather than cave bears, and there does not seem to have been the same collection of bears' skulls in special structures within the caves.

### Artistic activities; use of pigments

The use of pigments has a venerable antiquity in Europe going back at least to three hundred thousand years ago, for example at Terra Amata, Nice, France where seventy-five lumps of pigment from yellow to brown, red and purple were found mainly showing signs of abrasion. They must have been introduced to the site as they do not occur locally (Bahn & Vertut 1997: 24). It is thus not surprising to find that Neanderthals also collected lumps and crayons of ochre, manganese dioxide and iron oxide. For example in a single layer in the cave at Pech de L'Azé 1 there were 218 blocks of manganese dioxide (yielding a blue/black colour), and 23 pieces of iron oxide (red) (Bahn 1997: 26). In fact Mellars reports that fragments of ochre have been found in Neanderthal contexts in at least a dozen sites in SW France and manganese oxide is even more common (Mellars 1996: 370).

What were these materials being used for? The burial of a Neanderthal skeleton at Le Moustier was sprinkled with red powder, and red pigment was found round the head of the man buried at La Chapelle-aux-Saints. Two Neanderthal skeletons from Qafzeh, Israel had seventy-one fragments of ochre alongside their bones. The dismembered fallow deer at Nahr Ibrahim, Lebanon, was also sprinkled with red ochre (Solecki 1982: 47f). Apart from these documented examples we are left only with speculations. These were the same substances that were used in the Upper Palaeolithic to decorate cave walls, but so far we have no examples of Middle Palaeolithic cave art. They may well have been used to decorate the bodies of the living or to decorate animal skins and tools but so far we have no evidence.

## Decorated bones and stones

There have been a number of finds of animal bones from Neanderthal contexts with incised lines which have been claimed as having been decorated – for example in the Prolom II cave in the Crimea a large series of decorated bones included a horse canine with five parallel engraved lines and a saiga phalange with a fan-like engraved motif. La Quina yielded a bovid shoulder blade engraved with very fine parallel lines. Notched bones are known from La Ferrassie and the Cueva Morin in Spain whilst the Bulgarian cave of Bacho Kiro yielded a bone decorated with a zigzag motif and dated to 47,000 BP (Bahn & Vertut 1997: 25) A bone from Pech de l'Azé II had a similar zigzag motif (Stringer & Gamble 1993: 160). Whilst some of these marks may be the result of butchery (Chase 1991: 210), others may be decorative. Since they are abstract patterns they may appear meaningless to us although the marks may have had great significance to those who made them. Stringer and Gamble (1993: 160) claim that "they most probably lacked any symbolic rationale", but how can we tell?

The finds of decorated stones are equally enigmatic. The nummulite fossil from Tata in Hungary has a finely incised line running at 90 degrees to a natural crack to form a regular symmetrical cross (Mellars 1996: 374). A flint cortex from Quneitra, Israel, some 54,000 years old, is engraved with four concentric semi-circles carefully incised on its surface (Bahn & Vertut 1997: 25). A recent find of a large flint nodule in the likeness of a human face with a bone rammed through a natural hole and wedged in position with two small pebbles making it look as if it has two eyes was reported by Marquet and Lorblanchet in *Antiquity* (December 2003). It was found on the banks of the Loire at La Roche-Cotard and dates to 35,000 BP. It is a unique find quite unlike anything else from this period.

## Perforated bones and teeth

Some of the perforated bones found associated with Neanderthal deposits have been dismissed as the results of natural damage or carnivore gnawing: for example the perforated bone from Pech de l'Azé II and the perforated reindeer phalange from La Quina (Mellars 1996: 374f). The perforated teeth of a fox from La Quina, a wolf incisor from Repolusthöhle and the swan's vertebrae and wolf metapodial from Bocksteinschmeide, Germany are not so easily dismissed (Mellars 1996: 375). At the Grotte de Renne, Arcy-sur-Cure a collection of 36 personal ornaments of different kinds – perforated animal teeth, ivory beads and bones with perforations or grooves for suspension were found associated with a juvenile temporal bone of a Neanderthal child dating back 45,000 BP, and Châtelperronian stone tools. João Zilhão, Francesco d'Errico and colleagues claim that these represent an "independent development, not the product of trade, acculturation or imitation precipitated by cultural contact with modern humans" migrating into western Europe (Zilhão 2000: 30).

The find of a femur of a young cave bear with four perforations all in a row at Divje babe I in the Idrijca valley, Western Slovenia has been claimed to be a flute. The question has been raised as to whether the holes were made by the teeth of a carnivore or the pointed stone tools used by humans. Marcel Otte writing in *Current Anthropology*

(Vol. 41, No. 2, April 2000) says "The idea of Mousterian ineptitude is one of the deepest and one of the most perverse because it reassures us about ourselves. The destiny of the Mousterian flute discovered at Divje babe was preordained: it could be only disputable and doubtful *a priori*." So the evidence for personal decoration in the form of pendants and of musical instruments in the form of bone flutes and whistles is at best slight and at worst not accepted.

## Conclusions

This paper sets out some of the evidence which is currently available to the nonspecialist in Neanderthal studies that may be examined to indicate whether or not Neanderthals were capable of abstract thought and symbolic behaviour. Their human relations and values, their relationship with cave bears and other animals and their admittedly modest artistic activities do seem to indicate that they were capable of symbolic behaviour beyond the struggle for everyday survival. They seem to have been consistently underestimated and maligned since their first discovery in 1856. As Stringer and Gamble rightly say, "No other group of prehistoric peoples carries such a weight of scientific and popular preconceptions or has its name so associated with deep antiquity and lingering taints of savagery, stupidity and animal strength" (1993: 26). It is surely time that Neanderthals were given credit for some of their pioneering abstract thoughts.

**BIBLIOGRAPHY**

Adam K. D., 1985. The chronological and systematic position of the Steinheim skull, in *Ancestors: The Hard Evidence*, ed. E. Delson. New York: Alan R. Liss.

Bahn P. G., & J. Vertut, 1997. *Journey through the Ice Age*. London: Weidenfeld and Nicholson.

Berkowitz M., 1996. Neanderthal news. *Archaeology* **40**, 22.

Campbell B. G., & J. D. Loy, 1996. *Humankind Emerging*. New York: Harper Collins.

Chase P. G., 1991. Symbols and Palaeolithic artefacts: style, standardization and the imposition of arbitrary form. *Journal of Anthropological Archaeology* **10**, 193–214.

Coles J. M., & E. S. Higgs, 1969. *The Archaeology of Early Man*. New York: Frederick A. Praeger.

Constable G., 1973. *The Neanderthals* (consultant editor Ralph Solecki). Nederland: Time Life International B.V..

Coon C. S., 1972. *The Hunting Peoples.* London: Jonathan Cape.

Defleur, A. 1999. Neanderthal cannibalism at Moula-Guercy, Ardèche, France. *Science* **286** (5437), 128–31.

Gargett R. H., 1989. Grave shortcomings: the evidence for Neanderthal burial. *Current Anthropology* **30**, 157–90.

Jelinek J., 1989. *Primitive Hunters: A Search for Man the Hunter.* London: Hamlyn.

Johansen, D. & Edgar, B., 2006. *From Lucy to Language* (2nd Ed.). New York: Simon and Schuster.

Jones S., R. Martin & D. Pilbeam, 1994. *The Cambridge Encyclopedia of Human Evolution.* Cambridge: Cambridge University Press.

Klein R. H., 1989. *The Human Career.* Chicago: University of Chicago Press.

Marquet J. C., & M. Lorblanchet M., 2003. A Neanderthal face? The proto figurine from the Rock-Cotard, Langeais (Indre-and-Loire, France). *Antiquity* **77**, 661–70.

Mellars P., 1996. *The Neanderthal Legacy: An Archaeological Perspective from Western Europe.* Princeton: Princeton University Press.

Pettitt, P. B., 2002. The Neanderthal dead: exploring mortuary variability in Middle Palaeolithic Eurasia. *Before Farming* **1**, 1–26.

Pfeiffer J. E., 1985. *The Emergence of Humankind* (4th ed.). New York: Harper and Row.

Solecki R. S., 1982. A ritual Middle Palaeolithic deer burial at Nahr Ibrahim Cave, Lebanon. *Archéologie au Levant: Recueil a la mémoire de Roger Saidah.* Lyon: Maison de l'Orient, 47–56.

Stringer C., & C. Gamble, 1993. *In Search of the Neanderthals.* London: Thames and Hudson.

Trinkaus E., 1982. Artificial cranial deformation of the Shanidar 1 and 5 Neanderthals *Current Anthropology* **23**, 198–199.

Zilhão J., 2000. Fate of the Neandertals. *Archaeology* **53**, 25–31.

5

# Identifying ancient religious thought and iconography: problems of definition, preservation, and interpretation

*Paul S. C. Taçon*

## Origins

When did religious ideas first register in the minds of early humans? When did ideologically motivated depiction and other forms of art emerge? Do changes in art and material culture among ancient peoples reflect changes in religious thinking or orientation? How do we detect the earliest evidence or roots of human religious expression? And how do we avoid the trap of reading our own ways of thinking into the enigmatic records of the past? These are challenging questions that go right to the heart of any discussion concerning the origin of religion. They are also fundamental if we are ever to know how religion became such a dominant force the world over.

There are both broad and specific definitions of religion, with many people emphasising differences between the major organised world religions and various shamanistic, totemic, animistic and other beliefs held by various indigenous peoples past and present. This is not the place to review all of these (e.g. see Lessa and Vogt 1958). One of the more succinct but inclusive definitions of religion has been provided by Haviland (1989: 511):

> Religion may be regarded as the beliefs and patterns of behavior by which humans try to deal with what they view as important problems that cannot be solved through the application of known technology or techniques of organization. To overcome these limitations, people turn to the manipulation of supernatural beings and powers.
>
> Religion consists of various rituals – prayers, songs, dances, offerings, and sacrifices – through which people try to manipulate supernatural

beings and powers to their advantage. These beings and powers may consist of gods and goddesses, ancestral and other spirits, or impersonal powers, either by themselves or in various combinations. In all societies there are certain individuals especially skilled at dealing with these beings and powers, who assist other members of society in their ritual activities. A body of myths rationalizes or "explains" the system in a manner consistent with people's experience in the world in which they live.

Perhaps religion is a natural phenomenon. Once a certain amount of intelligence is attained, creatures question their being. In order to survive better they need to place their experience in a much wider universe. But once this universe is sought it needs to be explained. Thus religion is born – through insight, revelation, contemplation and self-reflection. But this is not enough, for in order to truly understand and to believe, religious ideas need to be shared and reaffirmed – transmitted across time and space to others but also reinforced through repetitive, out of the ordinary, action. Religious art and ritual was born to aid this process, reaffirming ideas but also conveying complexity in ways that are more easily managed. Visual symbols were also invented, as a form of short-hand and for restricted knowledge. Ultimately, the use of symbols made social statements about status and power. Rappaport (1999) argues religion is the inevitable consequence of language acquisition but perhaps it was the other way around. Others suggest religious experience is a consequence of the hard wiring of our brains (e.g. see Holmes 2001 for a review). Whatever the case, it appears a certain amount of evolutionary development – biological, cultural and social – was necessary for humans to be capable of religious experience.

There are many definitions of what it is to be human. Certainly we are one of the few creatures that can contemplate our own predicament of existence. Using our minds, we can reflect on experience and interpret the larger universe with a range of intellectual tools of religious and scientific natures. Also unlike other creatures, the gods and universal forces we define, think about and describe can be given material form – through drawing, painting, sculpting and, today, a range of multi-media techniques. Symbol transposed into and combined with other imagery is a very powerful form of communication but usually there is structure, grammar and coding (e.g. see Sauvet and Wlodarczyk 1995). Of course, imagery has also long been used to communicate a vast array of messages, never being restricted to the purely religious. One of the challenges is to find a way to better identify the truly religious and to separate this from design and imagery that resulted from other motivations and experiences. Other forms of archaeological evidence also need better evaluation.

## Early Surviving Evidence

### PIGMENT AND IMAGES

For at least 32,000 years humans have been highly productive and creative artistic beings, given the many accomplished works of parietal and portable imagery surviving across Western Europe and Siberia (e.g. see Bahn and Vertut 1997; Clottes 1998; Clottes et al. 1995; Hahn 1971). In Eastern Europe and much of Asia non-figurative art designs were also made for many tens of thousands of years (e.g. see Bednarik 2003). In Australia, used ochre is found throughout most levels of rock shelter excavations and is associated with the lowest levels of many of the continent's oldest dated sites (see Allen and O'Connell 2003; Taçon 1999). In South Africa, Henshilwood et al. (2002, 2004) found evidence for modern art behaviour at about seventy seven thousand years, in the form of shell beads and shaped pieces of red ochre incised with engraved cross-hatch designs. Are these the earliest surviving abstract symbols? Were they purely decorative in function or did they represent some spiritual idea or experience?

To help answer these questions, we need to further explore the global roots of art activity (Bednarik 2003). Recent evidence suggests pigment has been used to create colourful designs on bodies, if not objects or rock-shelter walls, for at least three hundred thousand years (Taçon 2003a). In parts of Zambia, India and even Europe archaeo- logical sites containing vast quantities of imported pigment – haematite, limonite, manganese dioxide and other substances – have been exca- vated and dated to between two hundred thousand and three hundred thousand years ago (e.g. see Barham 2002; Bednarik 1990; McBrearty and Brooks 2000; Mellars 1996; Taçon 2003a). In Africa, for instance, Barham (2002) found Middle Pleistocene hominids were using a range of mineral pigments from different parts of the landscape on a grand scale. He concluded 'Central and East African hominids had incorpo- rated colour into their lives by 270,000 years ago, and this addition to their behavioural repertoire would remain a feature of the African archaeological record until the historical present' (2002: 188–9). In

Europe, Neanderthals were also using manganese and red ochre since three hundred thousand years ago (Barham 2002: 188–9; McBrearty & Brooks 2000; Mellars 1996) while *Homo erectus* in India left used pieces of ochre, some with striations, at sites dated to two hundred thousand to three hundred thousand years ago (Bednarik 1990; Petraglia pers. comm. 2004).

This widespread pigment evidence, along with scattered instances of extremely ancient cupules, engraved stone tools, enhanced manuports, crystal collections and highly aesthetic handaxes (Figure 5.1, and e.g. see Bednarik 2003; Oakley 1972, 1981) suggests that it was during the Acheulean that art activity first blossomed. It soon went on to become an integral part of people's lives. Some of this activity would have been related to expressing individual and group identity, thus self-awareness and group awareness must have been important during the Acheulian. Whether the use of pigment was independently invented in widely separated places or stems from a single source, rapidly transmitted through culture contact

**5.1.** A symmetrical handaxe from Sterkfontein, South Africa, over seven hundred thousand years old. Handaxes may have had symbolic as well as practical significance. (Photo: P.S.C. Taçon)

and trade, we may never know. We may also never know if pigment was used as early as three hundred thousand years ago to express religious thinking. The evidence neither supports nor refutes such a hypothesis although, among peoples known ethnographically, ochre use is invariably associated with ritual. Thus, it does provide the possibility that religious expression *could* have occurred among archaic humans since at least three hundred thousand years ago. But is there other archaeological evidence to support such an early start to the expression of belief?

## BURIALS

There are many known forms of disposal or burial of the dead but the common element is that bodies were in some way ritually and/or habitually prepared, adorned, augmented or purposely placed, sometimes with material culture. In other words, they were not randomly dropped, left behind or otherwise discarded. And they were not disposed of from a purely practical, clinical, nutritional or sanitary point of view. Defleshing is practiced among some cultures as part of ritual burial practice and this is something that can be archaeologically visible. The oldest example, from Sterkfontein 5 in South Africa, is dated to 1.5 million years ago. Clear cut marks associated with defleshing are visible on the remains of a *Homo habilis* individual, STW53 (Pickering et al. 2000). There are other more recent examples (e.g. the Middle Pleistocene Bodo cranium) but the problem is that the marks on the bones may have resulted from cannibalism rather than burial practice. However, among recent modern humans cannibalism was rarely purely nutritional in nature. Instead, it more often was heavily ritualistic with formalised cultural elements.

It is not until about 320,000 years ago that more concrete evidence of the ritualised treatment of the dead emerges. For instance, at Atapuerca in Spain, it has long been argued that the 'Pit of Bones', resulting from *Homo heidelbergensis* bodies being purposely dropped down a deep shaft, is evidence of ritual burial. Almost three dozen skeletons have been dated to between 320,000 to 200,000 years ago (Bischoff et al. 1997). However, it was only recently that more conclusive evidence was found, in the form of a stone axe head placed among some of the oldest bones. Although the axe has sparked controversy and debate, Henry de Lumley, director of France's National Museum of Natural History, has declared the discovery is "proof of the birth of the first human myths" (see Tremlett 2003; De Lumley, this volume). Clark et al. (2003) claim anatomically modern human remains from Middle Awash, Ethiopia, recently dated to between 154,000–160,000 years ago (White et al. 2003), were ritually prepared. They note three crania "all bear cultural modification indicative of mortuary practice". Furthermore, they conclude "Polishing and intentional scraping modifications evident on two of these crania indicate that the Upper Herto hominids may have manipulated the crania of their dead in mortuary practices whose dimensions, context and meaning might be revealed only by further discoveries" (Clark et al. 2003: 751).

Pettit (2002: 2), on the other hand, suggests "The archaic skeleton of Skhûl 9 may be the oldest burial known as yet (Stringer 1998) although it is conceivable that the Tabun C1 Neanderthal is as old as 120 kys BP (e.g, McDermott et al 1993; Grün et al 1991)." At Qafzeh, in the Levant, there are at least four deliberate burials, one with possible grave goods. They have been confidently dated to between 90,000 and 120,000 years ago, using a range of techniques (Bar-Yosef 1998; McBrearty & Brooks 2000: 519; Vandermeersch 1981). Certainly, the Neanderthal were practicing ritualised burial on a regular basis since at least seventy thousand years ago:

> In the later Middle Pleistocene Neanderthals may have been caching the dead in unmodified natural surroundings. After 70 ka BP some Neanderthal groups buried infants, or parts of them, in pits, infants and adults in shallow grave cuttings and indulged in primary corpse modification and subsequent burial. It may have been on occasion too that certain enclosed sites served as mortuary centres, and that their function as such was perpetuated in the memory of Neanderthal groups either through physical grave markers or social tradition. In all it would seem that at least in some Neanderthal groups the dead body was explored and treated in socially meaningful ways. (Pettitt 2002: 1)

Significantly, in Australia both cremation and burial with ochre were practiced at least forty three thousand years ago (Bowler et al. 2003), and possibly as much as sixty five thousand years ago (Thorne et al. 1999). This suggests some forms of religious belief were well established, and that they had expression in fire, ochre and soil, in Asia before the arrival of humans in Australia. In other words, an organised religious and symbolic belief system was part of the cultural baggage the first immigrants to Australia brought with them.

## Therianthropes/Composite Creatures

What might we recognise as the oldest forms of depiction that reflect religious ideas, thinking or belief? Would it be abstract designs or figurative images? Perhaps the very act of creating images, representations, designs and so forth is reflective of a religious outlook in that it can involve belief, creativity, symbol-making, ritual and so forth. In terms of the old art of Europe, Ucko and Rosenfeld (1967) conclude that there likely were many motivations behind the production of Palaeolithic art. However, they suggest "some were used in acts of sympathetic magic (perhaps some of the representations pierced with holes)...and that some were illustrations of myths and traditions (perhaps those which contain imaginary creatures, anthropomorphs and unexpected combinations of animal species)" (1967: 239).

For the Aboriginal people of western Arnhem Land (Northern Territory, Australia), depictions of composite creatures, although relatively rare, are the most easily identifiable and most significant forms of old and recent rock-art that encode religious ideas. In most cases, they represent important Ancestral Beings associated with the Creation Era of the 'Dreamtime' and their composite 'unnatural' character makes them particularly potent as religious iconography (see Taçon & Chippindale 2001). These culture heroes "defined, shaped and transformed the world before and during the time of the First People" (Taçon & Chippindale 2001: 200). It is these images in Australian rock-art (including Dynamic Figures at least ten thousand and possibly as much as eighteen thousand years of age; Plates VI and VII) more than any other that can be identified, with a high degree of confidence, as being deeply religious in intent.

For instance, in May 2003 the Indigenous reaction to an important rock-art discovery made in Wollemi National Park, within the Blue Mountains World Heritage Area of New South Wales (Taçon 2003b; Taçon et al. 2003) was particularly revealing in the context of identifying religious iconography. The site, now known as Eagle's Reach, contains over two hundred drawings and stencils. There are a number of Ancestral Beings depicted, including one distorted creature identified as Daramulan, one of the more significant Creation Beings of southeast Australia. An incredible Eagle ancestor 'holding' a boomerang and hafted stone axe is featured (Plate VIII). There are also dozens of part animal/part human creatures, with either bird-like or macropod-like heads. Although the site was 'lost' to Aboriginal cosmology for perhaps 150 years, when Wiradjeri, Darug and Darkinjung elders saw photographs of the images, on separate occasions, they each arrived at the same conclusion – that this site was used to tell stories of creation. Indeed, all elders said important Ancestral Beings of the region were depicted. The images told of how life came into being, how some creatures were transformed from human to animal or vice versa, and the laws or rules of conduct humans were given to uphold.

Although it can be argued that the Aboriginal people associated with the site have had their cultures radically changed by over two hundred years of contact with European society it is interesting to note how consistent interpretations were with each other. They were also consistent with the scant early ethnographic record of southeast Australia and with the detailed ethnographic record of other parts of Australia. This suggests that the composite creatures, animals with artefacts and distorted figures provoke a common religious-oriented response among Australian Aboriginal people. But as was found in a larger study of therianthropes and composite creatures (Taçon & Chippindale 2001), prior to the Eagle's Reach discovery, this sort of response is much more universal. In a global survey of composite and other unusual creations six types of supernatural creature were identified in world oral history, art and literature, as well as Australian rock-art (Taçon & Chippindale 2001: 176–9). These are (a) animal-human combinations (Plates VI and VII); (b) composite animals (Plates IX and X); (c) double-headed animals (Plate XI); (d) creatures with different animal body parts; (e) animals with artefacts (Plates VIII and XII); and (f) distorted-deformed human-like creatures. It was also found that humans past and present the world over have used such imagery in similar ways – to illustrate, tell stories about and represent other forms of reality, religious belief and what Westerners more generally call the supernatural:

> Animal-headed beings also denote another world, another dimension of time and space that humans can sometimes tap into, through trance, ritual, ingestion of certain drugs or in other special contexts. Composite creature can be guides, messengers, helpers, friends, ancestors, gods, fools, villains, enemies, beings of great evil, symbols of the greater good. In a clinical, scientific sense they are symbols and tools used for teaching history, laws, lessons, norms of conduct and the rules of society. But they are also creatures of the Dreamtime – not the Australian Aboriginal

Dreamtime but the Dreamtime of humanity, that rich ancestral world of times long ago that every so often penetrates the present to provide insight and other-world experience. (Taçon & Chippindale 2001: 176)

The earliest surviving depictions of these creatures are indicative of the minimum age of this widespread expression of religious thinking. One of the most reliably dated of these is a portable piece, the human-feline Hohlenstein-Stadel statuette, about thirty-two thousand years of age (see Bahn & Vertut 1997: 100–1; Hahn 1971; De Lumley, this volume). However, a second human-feline carved figure has recently been reported from Hohle Fels Cave, not far from the earlier find. This much smaller piece, along with associated carvings of a water bird and probable horse head, is of comparable age and possibly a bit older (Conard 2003). The conclusion to be drawn is that this fundamental expression of religious thought, the existence of powerful supernatural creatures, has been a part of humanity for as long as the oldest surviving rock-art figurative pictures, also thirty-two thousand years, suggesting this global human belief has much more ancient origins.

## Conclusion

It is clear that the roots of both art and religion are very deep, extending back probably to at least three hundred thousand or more years ago. The earliest surviving evidence found to date consists primarily of used pieces of pigment – mainly red ochre or haematite but also limonite, manganese, and specularite – along with a range of purposely selected or fashioned stone. The evidence is widespread, from Africa, Asia and Europe. This suggests similar cultural pursuits among different types of archaic humans, spanning the evolutionary transition from various archaic *Homo* species to what we define as modern *Homo sapiens*. However, it is only from the past 160,000 years that clear-cut signs of religious thinking have survived, with purposeful human burial in several parts of the world, including cremation and with red ochre by forty-three thousand to sixty-five thousand years ago in Australia. The oldest surviving reliably dated form of abstract portable 'art' is about seventy-seven thousand years of age (Africa) while the oldest surviving religiously motivated figurative imagery we can recognise with confidence is dated to more than thirty-two thousand years ago (Europe).

Most of the early evidence of religion is associated with behaviourally, physically and cognitively modern humans but the early use of pigment and other potentially symbolic substances (e.g. quartz, fossils, colourful stone, manuports) was widespread among archaic humans. Furthermore, there is much definitive evidence Neanderthals practiced various forms of burial, and possibly figurative sculpture (e.g. Marquet & Lorblanchet 2003). What all of this suggests is that in many ways human ancestors have been behaviourally modern much longer than has generally been accepted and that it is probable *Homo erectus*, *Homo ergaster* and *Homo neanderthalensis* all questioned their position in the universe. As to which had divine insight or intervention is still a matter of debate but the religiously and scientifically inspired 'story' of Adam and Eve arising in a garden of Eden somewhere in Africa holds much weight among many scientists (e.g. see Shipman 2003).

My own view is that the world was changed forever by the increased contacts and interactions that occurred among archaic humans across Africa, Asia, and Europe, since at least 160,000 years ago. Further periods of intense migration and contact followed, one of them occurring between fifty thousand and thirty thousand years ago. These contacts would have radically changed group worldviews, regardless of their nature. Whether populations were replaced by invaders 'out of Africa', different groups interbred and/or there was an exchange of ideas, material culture and technology, the result of contact for all inevitably would have been a changed view of the world and one's place in it. Perhaps in those moments that followed revelation occurred and religious thinking as we know it began to blossom and take hold.

## Acknowledgements

I would like to sincerely thank the many Australian Aboriginal traditional owners and custodians of the various parts of Australia I have worked in for their generosity, patience, hospitality, permission to undertake field research and the time they took to teach me so much about art, belief, land and life. In particular, elders past and present of the Arrente, Darkingjung, Darug, Gagudju, Gundjebmi, Gurig, Jawoyn, Kunwinjku, Waanyi, and Wiradjuri communities are gratefully acknowledged for sharing their wisdom.

The Templeton Foundation is thanked for inviting me to present an earlier version of this paper at a symposium held at Les Eyzies, France, on

14–16 May 2004 and for funding my participation. I am especially grateful to Mary Ann Meyers for organising things for me and inviting me to submit this revised paper for publication.

Kirk Huffman, David Lewis-Williams, Mike Smith, and Alan Thorne are thanked for comments that improved this paper. Christopher Chippindale is thanked for many insights since we began working together in 1990. The Australian Museum has supported much of my research referred to in this paper, including work with Christopher Chippindale in Kakadu/Arnhem Land and Wayne Brennan, Shaun Hooper, Dave Pross, and Evan Yanna Muru in Wollemi National Park, NSW.

**REFERENCES**

Allen, J., & J. F. O'Connell, 2003. The long and the short of it: archaeological approaches to determining when humans first colonised Australia and New Guinea. *Australian Archaeology* **57**, 5–19.

Bahn, P. G., & J. Vertut, 1997. *Journey through the Ice Age*. London: Weidenfeld and Nicolson.

Bar-Yosef, O., 1998. On the nature of transitions: the Middle to Upper Palaeolithic and the Neolithic revolution. *Cambridge Archaeological Journal* **8**, 141–63.

Barham, L. S., 2002. Systematic pigment use in the Middle Pleistocene of South-Central Africa. *Current Anthropology* **43**, 181–90.

Bednarik, R., 1990. An Acheulian haematite pebble with striations. *Rock Art Research* **7**, 75.

Bednarik, R., 2003. The earliest evidence of palaeoart. *Rock Art Research*  **20**, 89–135.

Bischoff, J. L., J. A. Fitzpatrick, L. Léon, J. L. Arsuaga, C. Falgueres, J. J. Bahain, & T. Bullen, 1997. Geology and preliminary dating of the hominid-bearing sedimentary fill at Sima de los Huescos Chamber, Cueva Mayor of the Sierra de Atapuerca, Burgos, Spain. *Journal of Human Evolution* **33**, 129–54.

Bowler, J. M., H. Johnston, J. M. Olley, J. R. Prescott, R. G. Roberts, W. Shawcross, & N.A. Spooner, 2003. New ages for human occupation and climatic change at Lake Mungo, Australia. *Nature* **421**, 837–40.

Clark, J. D., Y. Beyene, G. WoldeGabriel, W. K. Hart, P. R. Renne, H. Gilbert, A. Defleur, G. Suwa, S. Katoh, K. R. Ludwig, J.-R. Boisserie, B. Asfaw & T. D. White, 2003. Stratigraphic, chronological and behavioural contexts of Pleistocene *Homo sapiens* from Middle Awash, Ethiopia. *Nature* **423**, 747–51.

Clottes, J., 1998. The 'Three Cs': fresh avenues towards European Palaeolithic art, in *The Archaeology of Rock-Art*, eds. C. Chippindale & P. Taçon, Cambridge: Cambridge University Press, 112–29.

Clottes, J., J.-M. Chauvet, E. Brunel-Deschamps, C. Hilliaire, J.-P. Daugas, M. Arnold, H. Cachier, J. Evin, P. Fortin, C. Oberlin, N. Tisnerat, & H. Valladas, 1995. Les peintures paléolithiques de la Grotte Chauvet-Pont-d'Arc, à Vallon-Pont d'Arc (Ardèche, France): datations directes et indirectes par la méthode du radiocarbone. *Comptes-Rendus de l'Académie des Sciences* series IIa **320**, 1133–40.

Conard, N. J., 2003. Palaeolithic ivory sculptures from southwestern Germany and the origins of figurative art. *Nature* **426**, 830–2.

Grün, R., C. B. Stringer, & H. P. Schwarcz, 1991. ESR dating from Garrod's Tabun Cave collection. *Journal of Human Evolution* **20**, 231–48.

Hahn, J., 1971. La statuette masculine de la grotte du Hohlenstein-Stadel (Württemberg). *L'Anthropologie* **75**, 233–44.

Haviland, W. A. 1989. *Anthropology*. Fort Worth: Holt, Rinehart and Winston.

Henshilwood, C. S., F. d'Errico, R. Yates, Z. Jacobs, C. Tribolo, G. A. T. Duller, N. Mercier, J. C. Sealy, H. Valladas, I. Watts, & A. G. Wintle, 2002. Emergence of modern human behavior: Middle Stone Age engravings from South Africa. *Science* **295**, 1278–80.

Henshilwood, C. S., F. d'Errico, M. Vanhaeren, K. van Niekerk, & Z. Jacobs, 2004. Middle Stone Age shell beads from South Africa. *Science* **304**, 404.

Holmes, R., 2001. In search of God. *New Scientist* 2287, 24–8.

Lessa, W. A., & E. Z. Vogt, 1958. *Reader in Comparative Religion: An Anthropological Approach*. New York: Harper and Row.

Marquet, J.-C., & M. Lorblanchet, 2003. A Neanderthal face? The proto-figurine from La Roche-Cotard, Langeais (Indre-et-Loire, France). *Antiquity* **77**, 661–70.

McBrearty, S., & A. S. Brooks. 2000. The revolution that wasn't: a new interpretation of the origin of modern human behaviour. *Journal of Human Evolution* **39**, 453–563.

McDermott, F., R. Grün, C. B. Stringer, & C. J. Hawkesworth, 1993. Mass-spectrometric U-Series dates for Israeli Neanderthal/early modern hominid sites. *Nature* **363**, 252–4.

Mellars, P., 1996. *The Neanderthal legacy*. Princeton: Princeton University Press.

Oakley, K., 1972. Skill as a human possession, in *Perspectives on human evolution*, eds. S.L. Washburn & P. Dolhinow. New York: Holt, Rinehart and Winston, 14–50.

Oakley, K., 1981. Emergence of higher thought, 3.0–0.2 Ma B.P. *Philosophical Transactions of the Royal Society of London* B 292, 205–11.

Pickering, T. R., T. D. White, & D. Toth, 2000. Cut marks on a Plio-Pleistocene hominid from Sterkfontein, South Africa. *American Journal of Physical Anthropology* **111**, 579–84.

Pettitt, P. B., 2002. The Neanderthal dead: exploring mortuary variability in Middle Palaeolithic Eurasia. *Before Farming* **1**, 1–26.

Rappaport, R., 1999. *Ritual and religion in the making of humanity.* Cambridge: Cambridge University Press.

Sauvet, G., & A. Wlodarczyk, 1995. Éléments d'une grammaire formelle de l'art pariétal paléolithique. *L'Anthropologie* **99**, 193–211.

Shipman, P., 2003. We are all Africans. *American Scientist* **91**, 496–9.

Stringer, C. B., 1998. Chronological and biogeographic perspectives on later human evolution, in *Neanderthals and modern humans in western Asia*, eds. T. Akazawa, K. Aoki, and O. Bar-Yosef, New York: Plenum, 29–37.

Taçon, P. S. C., 1999. All things bright and beautiful: the role and meaning of colour in human development. *Cambridge Archaeological Journal* **9**, 120–6.

Taçon, P. S. C., 2003a. Behaviourally modern at 300,000 B.P.: was my ancestor brighter than yours? Paper presented at the UNSW *Modern Human Origins: Australian Perspectives* Conference, Sydney, 30 September 2003 (in press, Proceedings Volume).

Taçon, P. S. C., 2003b. Wollemi rock-art: a new study reveals long lost secrets. *Muse* Nov./Dec. 2003-Jan. 2004, 10–11.

Taçon, P. S. C., W. Brennan, S. Hooper, D. Pross, & E. Gallard. 2003. The landscape of Blue Mountains rock-art: Wollemi Phase 1 results. Unpublished report. People and Place Research Centre, Australian Museum, Sydney.

Taçon, P. S. C., & C. Chippindale, 2001. Transformation and depictions of the First People: animal-headed beings of Arnhem Land, N.T., Australia, in *Theoretical perspectives in rock art research*, ed. K. Helskog. Oslo: Instituttet for sammenlignende kulturforskning.

Thorne, A., R. Grün, G. Mortimer, N. Spooner, J. Simpson, M. McCulloch, L. Taylor, & D. Curnoe. 1999. Australia's oldest human remains: age of the Lake Mungo 3 skeleton. *Journal of Human Evolution* **36**, 591–612.

Tremlett, G., 2003. Moment mankind's imagination came alive. *Sydney Morning Herald* 10 Jan. 2003, 8.

Ucko, P. J., & A. Rosenfeld, 1967. *Palaeolithic Cave Art.* London: Weidenfeld and Nicolson.

Vandermeersch, B., 1981. *Les hommes fossiles de Qafzeh (Israel).* Paris: CNRS.

White, T., B. Asfaw, D. DeGusta, H. Gilbert, G. D. Richards, G. Suwa, & F. C. Howell, 2003. Pleistocene *Homo sapiens* from Middle Awash, Ethiopia. *Nature* **423**, 742–7.

# 6

## Situating the creative explosion: universal or local?

*Colin Renfrew*

In this chapter, the intention is to reassess the significance of what has been termed the 'creative explosion' (Pfeiffer 1982), that is to say the appearance in Europe during the Upper Palaeolithic period of the cave art, and of the smaller carvings on bone and ivory (the so-called mobiliary art) which form the subject matter for so much of this book. As noted in the Introduction, and as authoritatively documented in the paper by Henshilwood, our notion of the 'human revolution' has recently been transformed. The emergence of *Homo sapiens*, and of most of the behaviours associated with the appearance of *Homo sapiens* is to be sought and found in Africa. With the out-of-Africa dispersal of our species around sixty thousand years ago, these sapient behaviour patterns were carried by the new population to Asia and along the southern route as far as Australia, and by forty thousand years ago to Europe. There is no reason to think that the cognitive capacities of one group of these new humans differed significantly from those of another group of the same species.

Yet in one specific area, in Europe, there came, before the end of the Pleistocene climatic period, an almost explosive proliferation of new activities and behaviours. In most earlier accounts, especially those which tended to locate the 'human revolution', in the sense of the emergence of the species *Homo sapiens* and the accompanying behaviours reflected in the new lithic industry and other ways, in Europe, the new creativity in painting and sculpture was viewed as an important component of that 'human revolution'. For this reason such products were often regarded as an integral part of that revolution, inextricably associated with the emergence and early existence of *Homo sapiens*.

It can now be demonstrated that this assumption was an error. We can indeed recognise that symbolic capacities were part of that 'human revolution' associated with the emergence of our species. They are seen in a modest way already at Blombos in Southern Africa, prior to the out-of-Africa dispersal, and then, not long after that dispersal, in Australia. But sculptures like those of the Gravettian culture of Europe are not, in general, seen elsewhere until after the end of the Pleistocene period. And it seems that cave art in the Franco-Cantabrian style, with large, some-times almost life-sized representations of mammals, often seen in profile, in a manner which might be described as 'naturalistic', were, during the Upper Palaeolithic period, found only in southern France, northern Spain and a few outlying sites, mainly in Italy. Cave art was not a general feature of the human revolution or of the Upper Palaeolithic, on a worldwide scale, but a very special phenomenon, restricted exclusively at that time to western Europe.

To say this is not, I hope, merely to develop a novel expression of Eurocentrism. And of course there will, over the years to come, be many important new discoveries elsewhere which may change that emerging picture. But the general soundness of this position should, I believe, be recognised and its implications noted. Instead it may be worth com-paring this creative explosion (of the Franco-Cantabrian Upper Palaeo-lithic) with another, perhaps even more significant explosion which occurred in Western Asia rather later, around 10,000 BC: the sedentary revolution. Both were localised phenomena, and both drew upon qualities which must have been latent within the more general human capacities which had been distributed widely over the world following the out-of-Africa dispersal.

In a later paper in this volume, Paul Mellars offers an interesting analysis, seeking an explanation for this localisation of Upper Palaeolithic cave art to the Franco-Cantabrian region. Here my intention is simply to stress the significance of that localisation, and to compare that creative episode with others which took place later in the human story.

## Relocating the human revolution: the shift to Africa

The astonishing antiquity of humankind was first established in France (Daniel & Renfrew 1988), in that remarkable year 1859, which also saw the publication of Darwin's *On the Origin of Species* (Darwin 1859). There the first finds of fossilised remains of early *Homo sapiens* were made at various sites in the Dordogne, which have given their name to

'Cro-Magnon man', and to the Aurignacian lithic industry which accompanied these early finds. In France, too, were first recognised the 'hand axes' and other early flint tools which are representative of the much earlier Lower and Middle Palaeolithic periods, and which we now associated with that much earlier hominid *Homo erectus*. And it was in Germany, at a site in the Neander Thal, that fossil remains of our immediate predecessor in Europe, *Homo neanderthalensis*, were first recognised. Indeed the social behaviour of these early hominids has been very well studied in France. Various important advances, such as the use of fire and the development of their skills in lithic manufacture, have also been investigated there, as Henry de Lumley's paper 'The emergence of symbolic thought' (this volume) indicates. Another feature of interest to the modern observer is the craftsmanship we see in some of the flint tools, particularly the hand axes, which are symmetrical and carefully produced in a manner which we find satisfying and sometimes beautiful. It is interesting to wonder whether the creator of objects which we admire in this way were themselves susceptible to such aesthetic feelings – and why not? But we ourselves are capable of seeing beauty in the natural world also, and must be careful not to fall into the 'pathetic fallacy' of ascribing our own human feelings and sentiments to the material things which provoke them.

Since the 1920s the remarkable discoveries in Africa, from the recognition of that very early ancestral form *Australopithecus* by Raymond Dart to the rich researches of Louis Leakey at Olduvai and the recovery of *Homo habilis*, the focus of attention has moved south. It is now well documented that our own species *Homo sapiens* developed in Africa from the ancestral *Homo erectus* or *Homo ergaster*, which indeed ultimately were themselves the descendents of *Australopithecus*. All of this has become increasingly clear in recent decades. But until recently it was still possible to take seriously the notion of multilineal evolution, with comparable processes taking place in East Asia, and perhaps also in Europe. The impact of DNA studies (Forster 2004) now documents in a much more detailed way the out-of-Africa expansion of our species around sixty thousand years ago.

Until recently, however, the behavioural changes which we see as accompanying the emergence of our species, or following from that emergence (see, for instance, Mellars 1991) were seen as emerging most clearly in Europe. This was the so-called human revolution (Mellars & Stringer 1989). Now, however, with the increase in our knowledge of the African Middle Stone Age, that perception has changed

(McBrearty & Brooks 2000). The finds at the Blombos Cave in southern Africa (Henshilwood, this volume) confirm that at least two important traits which we recognise as integral to that human revolution may be discerned in Africa as much as seventy thousand years ago. The first of these is the production of beads of pierced shell, which are among the very earliest indications of deliberate human adornment. Such body decorations are rightly regarded as an indication that personal identity was now finding expression in the form of material culture. These small artefacts are thus of very considerable significance for our understanding not only of the emergence of social relations of new kinds, but also of new kinds of attractiveness or even new perceptions of human beauty, a beauty which can be enhanced through bodily adornment.

The remarkable patterns incised on the small, carefully shaped block of red ochre at Blombos, for all their modesty, have comparably significant implications. They are not representational – to call them 'art' might be too ambitious: patterning is a sufficiently grand term. But here are markings, deliberately made by a human being, which we may at least regard as 'expressive'. They mark the first step of what Merlin Donald (1991) has termed 'external symbolic storage'. Meaningful marks are being made upon some object, so that their meaning can be revisited at a later date when that object is returned to. For the first time, a device is being created where elements of memory may be stored outside the brain. Of course the various tools that humans had made, well before that time, would have carried various memories with them or at least were able to kindle such memories in their maker on subsequent occasions. But they remained tools. Here we see the beginning of deliberate markings, which we can regard as the starting point in the long process which led to the development of art in the Upper Palaeolithic period, and very much later, to writing.

The salient elements of the 'human revolution' have been set out by Mellars (1991) in a much-quoted article in which he listed some of the behavioural changes which characterise the transition from Middle to Upper Palaeolithic, notably in France:

1. a shift in the production of stone tools, from a 'flake' technology to one which gives more regular and standardised forms of 'blade' manufacture;
2. an increase in the variety and complexity of the stone tools produced, with more obvious standardisation of production;

3. the appearance for the first time of artefacts made out of bone, antler and ivory which have been extensively shaped;
4. an increased tempo of technological change, with an increased degree of regional diversification;
5. the appearance for the first time of a wide range of beads, pendants and personal adornments;
6. significant changes in both the economic and social organisation of human groups;
7. the appearance for the first time of representational or 'naturalistic' art, seen both in small carvings, mainly on bone, antler or ivory, and in the remarkable painted animals seen in the painted caves such as Lascaux or Altamira, or earlier at the Grotte Chauvet;

We can now recognise that the first six of these were indeed a general feature of the human revolution, as seen first in Africa (McBrearty & Brooks 2000) and then subsequently in other parts of the globe, with the dispersal of our species (Mellars 2006). The seventh, however, was at that time specific to the 'creative explosion' of France and Spain. Instead one could insert a new and more modest claim in place of number 7:

7. the deliberate use of simple patterns inscribed on small objects (and sometimes painted) documenting an external expression, which might be considered a basic instance of external symbolic storage.

Later it will be appropriate to consider more carefully the repertoire of visible symbolic expression, patterning, representative figuration and other production of expressive form which might be subsumed under the notion of 'art', seen in different places worldwide during the Upper Palaeolithic period – that is to say before the end of the Pleistocene climatic regime around 9,500 or 10,000 BC. But first it is appropriate to seek to specify some of the features which were special to that much more localised creative explosion of the Franco-Cantabrian Upper Palaeolithic and its other European relatives.

## Special features of the 'creative explosion' of the European Upper Palaeolithic

Having separated these two major phenomena: the 'human revolution' (African genesis and worldwide dispersal of *Homo sapiens*) and the 'creative explosion' (proliferation of social products including sculpture and painting in the European Upper Palaeolithic), it may be useful to seek to define the latter rather more closely. As already acknowledged, there may be a limited range of creative expressions which might just be characterised as 'art' which were produced elsewhere in the world during the Upper Palaeolithic period, that is to say before the end of the Pleistocene climatic phase around 10,000 BC. We shall turn again to them in a moment. But first we can list some of the salient features which seem to have been in effect restricted to Europe at that time.

We may list, among the notable features of the European Upper Palaeolithic creative explosion (Bahn & Vertut 1988), the following features, some of them of restricted distribution:

1. Small, three-dimensional hand-sized human figurines of bone, ivory, stone and sometimes baked clay, often readily identified as female and then sometimes termed 'Venus' figurines. These occur with a well-defined time range in the Gravettian culture of Europe, from c. 28,000 BP to c. 21,000 BP with a distribution extending far beyond that of the Franco-Cantabrian cave art, extending through the Czech Republic to sites in the Ukraine (e.g. Kostenki) associated with mammoth hunters. Among the more celebrated examples are those from Willendorf in Austria (see Figure 6.1), and those from Brassempouy (Figure 6.2) and Lespugue in France (Figure 6.3). Their approximate distribution is shown in Figure 6.4 (Renfrew 1991; Gamble 1982).

There is an extensive literature upon these interesting sculptures. Belonging with them in the Gravettian culture, within the same time frame, are some of the earliest known figurations in baked clay, also from sites in Moravia, in the Czech Republic, such as Pavlov and Dolni Vestonice (Figure 6.5).

Their occurrence outside the Franco-Cantabrian area might be seen to support Mellars' suggestion that their genesis is due to a shift towards sedentism. For the finds from Pavlov and Dolní Věstonice, like those from Kostienki, suggest that they come from the camps of mammoth hunters. These were not permanent dwellings, but they were well-established encampments. The use of baked clay for the creation of these animal and human figurines is particularly notable at these sites. The very clear use of this technique for producing human figurations is seen at an early date in the Jomon culture of Japan towards the end of the Pleistocene period and at the beginning of the Holocene.

**6.1.** 'Venus' of Willendorf, Austria. Stone, height 11.1 cms., ca. 25,000 to 23,000 BP. One of the figurines of the Gravettian culture, the earliest established category of sculpture known. (Cast, Natural History Museum, London)

As noted earlier, the principal distribution of these small sculptures occurred during the Gravettian period. Their origins probably go back earlier, to the preceding Aurignacian phase. For it is to this early time, around thirty-two thousand years ago that the remarkable lion-headed anthropomorphic (therianthropic) figure from Hohlenstein-Stadel in Germany is dated (Plate II).

The purpose here, however, is not to discuss in detail these first representations of the human body in three dimensions, but to emphasise their exceptional place in world history. Their distribution is limited to Europe (including some Italian sites). (In saying this, brief reference should be made to two very much earlier objects from Tan-Tan in Morocco (Bednarik 2003) and Berekhat Ram in Israel (d'Errico & Nowell 2000), the former dated to some 300,000 years ago, the latter to 230,000 years ago. These are so far the only possible figurations which might be dated so early, far earlier than *Homo sapiens*, and indeed back to the time of *Homo erectus*. At the moment their status should be considered as uncertain.)

It is remarkable that, despite the undoubted capacity of *Homo sapiens* to produce such figures, as clearly documented by the objects mentioned, their distribution during the Palaeolithic period is restricted to Europe.

2. Small-sized carvings, usually on bone or ivory, of animals or animal heads, seen on small objects, as decoration, sometimes on what have been identified as 'spear throwers' (Garrod 1955). These are often referred to as 'mobiliary art'. They may be in relief or incised (Figure 6.6).

**6.2.** 'Venus' of Brassempouy, France. Ivory, height 3.6 cms., ca 28,000 BP. Found in a layer associated with Aurignacian material, and so presumably earlier than the Gravettian figurines. (Photo by Jean Vertut. From Bahn, P. *The Cambridge Illustrated History of Prehistory Art*, p. 82)

**6.3.** 'Venus' of Lespugue, France. Ivory, height 14.7 cms., ca. 25,000 to 23,000 BP. (Cast, Natural History Museum, London)

These are widely found in contexts of the Aurignacian culture in Franco-Cantabria and beyond (Figure 6.7), and are also a feature of the Gravettian period. They are not well-documented elsewhere during the Upper Palaeolithic. Simple figurations of this kind will, I suspect, be found more widely from contexts of this period. For some of the simpler figurations would seem to be quite a predictable occurrence quite early in the developmental trajectory of human culture. But, so far as I am aware, they have not been documented in the Upper Palaeolithic of Australia or the Americas. Some terracotta figures of animals have reportedly been found along with human figurines in contexts dating from the end of the Pleistocene period on the northern part of the Pacific coast of Asia. They may represent developments similar to those of the Jomon culture of Japan at this time.

3. Larger carvings, often-in low relief either remaining in situ on the cave wall, or on heavy stone slabs. The so-called Venus of Laussel offers a good example (Figure 6.8).

Relief carvings are a noted feature of Franco-Cantabrian art. They are not yet documented for the Upper Palaeolithic period outside its distribution.

4. Sculptures in clay, left remaining in situ (such as the famous bison at Tuc d'Audobert: Figure 6.9). Such figurations as these have again not been reported outside the Franco-Cantabrian area for the Palaeolithic period.

5. Paintings of animals on the walls of caves or rock shelters, approaching life size, with 'naturalistic' outlines and sometimes with polychrome infilling to give a vivid effect. They were first recognised at Altamira (Plate XIII) and then at numerous sites in France and Spain, including Le Portel (Plate XIV). The early dates for their occurrence at the Grotte Chauvet (Plate XV), some thirty-two thousand years ago, occasioned surprise in view of the accomplishment of the figurations.

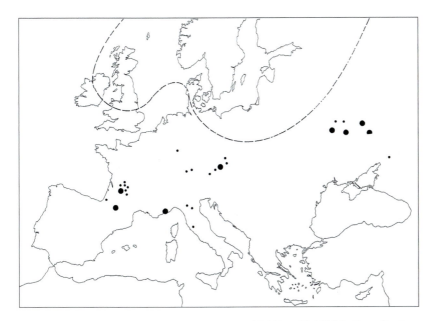

**6.4.** Map of the distribution of 'Venus' figurines, c. 25,000 to 23,000 BP. (From Renfrew 1991,9; after Gamble 1982)

**6.5.** 'Venus' of Dolní Věstonice, Moravia. Baked clay, 11.1 cms., ca 25,000 to 23,000 BP. (Cast, Natural History Museum, London)

Such splendid images as these naturally represent the paradigm case of what is meant by Palaeolithic cave art. Images of comparable scale, although differing in style, are found in the rock art of hunter-gatherer communities of the Holocene period, after 10,000 BC, in many parts of the world. These have been well studied in Australia (see Taçon, this volume), in South Africa (see Lewis-Williams, this volume), in North Africa (for instance in the Tassili area) and in the Americas.

The occurrences of animal paintings in the Pleistocene period are, however, few. Their very early occurrence in Australia is now well documented, as Taçon indicates. But it is not yet clear what the full range of subjects and styles may be, prior to the onset of the Holocene period some ten thousand years ago. So far nothing has been published which compares with the Franco-Cantabrian style.

This picture may yet change. The discovery of a painted plaque in the Apollo 11 Cave in Namibia (Plate XVI) well dated to before 25,000 years ago (Wendt 1976) is of particular interest. But so far, this is one of the very few cases of Palaeolithic painting outside of Australia and the Franco-Cantabrian distribution.

6. Paintings of hands on the walls of rock shelter or caves, resembling handprints, but often with the paint outlining the shape of the hand. These are a frequent feature of Franco-Cantabrian cave art (Plate XVII).

Superficially very similar paintings, but of the Holocene period, have been found in different parts of the world, for instance, in Borneo and in Argentina (Plate XVIII).

7. Paintings of schematic individual forms on the walls of caves or rock shelters, sometimes including 'tectiforms' and signs indicating the female sex (Figure 6.10).

**6.6.** Spear thrower from Mas d'Azil, France. Bone. Probably Magdalenian (ca. 15,000 BP). (Photo by Jean Vertut. From Bahn, P. & J. Vertut, 1997, *Journey Through the Ice Age*, p. 98)

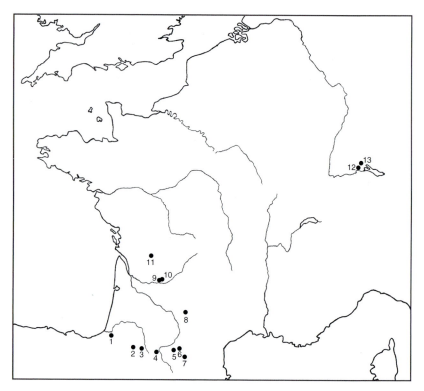

**6.7.** Map of find spots of spear throwers from Palaeolithic Europe, showing a similar distribution to the 'Venus' figurines seen in Figure 6.4. (After Garrod 1955, 21)

This is somewhat of a residual category, and it would be surprising if examples outside of Europe were not found, even for the Upper Palaeolithic period.

8. Incisions on the walls of caves and rock shelters showing animals in profile, often carved in the same place as earlier representations and so forming a palimpsest (Plate XIX).

Such figurations as these are very frequent in the caves and rock shelters of Franco-Cantabria. They occur also in the Côa valley in Portugal not only in rock shelters, but carved on rock surfaces in the open air. Their occurrence there has been securely dated to the Upper Palaeolithic period.

It is notoriously difficult to date rock art at open-air sites, and it may well be that Palaeolithic rock art will be found much more widely. At present, however, the main Palaeolithic cases remain Franco-Cantabria and Australia.

## Implications for the human story

This brief, and in some respects superficial survey has set out to document that the development of Franco-Cantabrian cave art represents what was in some respects a unique episode in human experience. The cave art in question and the associated material culture does not represent a general phase in the development of human culture, as has often been claimed.

**6.8.** 'Venus' of Laussel, France. Carved stone block, height 44 cms. Probably Gravettian (ca. 24,000 BP). (Photo by Jean Vertut. From Bahn, P. & J. Vertut, 1997, *Journey Through the Ice Age*, p. 113)

**6.9.** Modelled clay bison, Tuc d'Audobert, France. Length 63 and 61 cms. Probably Magdalenian (ca. 15,000 BP). (Photo by Jean Vertut. from Bahn, P. *The Cambridge Illustrated History of Prehistoric Art*, p. 139)

Such a claim can be made for the more modest products of the human revolution, such as are seen at Blombos, and then more widely. And such a claim could perhaps be sustained for the hunter-gatherer rock art so widely seen in the early Holocene period.

This particular creative explosion was something different. But although in its own way unique, as I have sought to emphasise, it may belong to a different class of event or process, which we can recognise at other places and times. For example, at about the time that the many millennia of cave art in Europe were falling into decline, around 10,000 BC, another creative explosion was building up in Western Asia. The very climatic changes that made no longer tenable the hunter-gatherer life mode which had sustained the European Upper Palaeolithic made possible new adaptations in Western Asia, documented for instance by the Natufian culture of the Levant, which soon developed into Pre-pottery Neolithic A, and then the full emergence of sedentism and domestication in Pre-Pottery Neolithic B. That was, of course, in a different part of the world. Its consequences were even more momentous, since the sedentary life which then developed was sustained by the domestication of wheat and barley, and the rearing of sheep, goat and cattle. This economy proved exceedingly durable, although we do not yet know whether the cycle of growth which it sustained will last as long as the creative cycle of the cave art of Franco-Cantabria.

Of course sedentism and the domestication of plants and animals occurred in different parts of the world also. Each of these might be regarded as a creative explosion in its own right, in what may be termed the 'tectonic' phase of human development (Renfrew 2006). Seen from a distance they were not so numerous (Bellwood 2005). And of course, at a micro level, we might seek to discern more numerous creative episodes, for instance of sedentism and domestication (Barker 2006). We could go on to apply the same approach to the urban revolutions which occurred independently in different parts of the world (Renfrew 2007). In each of

**6.10.** "Female sex"; carved in bas relief, Abri Cellier, France. Length of block 60 cms. Aurignacian (ca. 28,000 BP). (Photo by Jean Vertut. From Bahn, P. & J. Vertut, 1997, *Journey Through the Ice Age*, p. 104)

these, economic changes were accompanied, or perhaps preceded by spiritual developments, changes in belief systems which sometimes leave very clear traces, even if these are not always easy to interpret.

A notable example is offered by the discovery of what can be claimed as the world's first temple, or first built sanctuary, at Göbekli Tepe in south-east Turkey (Plates XX and XXI). Dating from c. 9000 BC, the buildings there precede the development of domesticated plants and animals (Schmidt 2001, 2006). Indeed the community cannot yet be regarded as fully sedentary, although in retrospect it can be seen that sedentism was on the way.

What is remarkable is that here an entirely new style is born, and seen exercised with great accomplishment on the relief stelae of the sanctuary. This, taken with the other developments in the Levant at this time was certainly another creative explosion.

It may be helpful to see the creative explosion of the European Upper Palaeolithic in this perspective. The notion of punctuated equilibrium has already been thoughtfully applied in prehistoric archaeology (Cherry 1984). Indeed the concept has its counterpart in catastrophe theory, with the 'anastrophe' of sudden creative development (Renfrew 1979). The Franco-Cantabrian creative explosion may be seen as perhaps the first great upsurge in human creativity – in material culture and, one may surmise, in spirituality. There are clear suggestions that a comparable development occurred in Australia at much the same time.

When scholars agree to shift the locus of the human revolution to Africa, as seems now to be widely agreed, the creative explosion documented for the European Upper Palaeolithic does not represent a worldwide phenomenon. It was intense and localised. It was the first of a number of such episodes in the human story. Each of them had its own context of origin and its own particularities. It is from these creative episodes that the human story was created.

**REFERENCES**

Bahn, P. G. & J. Vertut, 1988. *Images of the Ice Age*. Leicester: Windward.
Barker, G., 2006. *The Agricultural Revolution in Prehistory*. Oxford: Oxford University Press.
Bednarik, R. G., 2003. A figurine from the African Acheulian. *Current Anthropology* **44**, 405–13.

Bellwood, P., 2005. *First Farmers: The Origins of Agricultural Societies.* Oxford: Blackwell.

Cherry, J. F., 1984. The emergence of the state in the prehistoric Aegean. *Proceedings of the Cambridge Philosophical Society* **30**, 18–48.

Daniel, G. & C. Renfrew, 1988. *The Idea of Prehistory.* Edinburgh: Edinburgh University Press.

Darwin, C., 1859. *On the Origin of Species by Means of Natural Selection.* London: John Murray.

d'Errico, F. & A. Nowell, 2000. A new look at the Berekhat Ram figurine: Implications for the origins of symbolism. *Cambridge Archaeological Journal* **10**, 123–67.

Donald, M., 1991. *Origins of the Modern Mind: Three Stages in the Evolution of Culture and Cognition.* Cambridge (MA): Harvard University Press.

Forster, P., 2004. Ice ages and the mitochondrial DNA chronology of human dispersals: a review. *Philosophical Transactions of the Royal Society of London Series B* **359**, 255–64.

Gamble, C., 1982. Interaction and alliance in Palaeolithic society. *Man* **17**, 19–107.

Garrod, D., 1955. Palaeolithic spear-throwers. *Proceedings of the Prehistoric Society* **21**, 21–35.

McBrearty S. & A. S. Brooks, 2000. The revolution that wasn't: a new interpretation of the origin of modern human behaviour. *Journal of Human Evolution* **39**, 453–563.

Mellars, P., 1991. Cognitive changes and the emergence of modern humans in Europe. *Cambridge Archaeological Journal* **1**, 63–76

Mellars, P. M., 2006. Why did modern human populations disperse from Africa *ca.* 60,000 years ago? A new model. *Proceedings of the National Academy of Sciences of the USA* 103, 9381–6.

Mellars, P. & C. Stringer, 1989. *The Human Revolution.* Edinburgh: Edinburgh University Press.

Pfeiffer, J., 1982. *The Creative Explosion, an Inquiry into the Origins of Art and Religion.* New York: Harper and Row.

Renfrew, C., 1979. System collapse as social transformation: catastrophe and anastrophe in early state societies, in *Transformations: Mathematical Approaches to Culture Change*, eds. C. Renfrew & K. L. Cooke, New York: Academic Press, 481–506.

Renfrew, C., 1991. Before Babel, speculations on the origins of linguistic diversity. *Cambridge Archaeological Journal* **1**, 3–23.

Renfrew, C., 2006. Becoming human – the archaeological challenge. *Proceedings of the British Academy* **139**, 217–38.

Renfrew, C., 2007. *Prehistory: The Making of the Human Mind.* London: Weidenfeld and Nicolson.

Schmidt, K., 2001. Göbekli Tepe, Southeastern Turkey. A preliminary report on the 1995–1999 excavations. *Paléorient* **26**, 45–54.

Schmidt, K., 2006. *Sie Bauten die Ersten Tempel. Das Rätselhafte Heiligtum der Steinzeitjäger. Die Archäologische Entdeckung am Göbekli Tepe.* München: Verlag C. H. Beck oHG.

Wendt, W. E., 1976. 'Art mobilier' from the Apollo 11 cave, South West Africa: Africa's oldest dated works of art. *South African Archaeological Bulletin* **31**, 5–11.

# APPROACHES TO 'ART AND RELIGION'

# 7

# The roots of art and religion in ancient material culture

*Merlin Donald*

This chapter focuses on the functions served by art and religion in the context of human cognitive and cultural evolution. Art and religion are cultural achievements that can only be understood in terms of their complex cognitive functions. They are ultimately products of our own attempts at cognitive self governance.

Like every other major achievement of human thought and memory, they have emerged on the cultural level gradually, as biologically modern humans have struggled with their own intellectual and spiritual birth. The final evolutionary push of the human brain created a far more plastic cognitive system, with possibilities for future growth that culture is still exploring. In this respect, human culture is a gigantic search-engine that seeks out, and tests, various solutions to the many cognitive challenges faced by people living in symbolic cultures, with rapid information-flows, and high population densities. Art and religion are among the most important products of those cultural explorations.

## The cognitive importance of high culture

Art and religion can be viewed as closely related cognitive domains that constitute the foundations of what we might call traditional 'high culture'. Viewed strictly in terms of its function vis-à-vis the individual mind, the latter may be construed as a level of culture that endows its members with an articulated world-view that goes beyond the pragmatics of mere survival. World-views provide the imaginative engines that determine a great deal about how people live, what they value, and how they view reality. They take time, measured in many generations, and considerable communal effort to build.

In this context, the word 'art' refers to more than the visual image-making component of high culture; it includes many other expressive forms, such as music, dance, and theatrical performances, and aspects of the built environment, inasmuch as they serve the same cognitive ends. A complex tapestry of artistic expression defines the public surface of human social life, and I have referred to it as the 'mimetic' dimension of culture. The logic of mimetic culture is metaphorical; it works by an underlying logic of perceptual similarity. Mimesis extends beyond art, to encompass other nonverbal aspects of cultural life, including such things as public spectacle, athletic events, body-language, and the nonverbal transmission of skills. For a variety of reasons, which I have listed elsewhere (Donald, 1991, 1993, 1998, 1999, 2000, 2001, 2005), mimetic capacity is one of the basic building blocks of language, and must have preceded its evolution in hominid prehistory.

The word 'religion' refers broadly to a subcategory of high culture that comprises the fundamental beliefs that encapsulate and support the world-view of a society. In tracing the crucial role of language in constructing belief, I have called the governing representational form of traditional religious culture 'mythic', referring to its underlying logic of thought, which is based mostly on allegorical reasoning. Myths and mythologies are collectively remembered stories that tell people by example who they are, how to live, and what to value. Because their governing myths cut so deeply into the shared beliefs of a population, religions can shape the pattern of daily life in society, and dictate behaviour in such mundane areas as birth, marriage, the treatment and consumption of food, the proper progress of life, attitudes to death, and so on. These beliefs dominate other ideas. In the cognitive chain of command, myths rank at the top, in most societies.

In traditional societies, art is one of the principal means by which the mythic component of this hierarchy, religion, exerts its influence. In such societies, the uses and themes of art tend to be dominated by religion, and sacred artworks intrude into daily life, keeping the mind 'on track', that is, under constant cognitive regulation by the dominant worldview. For example, for many centuries Western art was dominated by the major themes and archetypes of the Judeo-Christian religious tradition; during that period, most arts and crafts, including all those that contributed to the building of cathedrals and shrines were dedicated primarily to purposes defined by the Church. This represented a collective pattern of self-regulation, a hierarchy of cognitive control that has often been repeated in human history. Such control in no way implies dictatorship; it resides in the entire population, and is no different in principle from many other methods of self-regulation, except that in this case, the 'self' that is regulated includes the notion of collective identity.

Art and religion have thus been closely interwoven during the emergence of modern culture, usually with art in an important subsidiary role, and religion (that is, the mythic component of cognitive regulation) in the dominant role. This is entirely understandable, since one of the major functions of art is the construction and advocacy of worldviews. Religions constitute the larger social-cognitive apparatus of the two; art provides one major means for that apparatus to exert regulatory control over thought and memory on the population.

It takes a great deal of communal intellectual work to build a society and a shared worldview. The collective intellectual apparatus of human society is very special, in evolutionary terms, because it is both more complex and more explicitly symbolic in nature than that of any other species, by far. Humanity is unique in the elaborate cultural structures it has created to smooth and coordinate the shared processes of cognition. Viewed in terms of their function in society, artists have traditionally played key roles in that social-cognitive apparatus.

## Art as a means of cognitive self-governance

From a cognitive standpoint, art is a uniquely human cognitive activity characterized by the following features (for more detail, see Donald, in press):

(1) art is aimed at influencing the minds of an audience, and as such, it might be called a form of 'cognitive engineering';
(2) art always occurs in the context of a distributed social network; and
(3) it is constructivist in nature, that is, aimed at the deliberate refinement and elaboration of some aspect of the worldview of the artist, which is usually derived from society; moreover,
(4) most art is metacognitive in function, that is, it engages in self-reflection, both individually and socially;
(5) the forms and media of art are technology-driven;

(6) neither the role of the artist, nor the local social definition of art, are fixed, and may change as a function of the state of the social-cognitive network in which the artist works; and finally,

(7) art, unlike most conventional physical engineering, is always aimed at a cognitive outcome, that is, at influencing the mind of an audience (even if the only audience were to be the mind of the artist).

Art grows from the simple fact of mutual attentional influence, which is an exquisitely evolved skill in human beings. People are expert at controlling one another's attention from infancy, and ultimately this extends to more elaborate means of influencing the ideas, beliefs, images, and ultimately world-views, of oneself and others, through the use of external representations. This culminates in various forms of art.

This quintessentially human game, of incessant mutual attentional influence, creates a fierce social competition for cognitive control, and imposes a tremendous burden on human memory. The resulting social networks elicit unending exchanges of knowledge and gesture throughout the lifespan. This exchange of influence is complex enough in small tribal and family groups; but in large societies, it generates too much complexity to remain informal and unstructured. In large groups, it can only attain a degree of coherence when it is supported by more formal institutional structures, which serve to govern and regulate it. The flow-patterns of that influence follow a pattern that reflects the lines of power, interest, and affiliation in any given society.

For this reason, eventually, cognitive regulation had to become concentrated in a unitary political and religious structure that included visual art as one of its means of governance. Historically, most cultures have not made an explicit distinction between religion and other aspects of cultural life, including visual art, music, and literature. Indeed, religion encompassed much of traditional cultural life, and the idea that the latter could become 'secular', and that religion could be hived off as an isolable component of the larger culture is recent, and marks a major shift in the Western tradition. Since the Enlightenment, religion has gradually been isolated from most other Western intellectual and artistic activity, and studied as an anthropological phenomenon. However, this is a misleading way to look at it, because it is the result of stripping religious institutions of many of their traditional functions. It is not clear that secular culture produces a type of government that is any less ideological or value-laden than those provided by so-called traditional religions in earlier times.

One might say that, for many cultures, art is the quintessence of religious expression. In many ways, secular high art is in a position vis-à-vis society that is remarkably similar to that of its more explicitly religious predecessors, because it usually expresses a world-view. This is true not only of artists whose work is obviously religious in nature, such as Rothko, Moreau, or Rouault, but also of those whose work is apparently focused on the surface of experience, such as Matisse or the Futurists.

Again, this raises questions of definition in modern society, which has superseded this ancient cognitive power structure with an open multi-cultural configuration that is unprecedented in human history. Within this new context, the influence of religion has often extended into what might be called secular space. For example, the term 'Hinduism' encompasses a widely subscribed system of myths and beliefs, including a caste system, numerous customs and rituals that define daily life, styles of dress and gesture, systems of architecture, music and art, as well as myriads of formal institutions, with sacred texts, organizations dedicated to education and welfare, and other spheres of influence that have par-allels in many secular governments. In a similar vein, terms such as 'Islam', 'Judaism', and 'Catholicism' are vast inclusive categories that cover much more than religious belief itself or its most common insti-tutional reflections in formal custom and ritual. Moreover, the influence of religions can carry far beyond their formal institutional reach. It remains possible today to identify oneself as culturally Muslim, Jewish, or Catholic, without acceding to any of the beliefs or dogmas that supposedly defined those religions in the first place. The same may be said of many nonreligious ideologies, some of which have tried to control art in most of its forms. Both communism and fascism tried to use art in a frankly propagandistic manner. The many nationalisms of the past cen-tury used art in a similar way, as have multinational corporations, in their own ways. The boundaries between religion, secular cultural identity, and art appear to be less clear today than in the past.

However, across these many forms of political and social control over cognition, the effectiveness of art is a constant. It speaks to the human mind in a particular way, with a logic of its own that is rooted in human evolution. Traditional religions have used art successfully to persuade, convert, remind, and guide the behaviour of their followers.

The metaphorical and allegorical styles of thought that are the hallmarks of religion have been well served by art, and the honoured place of art in many societies is a result of its firm association with religion and belief. The same is true of secular institutions, including that most secular of all institutions, the multicultural state. Artists are employed by the modern state for the same reason they have always been employed by the state: they, more than anyone else, have mastered the most powerful means of representation and persuasion.

More recently, nationalism and secular ideologies have served roughly the same social-cognitive organizing functions as traditional religion. Some things have changed, especially the openness and diversity of worldviews. But world-views are still composed with the same basic representational components, because the human mind can work only within the parameters of its own biological and cultural evolution.

Human societies are massive mindsharing networks that exchange knowledge and belief. In any society that enjoys a degree of cognitive unity, human beings share mind in certain crucial areas from a young age, and in doing this, they share the products of a long-standing, cumulative, and collective cognitive effort. Societies that lack this element of unity are always in danger of internal strife and collapse. However, there must also be enough diversity of ideas to satisfy the social need for innovation and creative adaptation to new circumstances. Maintaining a productive balance between unity and diversity is not easy, as the history of the Western experiment with diversity testifies. But it is essential.

## The special case of Franco-Cantabrian cave art

There is no reason to think that visual art in the Upper Palaeolithic came from a different creative source than it does today. The human brain is the biological constraint on, and ultimate source of, creativity. Culture provides the specific semantic fields that determine meaning.

Thus, we cannot expect that the inspiration for Upper Palaeolithic parietal art was somehow derived outside of the social-cognitive networks that have shaped its modern equivalents. Artists must work within a tradition. Images, technologies, and cultural archetypes do not spring fully formed from artists (if they did, they would not work, since the audience must share them). Total originality is an illusion, even in cases of great genius. It would be presumptuous to assume that the cultures of the Upper Palaeolithic were an exception to this rule. Therefore we must view the ancient images painted on the walls of caves in the Franco-Cantabrian region as reflections, however incomplete and indirect, of a religious worldview; that is, of myths and stories, archetypes and allegories, that gave human life meaning.

Moreover, given the extraordinary locations of these images, the tremendous effort that it took to create them and to develop the techniques for their creation, and the consistency of their themes, across time and place, for many millennia, a religious interpretation seems apt. In view of the similarity of these images and places to the religious imagery of some surviving New Stone Age societies, we have no alternative but to interpret them in the context of a very enduring mythic civilization, bound together by a common set of beliefs, whose reach was both wide and incredibly durable. I know of no other mechanism of cognitive control by which such consistency can be explained.

In my view, it is also legitimate to regard many of these images, and the larger corpus as a whole, as religious in motivation. It seems very likely that these images reflect a religious worldview that was essentially Animistic, like that of many other documented Stone Age cultures. An Animistic worldview is highly likely in this case because their artists were obsessed with animals and hybrid human-animal images, to the exclusion of many other common kinds of imagery. Moreover, the cave settings in which many of these images were found were generally not habitable, and in some cases, the surroundings showed clear evidence of ritualistic behaviour. Even though we know little about the specific beliefs of the Magdalenian and Gravettian cultures, it is a virtual certainty, in the absence of any credible alternative, that the long tradition of parietal art in the Dordogne Valley and adjacent regions reflects the presence of an influential Animistic religious worldview that was widely disseminated, and informally institutionalized in a hierarchy of ritual and social custom for thousands of years. This is scarcely an original conclusion, but its credibility is perhaps strengthened by the cognitive and evolutionary considerations raised in this paper.

The time-span bridged by these images is enormous. The cave-painting culture appears to have been maintained over tens of millennia, which suggests a very slow rate of change, when compared to the rapid turnover of modern civilizations. However, in Stone Age societies, the range of ideas and images available to their artists would have been very small, not for any lack of imagination on the part of artists, but simply because the technologies of image-making were limited, and writing was virtually nonexistent. Without these powerful technologies, reflection and radical revision would have been difficult, and the inertia created by existing informal institutions and rituals of such societies would have been hard to challenge.

In any case, this body of great parietal art constitutes a phenomenon of enormous cognitive significance for humanity, because it is at once so ancient, so modern in appearance, so visually skilled, and so enduring in its effects. The techniques underlying this art were undoubtedly the product of many years of experimentation, and suggest an apprenticeship system of some sort that carried a tradition of cultivating and transmitting such skills across many generations.

However, it did not endure forever. The conditions of life eventually changed, and Franco-Cantabrian cave art changed as well, and eventually disappeared. The fact that this tradition came to an end is not surprising, given the much shorter time span that most civilizations have enjoyed.

## Summary and conclusions

Ancient material culture contains the only incontrovertible evidence that art existed long before the invention of writing. This, combined with modern anthropological studies of New Stone Age societies, provides a sound evidential basis for the inference that the foundations of 'high culture', that is, art and religious belief, have existed since the 'symbolic explosion' began some fifty thousand years ago.

Viewed in terms of their cognitive functions, art and religion appear to be part of a social system of cognitive self-regulation whereby the ideas and images of a society can be coordinated and transmitted to the next generation, in a coherent and optimally understood form. They remain an immensely powerful means of social-cognitive coordination. In the recent past, the technology of symbolic representation has improved enormously, and the means of disseminating ideas and images has improved even more. As a result, art and religion are resurgent in their worldwide influence.

The rise to dominance of 'theoretic' culture during the post-Enlightenment period has shattered the pattern of traditional cultural-cognitive regulation. Its emergence has been rapid and seemingly unstoppable. Because of this shift, the artistic elites of the Western world have declared their independence of religion, and the uses of art have thus been split between secular and religious ends. However, only time will tell whether humanity as a whole will relax back into its more traditional cultural-cognitive mode wherein they are reunited. In that traditional mode, social coordination is achieved through a formal system of religious belief, and the latter is reinforced by the tools and techniques of arts employed largely in the service of enforcing those beliefs. The efficiencies of that system are considerable, and it has survived the test of time.

**REFERENCES**

Donald, M.W., 1991. *Origins of the Modern Mind: Three Stages in the Evolution of Culture and Cognition.* Cambridge (MA): Harvard University Press.

Donald, M.W., 1993. Précis of "Origins of the Modern Mind" with multiple reviews and author's response. *Behavioral and Brain Sciences* 16, 737–91.

Donald, M.W., 1998. Hominid enculturation and cognitive evolution, in *Cognition and Material Culture: the Archaeology of Symbolic Storage*, eds. C. Renfrew & C. Scarre. Cambridge: McDonald Institute Monographs, 7–17.

Donald, M.W., 1999. Preconditions for the evolution of protolanguages, in *The Descent of Mind*, eds. M.C. Corballis & I. Lea. Oxford: Oxford University Press, 120–36.

Donald, M.W., 2000. The central role of culture in cognitive evolution: a reflection on the myth of the isolated mind, in *Culture, Thought and Development*, eds, L. Nucci, G. Saxe, & E. Turiel, New York: Lawrence Erlbaum, 19–38.

Donald, M.W., 2001. *A Mind So Rare: The Evolution of Human Consciousness.* New York: Norton.

Donald, M.W. 2005. Imitation and Mimesis, in *Perspectives on Imitation: From Neuroscience to Social Science*, eds. N. Chater & S. Hurley. Cambridge (MA): MIT Press.

Donald, M.W., in press b. Art viewed in the light of cognitive evolution, in *The Artful Mind*, ed. M. Turner. Oxford: Oxford University Press.

# 8

# The archaeology of early religious practices:
a plea for a hypothesis-testing approach

*Francesco d'Errico*

## Religion and the origin of modern behaviour debate

The paradox of the archaeology of religion lies in the fact that while archaeologists are probably not the best scientific community whom to ask what religion is and how and when it arose, they retain in their hands the best information to answer these questions. To solve this paradox archaeologists should try to grasp the wide-ranging implications of the phenomenon. Historians of religion, on their side, should understand what role these and other related topics are playing among Palaeolithic archaeologists and evolutionary anthropologists in the debate on the origin of behavioural modernity. I hope that the questions I will address in this paper will be of interest for both communities and open the path for constructive collaborations.

In the last decade there has been a strong tendency among palaoan-thropologists to liken the biological origin of modern humans with the origin of modern behaviour and developed cognitive abilities (Mithen 1996; Mellars 1998; Foley & Lahr 1997; Klein 1999, 2000, 2003; Klein & Blake 2003; McBrearty & Brooks 2000). The idea behind this model, which is becoming a dominant paradigm, is quite simple. Since the publication of the 'Out of Africa' model for the origin of our species (Cann et al. 1987), based on mtDNA and Y-chromosome variation and confirmed by further studies (Ingman et al. 2000; Barbujani 2003), it has become generally accepted that Africa was the continent where our species emerged. The process that produced our species in Africa must also have granted this species a number of advantages (e.g. language, higher cognitive abilities, symbolic thinking) that have determined its spread out of Africa and favoured its eventual evolutionary success. If we were to assume from the start that these advantages were both dramatic and mainly determined by biological change, we might easily reach the surprising conclusion that the study of past material culture can cast little light on this issue. Populations would be considered smart, eloquent and symbolic simply according to their taxonomic status and not on the basis of material culture they have left behind. In contrast, if we see archaeology as an independent discipline (d'Errico 2003; d'Errico et al. 1998; 2003, in press; Zilhão 2001; Zilhão & d'Errico 2003; Jehs 2004) we should be able to assess issues which deal with cultural and behavioural change on primarily archaeological grounds, rather than limit ourselves to models shaped by current hypotheses of human biological evolution.

Following this reasoning it is legitimate to ask a question such as "is religion a species-specific or a trans-species phenomenon?". In the first of these two cases, religion would represent, together with language, symbolism, and advanced cognitive abilities, the behavioural outcome of the biological shift that created our species. In the second case, we may have shared this and possibly other of these behavioural traits with hominids such as Neanderthals or archaic *sapiens* populations. Should that be so, were the religious beliefs and associated practices of these ancestors comparable to those of contemporary or succeeding modern human populations, and were they significantly different from those of ethnographically known human societies? Does archaeology recognise universal trends in early religious beliefs and practices? Should we, for example, assume that all past hunter-gatherer societies had shamanic (Lommel 1970; Lewis-Williams & Dowson 1988, 1989; Lewis-Williams 2004) or totemic (Frazer 1890; Sollas 1911) beliefs or can we conceive early human societies capable of symbolic thinking but having a different way to conceive the Beyond? In the first case, the identification of an early symbolic material culture becomes synonymous with the identification of the first shamanic/totemic practices; in the second one, we face the difficult endeavour of hypothesizing what these very early beliefs could look like or whether we can say anything significant about them.

## What is religion? An operation definition

To answer these questions, we must explain what we mean by religion, establish how early religious practices may be identified in prehistoric material culture, critically interrogate the archaeological record in search for these traces, study their nature and occurrence in time and space, and investigate their association with different hominid populations. As young initiates in a fervent search for the truth, we must clear our mind of dominant paradigms, wishful thinking, and mainstream opinions and consider them as no more than working hypotheses we wish to test against the archaeological record. In other words, I consider all these topics as matters of scientific enquiry. This implies that contrary to those who see this as a dangerous field that is better to avoid, I consider, with Renfrew (1994), the emergence and characterisation of prehistoric religious beliefs proper subjects for archaeological study, that should not be left to lunatic fringe.

It is not among the goals of this paper to list and discuss all the definitions of religion (Tylor 1971; Durkheim 1915; Sollas 1911; Frazer 1890; Geerz 1985) or the lack of a need for a definition (Weber 1966) given by a distinguished tradition of scholars.

For the goals of this paper religion may be defined as a set of socially shared and transmitted beliefs encoding a group's understanding of the essence of reality. I would complement this first definition with that proposed by Geertz (1966) of "a system of symbols which acts to establish powerful, pervasive, and long-lasting moods and motivations in men by formulating conceptions of a general order of existence and clothing these conceptions with such an aura of factuality that the moods and motivations seem uniquely realistic." In simple words religion is about the deep symbolic content of life. Personal beliefs are of reduced interest here. They are rare, if any, in traditional societies and have little probability, even when associated with practice, to survive archaeologically. One may correctly argue that such a dry view underestimates the spiritual nature of the phenomenon. The reason for taking this stand is operational. In archaeology we need to concentrate on people's actions and their outcome in the material culture rather than on beliefs since the former are more within the realm of the discipline than the latter.

Heuristic tools to archaeologically investigate the emergence of this behaviour and characterise its early stages of development may come, in general, from the analysis of how religion changes people's view of the world and how this is mirrored by and may survive in the archaeological record. In particular, cross-cultural analysis of the material culture involved in religious performances may provide criteria by which to assess the nature and significance of possible early religious practices.

This approach may be complemented by the analysis of other categories of material culture. Because of the eminently symbolic character of all known religious beliefs, modern language and symbolic thinking must be considered as necessary prerequisites for the emergence of religion. Human language is essential to conceive, communicate, and pass from one generation to another religious complex understandings. Human language is the only means of communication that has a built-in meta-language enabling us to create and socially share a multitude of symbolic codes, including those that make possible the creation and transmission of religious practices (Aiello 1998). Language does not fossilize. The use of symbolic codes, in contrast, may leave archaeological traces when these codes are embodied in long-lasting material culture. Beliefs have more probability of becoming stable traditions when they involve the use of long-lasting symbolic items. In sum, although symbolic material culture cannot be considered as a direct proxy for religion, it is clear that it is in such a social, cultural, and cognitive environment that religion may rapidly spread and take hold.

## The archaeology of the earliest religious practices, a breviarium

Many authors have proposed criteria by which to assess the symbolic status of prehistoric material culture (Byres 1994, 1999, 2001; Chase 1991, 1999; Chase and Dibble, 1987; McBrearty & Brooks 2000; Henshilwood & Marean 2003; d'Errico et al. 2003; Donald 1991; Lock & Peters 1999; Buissac 2003). Complex technologies, regional trends in the style and decoration of tools, systematic use of pigments, abstract and representational depictions on a variety of media, burials, grave goods, and personal ornaments are among the more common long-lasting creations that attest to the complex symbolic nature of ethnographically recorded human cultures. These features may be reasonably seen as archaeological proxies for the emergence of religious beliefs. However, views diverge on the significance of each of these categories and on the interpretation of individual finds.

A symbolic interpretation has been formally discarded for a number of objects as it has been demonstrated that the modifications described as anthropogenic and bearing symbolic meaning were in fact natural in origin. Cases in point are grooved and perforated objects from Lower and

Middle Palaeolithic sites from Europe and North Africa, interpreted as purposely engraved items, personal ornaments, musical instruments or elaborated bone tools, that when submitted to a close scrutiny have appeared to be (Figures 8.1 and 8.2) bones bearing vascular grooves (d'Errico & Villa 1997) or variously damaged by carnivores (d'Errico 1991; d'Errico et al. 1998; Chase & Nowell 1998; d'Errico & Lawson 2006). In other cases such as for a number of Neanderthal burials (Gargett 1989, 1999; but see d'Errico 2003; d'Errico et al. 2003) a natural origin is not demonstrated but rather suggested as an alternative interpretation of the evidence in the absence of contextual data demonstrating clear human intervention. Still in others, as for the use of pigment by Middle Stone Age and Mousterian populations or some shaped representations (d'Errico & Nowell 2000), human utilisation is widely accepted but a symbolic intention ruled out by some authors on the ground that pigments might have been used for purely functional reasons (Klein 1999, 2000; Wadley 2001, 2002). Abstract or depictional representations and personal ornaments are the only unquestioned evidence for the emergence of symbolism.

If the emergence of these innovations was determined by a biological change, such as a genetic mutation or a speciation process that would have 'switched on' the light of humankind we should expect to find them reflected in the material culture produced by early, anatomically modern populations. Specifically, we should find such archaeological evidence at

**8.1.** Bovid rib from the Pech de l'Azé II Mousterian site bearing grooves interpreted by some authors as deliberate engravings. Microscopic analysis of these grooves and their comparison with reference collections have demonstrated that they are impressions of blood vessels. (Modified after d'Errico & Villa 1997) Scale bars = 1 cm

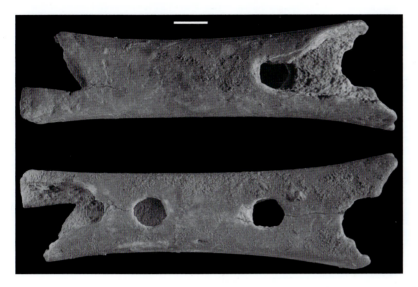

**8.2.** Perforated cave-bear femur from Divje babe II Mousterian site, Slovenia, interpreted by some authors as a Neanderthal flute. Taphonomic analyses of cave bear bone accumulations and microscopic analysis of the object clearly indicate that the perforations are the result of carnivore damage. (Modified after d'Errico & Lawson 2006) Scale bars = 1 cm

sites in Africa from between two hundred thousand and one hundred thousand years ago, and see it rapidly spreading within this continent. If this was the case one could speculate that early religious beliefs originated at a given time and place, in conjunction with the origin of modern humanity and it could even be possible in the future to identify the most likely area and period when this cognitive revolution took place. Things, however, are more complicated. Archaeologically, what we see instead is a gradual emergence of behavioural innovations in and outside Africa between three hundred thousand and twenty thousand years ago. Moreover, anatomically modern populations shared a number of these innovations with Neanderthals, which many anthropologists and geneticists consider a different species, or a human type inherently incapable of reaching our cognitive level (Figure 8.3).

For example, elongated stone blades are found not only at Neanderthal sites in Europe and the Near East, but also at sites inhabited by Moderns in the Near East and Africa since at least one hundred thousand years ago. Blade technologies then disappeared and reappeared cyclically in these areas, and in some regions, such as Australia, they only appeared a few thousand years ago, in spite of them being colonised by modern humans at least fifty thousand years earlier.

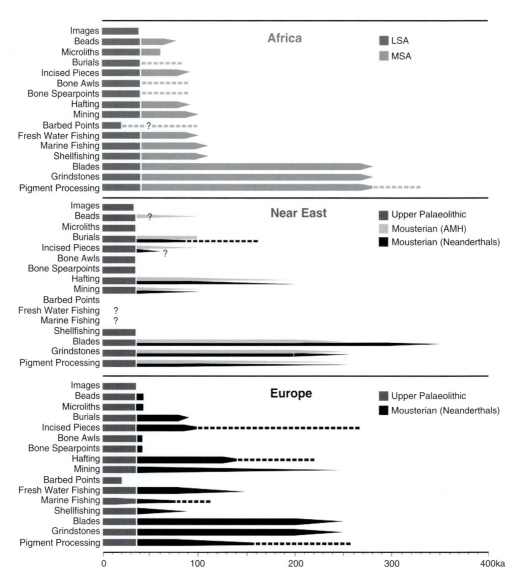

**8.3.** Occurrence of "modern" traits in the African, Near Eastern, and European archaeological records. Interrupted lines indicate discontinuous presence. (Modified after d'Errico 2003)

Similarly, standardized tools produced by both Neanderthals and Moderns appeared eighty thousand years ago. Pigments (Plate XXII), probably used in symbolic activities such as tattooing or body painting, are found at Southern African sites since three hundred thousand years (Barham 1998, 2002), but also at contemporaneous and more recent Neanderthal sites in Europe and the Near East (Hovers et al. 2003).

The intentional character and symbolic significance of burials prior to thirty thousand years ago, especially those of Neanderthals, remain the subject of intense debate (d'Errico et al. 2003). But there is enough evidence to believe that both anatomically modern humans and Neanderthals began burying their dead one hundred thousand years ago – and probably before, as suggested by the recent dating at 160,000 years of a Neanderthal burial site at Tabun, Israel.

Sophisticated bone tools, such as harpoons, spear points, and awls, seem to have appeared in Africa ninety thousand years ago, much earlier than in the rest of the world (Henshilwood et al. 2002). This also applies to personal ornaments, with recently discovered shell beads from Blombos Cave, South Africa (Figure 8.4, also Plate V), dated at seventy five thousand years ago (Henshilwood et al. 2004; d'Errico et al. 2005, Vanhaeren 2005).

But these innovations do not seem to have been widespread. Bone tools and beads are virtually absent from sites in Africa and the Near East inhabited by modern humans beginning one hundred thousand years ago, and few abstract engravings on bone and on fragments of ochre are found at African sites dated to seventy-five thousand years ago. Depictions of animals, human beings, and other natural features do not occur

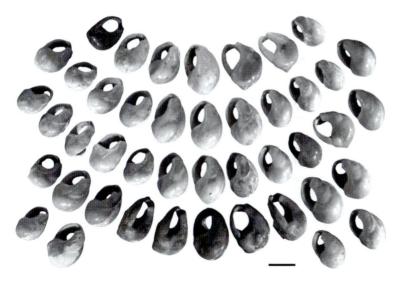

**8.4.** *Nassarius kraussianus* shell beads from Middle Stone Age layers of Blombos Cave dated at seventy-five thousand years ago. (Modified after Henshilwood et al. 2004) Scale bars = 1 cm

in the three records – Africa, Europe, and the Near East – before forty thousand to thirty thousand years ago, and they appear much later in some areas than others.

In sum, some behavioural innovations seem to appear in Africa between ten thousand and thirty thousand years before Neanderthals express them. But one can doubt that this gap represents the evidence of significantly different cognitive abilities. After all, it took seven thousand years for agriculture to arrive in Britain from the Near East, and nobody would argue that the cognitive abilities of Mesolithic hunter-gatherers from Britain were inferior to those of early agriculturalists.

In other words if the emergence of the modern traits listed above, and in particular those indicating the emergence of symbolic thinking reflect, as one may reasonably argue, the raising of a comprehensive and socially shared symbolic view of the world, one must conclude that religious practices developed gradually, at different places, and among a number of human populations, probably including Neanderthals and Archaic sapiens. This is the only take-home message the reader of this contribution must retain. But this is not the end of the story.

During this long timespan religious beliefs certainly took a variety of forms, perhaps involving a number of stages in the way they have pervaded the human soul. Religion as we know it probably originated in an attempt to order shared beliefs and symbols arising in response to direct experience of the spiritual. As this attempt expands in its elaboration, it becomes a process that creates meaning for itself on a sustaining basis.

The main challenge that faces the archaeology of religion is to propose reliable scenarios for this complex process and find means to test those scenarios on the archaeological and paleoanthropological records.

In my view, five types of inferences may help us to speculate about the earliest phases of this process, but also caution us against reaching excessively hasty conclusions: (1) the observation of those among our close relatives that possess, to some extent, the capacity or the potential for symbolic behaviours; (2) the cross-cultural comparative analysis of symbolic behaviours produced by modern and submodern traditional societies; (3) the study of the material culture of past symbolic societies; (4) the identification of natural phenomena that can be erroneously interpreted as the result of symbolic human behaviours; and (5) the experimental reproduction of human behaviours producing on durable material culture features that may have had symbolic purposes.

Although criteria relative to each of the above categories of data were published in the literature, few attempts have been made so far to unify them in a comprehensive research strategy and refine them through application to concrete archaeological case studies. This is mainly due to the fact that each of these potential sources of reflection falls within the competence of a different discipline (ethology, cross-cultural anthropology, taphonomy, experimental archaeology, semiotics, etc.) approaching the issue from a different viewpoint, and often with a limited understanding of the potential contribution offered by the others.

## Ethology

Trained chimpanzees seem fully capable of learning and transmit complex systems of signs and, to some extent, understand articulated and, by definition, highly symbolic human language (Premark 1986; Savage-Rumbaugh et al. 1998). Wild chimpanzees, however, show little interest in using these cognitive capacities to transform their gestural conventions in proper systems of signs and embody them in their material culture. What are the implications of chimpanzee symbolic abilities for the elaboration of predictive models about the origin of religion that archaeologists could test against the empirical evidence? The first implication is that hominid cultures may have existed with rather complex systems of signs, transmitted from generation to generation, that have left no durable traces of their existance. After all oral traditions were responsible until recently for the transmission of the more peculiar aspects of human cultural traditions. This means that the absence of symbolic material culture does not imply the absence of symbolic thinking or religion. It only indicates that it was, perhaps, not there or it was there at such a level of consciousness as not to need a degree of formulation and elaboration involving a material expression and a formalised ritual.

## Cultural anthropology

Modern cultural anthropology abhors evolutionary models for the origin of universals such as symbolism since it fears that they may be used, as they were by nineteenth century ethnology, to classify societies according to their 'stage of civilisation' or the nature of their way of thinking (Tylor 1891; Lévy-Bruhl 1922). Claude Lévi-Strauss is one of the very few cultural anthropologists of the second half of the twentieth century who has developed an anthropological theory comprising a mechanism for the origin of the symbolic function and predicting social behaviours that would demonstrate its acquisition. Although some of these behaviours may be reflected in the archaeological record thus paving the way for the creation of predictive archaeological models, little interest has been paid by archaeologists to Lévi-Strauss's contribution in this field.

The taboo of incest, on which basis, according to Lévi-Strauss, symbolic societies organise their social structure and symbolic systems, implies the existence of links of solidarity between males reinforced by ritualised exchange of gifts (Mauss 1923–24). In a number of societies these gifts take the form of mere symbolic objects, often made in exotic or rare raw material or, when functional, of items which differ for their quality of manufacture and design from every-day tools. When did objects that may be reasonably interpreted as such gifts appear in the archaeological record?

I believe there is no proof that shamanism should be considered to be a universal of hunter-gatherers societies nor, as a consequence, that the origin of symbolism and shamanism should necessarily be linked. I also realize that shamanism is a complex and articulated phenomenon, encompassing very different realities. It is a fact, however, that this way of conceiving the outside world and interacting with it characterises most hunter-gatherers societies, living in very different regions of the planet and adapted to dramatically different environments. Thus, we may expect that a number of early symbolic societies were shamanic.

In many shamanic societies the power of the shaman is materialised by his dress and tools. These objects are an integral part of his/her activities. At the end of his life, the well-known Siberian shaman Tubiaku refused to treat very ill patients saying that without his dress and drum, sold to a museum, he could only work with nearby spirits, not powerful enough to treat mortal illnesses. Although no extensive comparative ethnoarchaeological study of these artefacts has been conducted so far, my preliminary cross-cultural survey identifies three basic categories: unmodified natural objects, natural objects carrying anthropic or natural perforations used to include them in a chain, put them on a hat belt and so on, and a large variety of fully manufactured artefacts such as dolls, often wearing personal ornaments, miniatures of tools and animals (Plate XXIII). These objects are generally of small to very small size and when unmodified they are kept in skin bags, nets or boxes. Composite shamanic tools are generally made of a variety of objects strung together. Wear from transport or prolonged manipulation which may or may not be associated with traces of pigments are a common feature on these objects. Considering the trans-cultural occurrence of such objects, we may reasonably expect to find a number of them in the material culture left by early symbolic societies.

Lévi-Strauss's theory predicts other features on which archaeologists may build. Traditional societies pay much attention to details of the natural world, including the human body itself, in search of features – colours, flavours, shapes, rhythms – on which systems of signs and, by extension, of beliefs can be based. The importance fulfilled by pigments among MSA and Neanderthal populations at some stages of their cultural evolution might well reflect the emergence of this new way of looking at the natural world. Lévi-Strauss's distinction between 'sociétés froides', living in an eternal present and 'sociétés chaudes' attributing more importance to events creating a 'cumulative history' is also relevant here: it provides an explanation for the apparent low rate of innovation that archaeologists observe when they study early symbolic systems.

## Semiotics

A paradox appears when we compare the powerful means that, in principle, semiotics should provide for recognising early systems of signs, including those closely linked to religious practices, and the little factual contribution this discipline has given so far to the debate on the emergence of symbolic thinking. Semioticians may claim that in order to demonstrate the symbolic nature of prehistoric societies we must, ideally, find in the archaeological record systems of signs comparable, in their organisation, to those observed in modern and ethnographically known human societies. That is a material culture with a range of deliberate human-made representations. The term 'range' is used because a system of signs is by definition based on a variety of meaningful representations. While all symbolic societies use elements of the natural world in their symbolic systems there is no way to establish that this was indeed the case for a past society in absence of other indications of its symbolic nature. We may also expect to find these systems of signs shared by a number of close contemporary human groups. Archaeologically this should take the form of a cluster of neighbouring sites characterised by similar representations, artefact style and decoration. A symbolic culture can hardly survive in isolation. A powerful function of symbolic material culture is that of transmitting, reinforcing and preserving cultural identity. This means that the above-mentioned cluster of sites should be surrounded by other clusters, characterised by different symbolic material cultures and, possibly, by meaningful gradients toward the periphery of each region. Even in Lévi-Strauss's 'cold societies' systems of sign evolve, change dramatically or disappear according to historical and ecological contingencies. These changes should also, in principle, be detected by archaeologists either within a particular site stratigraphy or when correlating contemporaneous sites. Symbols are never displayed randomly. They always appear in meaningful contexts, that is, on media (objects, the human body, walls etc.) and at times (periods of the year, moments of the individual life . . .) which grant them communicating power. Although such locations may be lost in the majority of the cases, it is possible that some of these regularities may survive archaeologically and be detected as consistent patterns.

## Experimental archaeology

In the absence of reliable predictive models, some meaningful information, once the anthropic origin of the modification is warranted by contextual and actualistic data, is provided by technological analysis of the object. The use of this analogy is based on the assumption that our ancestors shared with us most neuromotor constraints, thus enabling us to reconstruct the motions resulting in certain modifications. Of course one cannot tackle meaning through technological analysis nor will the result of such analysis directly account for the development of symbolism. It will nevertheless provide factual information on the type of tool used, on possible changes of tools, on the chronology of the anthropic modifications, and on the time taken to produce them. This information will help us to evaluate the degree of intentionality of the makers and try to make sense of the sequence of choices and decisions behind their acts in terms of cognitive processes at work. These technical choices, in particular when they can be examined on a number of similar objects, may become integral to any argument on the significance of early symbolic behaviour and they can by a step-by-step process generate testable theories on the first stages of development of this capacity.

However, archaeologists face a final difficulty when it comes to using this evidence. The link between technical actions and the recognition of the symbolic nature of an artefact possibly involved in symbolic activities is ambiguous. The discovery of pigments with traces of use in the form of ground facets, scraping marks and grooves is generally not considered as formal proof that these pigments were used in symbolic activities. The reason is that the activities in which pigments were used (colouring on a variety of media, body painting, camouflage, hide preparation, etc.) are considered difficult to infer from the mineral fragments found at archaeological sites. Engraved lines, especially when they create regular abstract patterns, such as those from Blombos, or those that may be interpreted as depictions of objects or beings, are generally seen as more powerful arguments in favour of the symbolic nature of a material culture.

The problem is that each artefact is the reflection of actions we know little about and that the criteria used to attribute to the evidence a more or less convincing power are rarely made explicit. To find reliable criteria of symbolicity it is necessary to create an interpretive framework in which we explain in detail the relationship between technical action or, better, sequences of technical actions and their implications for the interpretation of an artefact in term of symbolicity.

The next question must concern when repetition of actions becomes a 'consistent pattern'? It is dangerous to equate the frequency of a type of archaeological material with its ancient social significance. The amount of pigment recovered from an excavation depends on taphonomic factors, including the technique used to prepare the pigment, the media on which the pigment was applied, and the frequency of the activities in which pigments were used. The presence of used pigment indicates that other colourants may also have been used but did not survive archaeologically.

## Conclusion

Contrary to a popular belief, archaeology has the means to conduct investigations on the earliest religious practices and integrate results of this search on the broader debate concerning the origin of modern cognition (Renfrew 1994). The 'Out of Africa' model for the origin of our species implies that the emergence of modern cognition was a stocastic event. Thorough analysis of current archaeological evidence from Africa and Europe shows that an alternative scenario is consistent with the empirical data. Features used to define modern behaviour arose over a long period of time among different human populations including Neanderthals. Our anatomically modern ancestors certainly shared with Neanderthals and other contemporary populations many traits that we have for long preferred to consider the monopoly of our species, including religion. The nature of these early religious practices and their variability in time and space is still a topic we know little about. Research strategies that may enable us to gain a better insight into this crucial phenomenon exist though, and will certainly provide new relevant data in the next few years.

## Acknowledgements

Many thanks to the holders of image copyrights who kindly gave permission for figures to be reproduced here. They are listed in the acknowledgements at the front of the book.

### REFERENCES

Aiello, L. C., 1998. The foundation of human language, in *The origin and diversification of language*, eds. N. G. Jablonski & L. C. Aiello. San Francisco: California Academy of Science, 21–34.

Barbujani, G., 2003. Genetics and the population history of Europe, in *Encyclopedia of the Human Genome*. Nature Publishing Group, 1–5.

Barham, L. S., 1998. Possible early pigment use in south-central Africa. *Current Anthropology* **39**, 703–10.

Barham, L. S., 2002. Systematic pigment use in the Middle Pleistocene of south-central Africa. *Current Anthropology* **43**, 181–90.

Beffa M.-L. & L. Delaby, 1999. *Festins d'âmes et robes d'esprits. Les objets chamaniques sibériens du Musée de l'Homme*. Paris: Publications scientifiques du Muséum.

Byers, A. M., 1994. Symboling and the Middle-Upper Palaeolithic transition: a theoretical and methodological critique. *Current Anthropology* **35**: 369–400.

Byers, A. M., 1999. Communication and material culture: Pleistocene tools as action cues. *Cambridge Archaeological Journal* **9**: 23–41.

Byers, A. M., 2001. A pragmatic view of the emergence of Paleolithic symbol-using, in *In the Mind's Eye: Multidisciplinary Approaches to the Evolution of Human Cognition*, ed. A. Nowell. Ann Arbor: International Monographs in Prehistory, 50–62.

Bouissac, P., 2003. Criteria of symbolicity: intrinsic and extrinsic formal properties of artifacts. Paper presented at the *9th Meeting of the European Archaeologists Association.* 10–14 Sept. 2003, St. Petersburg. Available at http://www.semioticon.com/virtuals/symbolicity/intrinsic.html

Cann, R. L., M. Stoneking & A. C. Wilson, 1987. Mitochondrial DNA and human evolution. *Nature* **356**, 389–90.

Chase, P. G., 1991. Symbols and Paleolithic artifacts: style, standardization, and the imposition of arbitrary form. *Journal of Anthropological Archaeology* **10**, 193–214.

Chase, P. G. & H. Dibble, 1987. Middle Palaeolithic symbolism: a review of current evidence and interpretations. *Journal of Anthropological Archaeology* **6**, 263–96.

Chase, P. G. & A. Nowell, 1998. Taphonomy of a suggested Middle Paleolithic bone flute from Slovenia. *Current Anthropology* **39**, 184–94.

Chase, P. G., 1999. Symbolism as reference and symbolism as culture, in *The Evolution of Culture: An Interdisciplinary View*, eds. R. I. M. Dunbar, C. Knight & C. Power. Edinburgh: Edinburgh University Press, 34–49.

d'Errico, F. & G. Lawson 2006. The sound paradox. How to assess the acoustic significance of archaeological evidence?, in *Archaeoacoustics*, G. Lawson & C. Scarre. Cambridge: McDonald Institute Monographs, 41–57.

d'Errico, F. & A. Nowell. 2000. A new look at the Berekhat Ram figurine: implications for the origins of symbolism. *Cambridge Archaeological Journal* **10**, 123–67.

d'Errico, F. & P. Villa, 1997. Holes and grooves: the contribution of microscopy and taphonomy to the problem of art origins. *Journal of Human Evolution* **33**, 1–31.

d'Errico, F., 1991. Carnivore traces or Mousterian skiffle? *Rock Art Research* **8**, 61–3.

d'Errico, F., 2003. The invisible frontier. A multiple species model for the origin of behavioural modernity. *Evolutionary Anthropology* **12**: 188–202.

d'Errico, F., C. Henshilwood, G. Lawson, M. Vanhaeren, A.-M. Tillier, M. Soressi, F. Bresson, B. Maureille, A. Nowell, J. Lakarra, L. Backwell, & M. Julien., 2003. Archaeological evidence for the origins of language, symbolism and music: an alternative multidisciplinary perspective. *Journal of World Prehistory* **17**, 1–70.

d'Errico, F., C. Henshilwood, M. Vanhaeren & K. Van Niekerk, 2004. *Nassarius kraussianus* shell beads from Blombos Cave: evidence for symbolic behaviour in the Middle Stone Age. *Journal of Human Evolution* **48**, 3–24.

d'Errico, F., M. Vanhaeren, C. Henshilwood, G. Lawson, B. Maureille, D. Gambier, A.-M. Tillier, M. Soressi, & K. Van Niekerk, in press. From the origin of language to the diversification of languages: what can archaeology and palaeoanthropology say? In *The Origin of Man, Language and Languages*, eds. J.M. Hombert & C. Renfrew. European Science Foundation.

d'Errico, F., J. Zilhão, D. Baffier, M. Julien & J. Pelegrin, 1998. Neanderthal acculturation in western Europe? A critical review of the evidence and its interpretation. *Current Anthropology* **39**, S1–S44.

d'Errico, F., P. Villa, A. Pinto, & R. Ruiz-Idarraga, 1998. A Middle Palaeolithic origin of music? Using cave-bear bone accumulations to assess the Divje Babe I bone 'flute'. *Antiquity* **72**, 65–79.

Derwent, S., R. de la Harpe & P. de la Harpe, 2000. *Zulu.* Cape Town: Struik.

Donald, M., 1991. *Origins of the Modern Mind: Three Stages in the Evolution of Culture and Cognition.* Harvard: Harvard University Press.

Dubin, L. S., 1999. *North American Indian Jewelry and Adornment: From Prehistory to the Present.* New York: Abrams.

Durkheim, E., 1915. *The Elementary Forms of the Religious Life: A Study in Religious Sociology.* New York: Macmillan.

Foley, R. & M. M. Lahr, 1997. Mode 3 technologies and the evolution of modern humans. *Cambridge Archaeological Journal* 7, 3–36.

Frazer, J. G., 1890. *The Golden Bough.* London: Macmillan.

Gargett, R. H., 1989. Grave shortcomings: the evidence for Neanderthal burial. *Current Anthropology* **30**, 157–90.

Gargett, R. H., 1999. Middle Palaeolithic burial is not a dead issue: the view from Qafzeh, Sainte-Césaire, Kebara, Amud, and Dederiyeh. *Journal of Human Evolution* **37**, 27–40.

Geertz, C., 1966. Religion as a cultural system, in *Anthropological Approaches to the Study of Religion*, ed. M. Banton. London, Tavistock, 1–46.

Henshilwood, C. S., J. C. Sealy, R. J. Yates, K. Cruz-Uribe, P. Goldberg, F. E. Grine, R. G. Klein, C. Poggenpoel, K. Van Niekerk & I. Watts, 2001. Blombos Cave, Southern Cape, South Africa: preliminary report on the 1992–1999 excavations of the Middle Stone Age levels. *Journal of Archaeological Science* **28**, 421–448.

Henshilwood, C. S. & C. W. Marean, 2003. The origin of modern human behaviour: A review and critique of models and test implications. *Current Anthropology* **44**, 627–51.

Henshilwood C. S., F. d'Errico, M. Vanhaeren, K. Van Niekerk & Z. Jacobs, 2004. Middle Stone Age shell beads from South Africa. *Science* 304, 403.

Hovers E., S. Ilani, O. Bar-Yosef & B. Vandermeersch, 2003. An early case of colour symbolism: ochre use by modern humans in Qafzeh Cave. *Current Anthropology* **44**, 492–522.

Ingman, M., H. Kaessmann, S. Pääbo, U. Gyllensten, 2000. Mitochondrial genome variation and the origin of modern humans. *Nature* **408**, 708–13.

Jehs, D., 2004. Gauging Neanderthal cognition: problems and perspectives. *Ghent Archaeological Studies* **1**, 85–99.

Klein, R. G., 1999. *The Human Career* (2nd ed.). Chicago: Chicago University Press.

Klein, R. G., 2000. Archaeology and the evolution of human behaviour. *Evolutionary Anthropology* **9**, 17–36.

Klein, R. G., 2003. Whither the Neanderthals? *Science* **229**, 1525–7.

Klein, R. G. & E. Blake, 2003. *The Dawn of Human Culture*. New York: John Wiley & Sons.

Lévi-Strauss, C., 1960. *Leçon inaugurale au collège de France*, 5 January 1960.

Lévi-Strauss, C., 1967. *Les Structures élémentaires de la parenté*. Paris: Mouton.

Lévy-Bruhl, L., 1922. *La mentalité primitive*. Paris: P.U.F.

Lewis-Williams, J. D. & T. A. Dowson, 1988. Signs of all times: entoptic phenomena in Upper Palaeolithic art. *Current Anthropology* **29**, 201–45.

Lewis-Williams, J. D. & T. A. Dowson, 1989. *Images of Power: Understanding Bushman Rock Art*. Johannesburg: Southern Book.

Lewis-Williams, J. D., 2002. *The Mind in the Cave: Consciousness and the Origins of Art*. London: Thames & Hudson.

Lock A. & C. Peters, 1996. *Handbook of Human Symbolic Evolution*. Oxford: Clarendon Press.

Lommel, A., 1970. *Shamanism: The Beginning of Art*. New York: McGraw-Hill.

Mauss, M., 1923–1924. Essai sur le don. Forme et raison de l'échange dans les sociétés archaïques. *L'Année Sociologique* **1**: 30–186.

McBrearty, S. & A. S. Brooks, 2000. The revolution that wasn't: a new interpretation of the origin of modern human behaviour. *Journal of Human Evolution* **39**, 453–563.

Mellars, P., 1998. Neanderthals, modern humans and the archaeological evidence for language, in *The Origin and Diversification of Language*, eds. N. G. Jablonski & L. C. Aiello. San Francisco: California Academy of Sciences, 89–115.

Mithen, S. J., 1996. *The Prehistory of the Mind: A Search for the Origins of Art, Religion and Science*. London: Thames & Hudson.

Premark, D., 1986. *Gavagai! The Future of the Animal Language Controversy*. Cambridge (MA): MIT Press.

Renfrew, C., 1994. The archaeology of religion, in *The Ancient Mind: Elements of Cognitive Archaeology*, eds. C. Renfrew & E. Zubrow. Cambridge: McDonald Institute Monographs, 47–54.

Savage-Rumbaugh, E. S., G. S. Stuart & J. T. Talbot, 1998. *Apes, Language and the Human Mind*. Oxford: Oxford University Press.

Sollas, W., 1911. *Ancient Hunters and Their Modern Representatives*. London: Macmillan.

Tylor, E. B., 1891. *Primitive Culture*. London: Murray.

Vanhaeren, M., 2005. Speaking with beads: the evolutionary significance of bead making and use, in *From Tools to Symbols from Early Hominids to Modern Humans*, eds. F. d'Errico & L. Backwell. Johannesburg: Wits University Press.

Van Peer, P. & P. Vermeersch, 2000. The Nubian complex and the dispersal of modern humans in North Africa, in *Recent researches into the Stone Age of Northeastern Asia*, ed. L. Krzyzaniak. Poznan: Poznan Archaeological Museum, Polish Academy of Sciences, 47–60.

Wadley, L., 2001. What is cultural modernity? A general view and a South African perspective from Rose Cottage. *Cambridge Archaeological Journal* **11**, 201–21.

Wadley, L., 2003. How some archaeologists recognize culturally modern behaviour. *South African Journal of Science* **99**, 247–50.

Weber, M., 1966. *The Sociology of Religion*. London: Methuen.

Wurz, S. 2000, *The Middle Stone Age sequence at Klasies River, South Africa*. University of Stellenbosch.

Zilhão, J., 2001. *Anatomically Archaic, Behaviourally Modern: the Last Neanderthals and Their Destiny*. Amsterdam: Enshedé.

Zilhão, J. & F. d'Errico, 2003. The chronology of the Aurignacian and transitional technocomplexes: where do we stand?, in *The Chronology of the Aurignacian and of the Transitional Technocomplexes: Dating, Stratigraphies, Cultural Implications*, eds. J. Zilhão & F. d'Errico. Lisboa: IPA, 313–49.

9

# Out of the mind: material culture and the supernatural

*Steven Mithen*

## 1. Cognitive evolution and Upper Palaeolithic art

My concern is with the contribution that an evolutionary perspective on the human mind provides to our understanding of the relationship between Upper Palaeolithic art and religion. I will draw on the ideas of two social anthropologists, Harvey Whitehouse (2000, 2004) and Pascal Boyer (1994, 2001), and two philosophers, Peter Carruthers (2002) and Andy Clark (1997, 2003; Clark & Chalmers 1998). Their ideas will be embedded within my own work (Mithen 1996, 1998, 2004) concerning the evolution of the human mind with regard to the two cognitive developments that resulted in religion and art – the emergence of cognitive fluidity and the extension of the human mind beyond the brain into material culture. I will characterise the paintings and carvings of the ice age as part of the Upper Palaeolithic mind: the art played an active role in generating, manipulating and transmitting ideas about the supernatural beings of the ice age world. Such ideas are inherently difficult for human brains alone to comprehend. This is used as just one example of the larger phenomenon of people using material and other types of culture including song and dance to make religious ideas tangible so that they can be more easily manipulated in the mind and transmitted to other individuals.

## 2. What is religion?

For the purposes of this article I will use the definition of religion recently employed by Whitehouse in his 2004 book *Modes of Religiosity*: "any set of shared beliefs and actions appealing to supernatural agency". This begs the question of what constitutes 'supernatural agency' and why this concept is so widespread within human society. Indeed, belief in supernatural beings is a universal feature of recent human communities and we have no reason to think that this was not also the case in pre-history, at least back to the origin of the first modern humans c. 170,000 years ago. A significant and ever-growing number of individuals in modern western society express disbelief in supernatural beings, but these remain in the minority and the possession of such views seems to involve a greater mental effort than does the converse. I assume that atheism was rare, if not absent, in traditional and especially prehistoric society. In most, if not all, religions, supernatural beings require that rituals are practiced and are associated with stories about a mythological world. So when faced with the art of the Upper Palaeolithic we can hardly doubt that it depicts the supernatural beings of the ice age – either directly or via metaphor – and the mythological worlds with which those beings were associated. Moreover, it is natural to assume that the paintings, engravings and carvings had been either made or utilised during the rituals practiced by ice age hunter-gatherers.

If Upper Palaeolithic art is evidence for ice age religion, then that religion is likely to fall into the 'imagistic' mode rather than the 'doctrinal' mode as defined by Whitehouse (2000, 2004). This dichotomy is similar to that drawn by other social anthropologists such as Max Weber (1947, charismatic vs. routinized religion), Jack Goody (1968, unliterate vs. literate religion) and Fredrik Barth (1990, 'guru' vs. 'conjurer' religious regimes). In Whitehouse's terms, the imagistic mode of religion is characterised by practices that are rarely enacted, highly arousing and lead to 'spontaneous exegetical reflection'. Such practices result in a diversity of religious experiences: while those of different individuals may converge on a similar theme they are likely to lack any explicitly shared meaning even though there is agreement about the ritual procedures themselves. Whitehouse relates this religious mode to a specific set of social circumstances that include an absence of dynamic leadership and the presence of intense social relationships.

The 'doctrinal mode' of religiosity involves the highly routinized transmission of religious teachings and explicit doctrines about the nature of supernatural beings that constitutes a formal theology (Whitehouse 2000). Such religions rely on the presence of religious leaders and 'orthodoxy checks' to ensure that highly standardized versions of religious teachings become widely shared and accepted via public rehearsal and frequent repetition. As with the imagistic mode, certain social circumstances are consistently related to doctrinal modes of religion, either as cause or effect: centralisation, formal leadership and 'open communities' in the sense that one can join them simply by ascribing to the religious doctrine. Doctrinal religions are characteristic of literate societies in which the teachings are written down in sacred texts.

The characteristics of ice age religion as inferred from Upper Palaeolithic art by scholars such as Jean Clottes and David Lewis Williams (Clottes et al. 1998; Lewis-Williams 2002) are consistent with White-house's concept of the imagistic religious. These include traumatic or violent initiation rituals, experiences of collective possession and altered states of consciousness. The specific role that the art played in such ice age religion remains unclear. Similarly, it remains questionable as to whether we can draw any specific inferences about the nature of ice age super-natural beings from that art and associated archaeological data. Before addressing such questions, we must consider the origin of religious thought. This requires a concern with the evolution of the human mind.

## 3. Origin of religion

The extent to which pre-modern humans undertook ritual activities and had religious beliefs has been a subject of substantial debate. Most of this debate has focused on the Neanderthals and what inferences can be drawn from the fact that they buried some of their dead. The literature regarding this subject is immense (e.g. Gargett 1989; Mellars 1996; and references therein) and the conclusions that I draw are: (1) some Neanderthals were deliberately buried, and (2) there is no evidence for graveside ritual or the presence of grave goods.

The absence of such ritual, symbolic artefacts in general, and other characteristics of the Neanderthal archaeological record, indicates that they lacked religious thought and did not conceive of supernatural beings (Mithen 1996). They were, I believe, very literal minded humans for reasons I have explained at length in my 1996 book *The Prehistory of the Mind*. Within that work I argued on the basis of both theory (from evolutionary psychology) and data (from archaeology) that the Neanderthals had a domain-specific mentality. By this, I mean that the Neanderthal mind had mental modules that had been selected during the course of evolution to solve the problems posed by a hunter-gathering and highly social way of life. In this regard the Neanderthal had botanical and zoological knowledge equivalent to that of modern hunter-gatherers within their domain of natural history intelligence, a theory of mind and at least third order intentionality within their social intelligence, and an understanding of fracture mechanics and basic physics within their technical intelligence. But they were unable to combine ways of thinking and stores of knowledge from different cognitive domains/intelligences as is characteristic of *H. sapiens*. In other words, they lacked the ability for metaphor and had limited imagination.

As I will explain later, the mental conception of a supernatural being requires cognitively fluid thought – that which makes such connections between cognitive domains. One reason why the Neanderthals lacked cognitive fluidity was the nature of their vocal communication. This was, I believe, complex and sophisticated but lacked symbols and syntax. In my recent book on the origin of language and music (Mithen 2005) I refer to Neanderthal communication by the acronym 'Hmmmmm' as I argue that it was Holistic multi-modal, manipulative, musical and mimetic. As such it played a major role in expressing and inducing emotion.

While the Neanderthals lacked religious thought, their burial activities would have been events of intense emotional experience. In light of their large brains, their complex material culture, and the challenging environmental conditions in which they survived, it seems likely that the Neanderthals lived in groups with strong social bonds to facilitate cooperation. On the basis of mortality data (Trinkaus 1995), their populations appear marginally viable. Hence the loss of any member of the social group would have been of considerable significance. Their burial would have been highly emotional events, most likely associated with expressive Hmmmmm 'song' and 'dance'. As such, these events would have served as precursors to those that are characteristic of the imagistic religious mode. But they were not religious events themselves, because the Neanderthals had no concept of the supernatural. Similarly, I am sympathetic to the idea that Neanderthal music may have been used for the same 'healing' purposes for their sick and injured, as found amongst many hunter-gatherers today (e.g. Roseman 1991; Gouk 2000); but again it would have lacked the religious dimension that is often found today.

Hmmmm type communication and domain-specific mentality would have also been characteristic of the immediate ancestor to *H. sapiens* in

Africa, although in a less extreme form than found amongst the Neanderthals. That ancestor is generally referred to as *H. helmei*, which may have also been the direct ancestor to the Neanderthals (Foley & Lahr 1993). During the last five years the genetic and fossil archaeological evidence have converged to suggest that *H. sapiens* had evolved in Africa by 170,000 years ago (White et al. 2003; Ingman et al. 2000). Moreover, studies of the FOXP2 gene (Lai et al. 2001) have been used to suggest that language evolved within that same time frame (Enard et al. 2002; Bishop 2002), while there are traces in the form of pigment usage that symbolic activity might reach back beyond one hundred thousand years ago in Africa (McBrearty & Brooks 2000). Consequently, I will assume that the speciation event of *H. sapiens* involved the origin of language and symbolic thought.

Language is the key to the transition from domain-specific thought to cognitive fluidity, which, in turn, is necessary for conceiving of supernatural beings. In my book, I argue that language evolved from Hmmmm by the process of segmentation that has been described by Alison Wray (1998, 2000) and formed the basis for the computational models of Simon Kirby (2000, 2002). Indeed, I suggest that Hmmmmm formed the basis for the two modern aural communication systems: language and music (Mithen 2005).

Language provides the vehicle for the flow of knowledge and ways of thinking from one cognitive domain to another (Mithen 1996). The philosopher Peter Carruthers (2002) has argued this in greatest detail and length within his important 2002 paper on the 'Cognitive Functions of Language'. He argued that the 'imagined sentences' we create in our minds allow the outputs from one intelligence/module to be combined with those from one or more others, and thereby create new types of conscious thoughts. The consequence is that we can imagine entities that do not – and cannot – exist in the real world. Perhaps the most pervasive consequence of cognitive fluidity has been for modern humans to imagine that all events have intentionality and meaning. A key element of the pre-modern human social intelligence was to infer the intentions behind another person's actions. Once that way of thinking became accessible to natural history and technical intelligence, people began to wonder what the intention was behind natural phenomena, such as thunderstorms, earthquakes and the sight of rare animals. As Guthrie (1993) has argued, such anthropomorphising of the natural and inanimate world is a pervasive feature of religious thought, and perhaps a defining characteristic. A more specific consequence of cognitive fluidity was the ability to imagine the existence of supernatural beings.

The cognitive anthropologist Pascal Boyer (1994, 2001; Boyer & Ramble 2001) has made extensive cross-cultural studies of such beings. As with Mithen (1996) he argues that they combine features of different cognitive domains (or in his terminology, intuitive ontologies). Ghosts, for instance, are often envisaged as being just like humans, except that they can pass through solid objects in the manner that sound or vibrations are able to do. A statue of the Virgin Mary is an inanimate object but has somehow acquired the psychological propensities of a person because it/she can hear prayers. Through his anthropological and experimental studies, Boyer has found that the types of supernatural beings that are most prone to be believed and most resilient to cultural transmission are those that are only 'minimally counterintuitive'. They must have counter-intuitive properties to have salience – such as a 'man' that can rise from the dead, does not need to feed, or lives in some other reality such as 'heaven' or the Dreamtime. On the other hand, they must have sufficient contact with an evolved cognitive domain for them to be conceived at all and to be transmitted across generations: hence the Classical Greek Gods, Aboriginal Ancestral Beings and the vast majority of supernatural beings recorded by anthropologists have often behaved and thought like 'real' people.

The chain of argument is, therefore, that the origin of language led to cognitive fluidity and this enabled the mental conception of supernatural beings (along with many other new types of ideas) and hence formed the basis for religious thought.


## 4. The role of material symbols within religion

Although modern humans, language, cognitive fluidity and symbolic thought are likely to have been present in Africa by 170,000 years ago, it is not until 70,000 years ago that the first symbolic artefacts have been found – the incised ochre fragments and shell beads from Blombos Cave (Henshilwood et al. 2002; Henshilwood et al. 2004). The most dramatic changes in material culture do not occur until after fifty thousand years ago (McBrearty & Brooks 2000). The most likely explanation for this seeming time lapse between the origin of new cognitive capacities and their manifestation in material culture is demography. Both the genetic (Ingman et al. 2000) and archaeological evidence (McBrearty & Brooks 2000) suggest a significant population expansion at around fifty thousand years, which may have had profound consequences for the process of cultural transmission and the 'fixing' of new ideas, technologies and symbols within human communities (Shennan 2001).

Early *H. sapiens* had dispersed into the Near East by one hundred thousand years ago, as evident from the caves of Qafzeh and Skhul where ritualised burial took place. I do not consider those early *H. sapiens* as fully cognitively modern, arguing that they had only achieved partial cognitive fluidity (Mithen 1996) and linguistic abilities (Mithen 2005) The direct ancestors of the first *H. sapiens* in Europe appear to have left Africa only fifty thousand years ago, and then rapidly dispersed throughout Europe, out-competing the resident Neanderthal populations for resources. The *H. sapiens* competitive edge was provided by the cognitive advantages delivered by having language and cognitive fluidity as oppose to Hmmmmm and domain-specific thought that characterised the Neanderthals. Whether or not having religion provided selective benefit to the incoming *H. sapiens* is debatable: it can be argued that having faith in supernatural beings provides a confidence in decision making that is of adaptive value.

The materialisation of religious ideas by material symbols is a pervasive, if not universal, feature of human societies. It is evident that some societies undertake such materialisation to a far greater extent than others, for reasons that remain unclear. The Upper Palaeolithic of South-West Europe is certainly one such example and we must be cautious against thinking that other hunter-gatherer societies, such as those of the early Holocene in Europe, did not have as complex religious beliefs just because they did not create such a striking material record. We face, of course, the problem that some societies might predominantly make their art objects out of organic or non-durable materials (e.g. sand paintings), which are unlikely to survive in the archaeological record. There is, however, an important question for archaeologists to address: why should some communities such as those of the Upper Palaeolithic in Europe or Early Neolithic in south-east Turkey, choose to represent their religious in material form to a greater extent than other societies have chosen to do?

The first step in answering this question is to ask why should people in general have a compulsion to represent religious ideas in material form? I believe this relates to the evolution of the mind, and the relatively recent emergence of cognitive fluidity in human evolution. Ideas about supernatural beings are 'unnatural' in the sense that they conflict with our deeply evolved domain-specific understanding of the world and are hence difficult to hold within our minds and transmit to others. So humans have learnt to use material symbols as an anchor for such unnatural ideas (Mithen 1998). Such anchors function to help formulate, maintain or retrieve the idea of a supernatural being within the mind, and to enable that idea to be shared with other members of one's community. In this regard the material symbols are not mere passive reflections of ideas within the mind, they are formative of those ideas. In a very real sense such material symbols form an extension of the mind.

The extension of the mind beyond the bounds of brain, bone and skin by using material culture may have been as important as the appearance of language for cognitive evolution. Merlin Donald (1991) identified the significance of 'external symbolic storage'. My concern, however, is with something rather more profound – material culture as an extension of mind in terms of providing an ability to manipulate ideas and to 'think thoughts' that could simply not have been possible by the use of the brain alone. The philosopher Andy Clark has recently used the term 'natural born cyborgs' to characterise the manner in which twentieth-century humans have extended their mental abilities by the use of new technology. I believe that term is also appropriate for the *H. sapiens* in prehistory (Mithen 2004) who used art as a cognitive anchor and as a means to manipulate ideas about supernatural beings that were formed by cognitive fluidity and which had no 'natural home' within the mind because they violated domain specific knowledge.

## 5. Upper Palaeolithic art and religion

When Clark (2003: 53) writes about "augmented technology" in which "information might appear attached to the space around an individual" he could be just as effectively writing about Upper Palaeolithic art rather than the twenty-first-century technology to which he is in fact referring. Similarly ice age paintings of bison, horse and supernatural beings (see Plates III and XIII–XV) appear to have added "new layers of meaning and functionality to the daily world itself . . . a kind of deliberate blurring of the boundaries between physical and informational space" (Clark 2003: 53). Indeed we can see the first appearance of art, and especially that of supernatural beings such as the lion-man of Hohlenstein-Stadel (see Plate II) as "freezing a thought" not in words but as a material object which then opens up what Clark calls "second-order cognitive dynamics" (2003: 79).

My argument is, therefore, that the materialisation of the religious ideology of the Upper Palaeolithic played an active role in the formation of that ideology and its transmission between generations. As we are dealing with an imagistic religious mode that ideology would have been ill-defined: while sharing some basic ideas, each person would have had their own particular conception of the supernatural beings that were represented in their art. The paintings and carvings should be considered as a shared part of their Upper Palaeolithic minds rather than as mere products or expressions of their minds. This is, of course, no more than Leach (1976: 37) argued thirty years ago when he explained that we convert religious ideas into material form to give them relative permanence so that they can be subjected to operations which are beyond the capacity of the brain alone. We can now understand why this is the case in terms of the three arguments I have presented: (1) the human mind has a deeply evolved domain-specific structure; (2) this has been subverted by language that delivers cognitive fluidity resulting in the formation of ideas that have no natural place within the brain; (3) to help form, manipulate and transmit such ideas, they are represented in material form that constitutes an extension of the mind.

The evolutionary perspective on the mind informs the work of Whitehouse and Boyer and allows us to draw further inferences about the ice age supernatural beings that would otherwise be the case. When we see the paintings of the 'Venus'/bison-man from Chauvet Cave or the lion-man from Hohlenstein-Stadel (see Plate II) we should be confident that these represent entities that had the "minimally counter-intuitive properties" that Boyer (2001) has found characteristic of supernatural beings in general. Such beings may have had partial animal form, but it would be surprising if they did not have human-like psychological properties, especially those that allow 'mind reading', frequently referred to as theory of mind. Indeed, I think it likely that such beings were the 'complete strategic agents' that Boyer (2001) has claimed to be characteristic of many religions – beings that had total knowledge of the world including the thoughts and behaviour of all people. In this regard, they are still watching and listening to us today.

While my concern has been the art of the Upper Palaeolithic, my argument is of general relevance to the role of material culture in religious thought. Day (2004), a Professor of Religion from Florida State University, has recently addressed the relationships between 'off-line' cognition, the extended mind and religious thought in general, drawing not only on my own work and that of Clark (1997, 2003), but also Dennett (1996) and Hutchins (1995), both of whom have contributed to the idea of the extended mind. Dennett has stressed how tools not only require intelligence to be made but also confer intelligence on the user, while Hutchins has focused on the idea of distributed cognition. Day finds a common thread through this work and summarises it as follows, which provides me with an appropriate concluding statement:

> The broad spectrum of rituals, relics, scriptures, statues and buildings typically associated with religious traditions are no longer seen as mere ethnographic icing on the computational cake. Rather than thin cultural "wrap arounds" that dress up real cognitive processes going on underneath, they begin to look like central components of the relevant machinery of religious thought...Without these elaborate layers of cognitive technology the gods would be, to one degree or another, unthinkable. (Day 2004: 116–17)

**REFERENCES**

Barth, F., 1990. The Guru and the Conjurer: transactions in knowledge and the shaping of culture in Southeast Asia and Melanesia. *Man (N.S.)* **25**, 640–53.

Bishop, D.V.M., 2002. Putting language genes in perspective. *Trends in Genetics* **18**, 57–9.

Boyer, P., 1994. *The Naturalness of Religious Ideas: A Cognitive Theory of Religion*. Berkeley: University of California Press.

Boyer, P., 2001. *Religion Explained: The Evolutionary Origin of Religious Thought*. New York: Basic Books.

Boyer, P. & C. Ramble, C., 2001. Cognitive templates for religious concepts: cross cultural evidence for recall of counter-intuitive representations. *Cognitive Science* **25**, 535–64.

Carruthers, P., 2002. The cognitive functions of language. *Brain and Behavioral Sciences* **25**, 657–726.

Clarke, A., 1997. *Being There: Putting Brain, Body and World Together Again*. Cambridge (MA): MIT Press.

Clarke, A., 2003. *Natural Born Cyborgs: Minds, Technologies, and the Future of Human Intelligence*. Oxford: Oxford University Press.

Clarke, A. & D. Chalmers, 1998. The extended mind. *Analysis* **58**, 7–19.

Clottes, J., D. Lewis-Williams & S. Hawkes, 1998. *The Shamans of Prehistory: France and Magic in the Painted Caves*. New York: Abrams.

Day, M., 2004. Religion, off-line cognition and the extended mind. *Journal of Cognition and Culture* **4**, 101–21.

Dennett, D., 1996. *Kinds of Minds: Towards an Understanding of Consciousness*. New York: Basic Books.

Donald, M., 1991. *Origins of the Modern Mind*. Cambridge (MA): Harvard University Press.

Enard, W., M. Przeworski, S.E. Fisher, C.S. Lai, V. Wiebe, T. Kitano, A.P. Monaco & S. Paabo, 2002. Molecular evolution of FOXP2, a gene involved in speech and language. *Nature* **418**, 869–72.

Foley, R. & M.M. Lahr, 1997. Mode 3 technologies and the evolution of modern humans. *Cambridge Archaeological Journal* **7**, 3–36.

Gargett, R.H., 1989. Grave shortcomings: the evidence for Neanderthal burial. *Current Anthropology* **30**, 157–90.

Goody, J., 1968. Introduction, in *Literacy in Traditional Societies*, ed. J. Goody. Cambridge: Cambridge University Press.

Gouk, P., 2000. *Music healing in cultural contexts*. Aldershot: Ashgate.

Guthrie, S., 1993. *Faces in the Clouds: A New Theory of Religion*. Oxford: Oxford University Press.

Henshilwood, C.S., F. d'Errico, R. Yates, Z. Jacobs, C. Tribolo, G.A.T. Duller, N. Mercier, J.C. Sealy, H. Valladas, I. Watts & A.G. Wintle, 2002. Emergence of modern human behavior: Middle Stone Age engravings from South Africa. *Science* **295**, 1278–80.

Henshilwood, C.S., F. d'Errico, M. Vanhaeren, K. van Niekerk, Z. Jacobs, 2004. Middle stone age shell beads from South Africa. *Science* **304**, 404.

Hutchins, E., 1995. *Cognition in the Wild*. Cambridge (MA): MIT Press.

Ingman, M., H. Kaessmann, S. Paabo, & U. Gyllensten, 2000. Mitochondrial genome variation and the origin of modern humans. *Nature* **408**, 708–13.

Kirby, S., 2000. Syntax without natural selection: how compositionality emerges from vocabulary in a population of learners, in *The Evolutionary Emergence of Language: Social Function and the Origins of Linguistic Form*, eds. C. Knight, M. Studdert-Kennedy & J.R. Hurford. Cambridge: Cambridge University Press, 303–23.

Kirby, S., 2002. Learning, bottlenecks and the evolution of recursive syntax, in *Linguistic Evolution through Language Acquisition: Formal and Computational Models*, ed. E. Briscoe. Cambridge: Cambridge University Press, 173–204.

Lai, C.S.L., S.E. Fisher, J.A. Hurst, F. Vargha-Khadem, & A.P. Monaco, 2001. A forkhead-domain gene is mutated in a severe speech and language disorder. *Nature* **413**, 519–23.

Leach, E. 1976. *Culture and Communication*. Cambridge: Cambridge University Press.

Lewis-Williams, D. 2002. *The Mind in the Cave*. London: Thames & Hudson.

McBreaty, S. & A. Brooks, 2000. The revolution that wasn't: a new interpretation of the origin of modern human behavior. *Journal of Human Evolution* **38**, 453–563.

Mellars, P., 1996. *The Neanderthal Legacy*. Princeton: Princeton University Press.

Mithen, S.J., 1996. *The Prehistory of the Mind: A Search for the Origin of Art, Science and Religion*. London: Thames & Hudson.

Mithen, S.J., 1998. The supernatural beings of prehistory and the external storage of religious ideas, in *Cognition and Material Culture: The Archaeology of Symbolic Storage*, eds. C. Renfrew & C. Scarre. Cambridge: McDonald Institute Monographs, 97–106.

Mithen, S.J., 2004. Review of 'Natural-Born Cyborgs' by A. Clarke. Metascience 13, 163–9

Mithen, S.J., 2005. *The Singing Neanderthals*. London: Weidenfeld and Nicolson.

Roseman, M., 1991. *Healing sounds from the Malaysian Rainforest: Temiar Music and Medicine*. Berkeley: University of California Press.

Shennan, S.J., 2001. Demography and cultural innovation: a model and some implications for the emergence of modern human culture. *Cambridge Archaeological Journal* **11**, 5–16.

Trinkaus, E., 1995. Neanderthal mortality patterns. *Journal of Archaeological Science* **22**, 121–42.

Weber, M., 1947. *The Theory of Social and Economic Organization*. Oxford: Oxford University Press.

White, T.D., D. Asfaw, D. DeGusta, H. Tilbert, G.D. Richard, G. Suwa, F.C. Howell, 2003. Pleistocene Homo sapiens from the Middle Awash, Ethiopia. *Nature* **423**, 742–7.

Whitehouse, H., 2000. *Arguments and Icons: Divergent Modes of Religiosity*. Oxford: Oxford University Press.

Whitehouse, H., 2004. *Modes of Religiosity: A Cognitive Theory of Religious Transmission*. Walnut Creek, CA: Altamira Press.

Wray, A., 1998. Protolanguage as a holistic system for social interaction. *Language and Communication* **18**, 47–67.

Wray, A., 2000. Holistic utterances in protolanguage: the link from primates to humans, in *The Evolutionary Emergence of Language: Social Function and the Origins of Linguistic Form*, eds. C. Knight, M. Studdert-Kennedy & J.R. Hurford. Cambridge: Cambridge University Press, 285–302.

# 10

# Of people and pictures: the nexus of Upper Palaeolithic religion, social discrimination, and art

*David Lewis-Williams*

Today much archaeological debate centres on the evolutionary status of the Neanderthals, especially as they were at the beginning of the Upper Palaeolithic period in Western Europe (the entire period lasted from ±40,000 to ±10,00 years BP). Although evidence from genetics has discounted the formerly supposed direct descent of modern humans from Neanderthals and the related hypothesis that archaic and modern forms were different but related populations within a single evolving species, there is still dispute about how different – if at all – they were from anatomically modern *Homo sapiens* populations (Krings et al. 1997, 1999; Hublin 2000; Mellars 1990, 1996, 2000; Caramelli et al. 2003).

This controversy is interesting from three perspectives:

- First, there are major substantive issues: Were Neanderthals the intellectual equals of modern humans? Did they have the mental capacity to live – and make pictures – as modern people undoubtedly do?
- Secondly, the debate is interesting for the way in which some researchers conduct it. Recently, there has been a tendency to draw in moral issues. To put it as bluntly as some researchers indeed do, are those who doubt the ability of Neanderthals to achieve certain things closet racists? On the other hand, are we morally liberated if we claim Neanderthals as intellectual equals?
- Thirdly, the debate illustrates the pivotal role that archaeology has to play in the development of understanding between religion and science. If there is to be any rapprochement, religionists and scientists need to confront, frankly and without any papering over of cracks, the thought-lives of the earliest people, for it is there that we

encounter the seeds of modern thought and religious belief. Archaeology goes to the heart of the matter.

In this contribution to the debate I consider, first, a few of the debilitating platitudes, sometimes laced with moral strictures, that have established themselves in the literature. Then, I move on to examine the west European Upper Palaeolithic origins of two-dimensional image-making that produced the stunning subterranean pictures of, largely, animals such as bison, horse and aurochs. This second, and major, part of the chapter, stands independently of what we may think about Neanderthal abilities, though I offer suggestions as to what might have happened when incoming *Homo sapiens* groups were living beside long-established Neanderthal communities. Finally, I point to some of the implications of Upper Palaeolithic evidence for an understanding of religion in twenty-first-century, science-oriented society. This evidence shows that the Neanderthal debate is not merely an esoteric dispute among inhabitants of an ivory tower: it has major implications for the way in which we see life today.

## A moral morass

The overtly moral position assumes that the view of Neanderthals as mentally less than equal to *Homo sapiens* is a 'construct'. It is said that late nineteenth-century writers, trapped in a Eurocentric, evolutionary paradigm, set a trend when they published imaginative pictorial reconstructions of what Neanderthals looked like, how they walked and behaved. They were (and sometimes still are) depicted as dim, low-browed, shambling 'cave men'; the argument parallels the feminist position that detects the subordination of women in accounts of the deep past. This dual perspective was taken up by cartoonists who sketch club-wielding Neanderthal men dragging their women by the hair. That images of this kind are lodged in the public imagination is, quite possibly, true. But to imply that imaginative reconstructions and cartoons likewise influence archaeologists in their perceptions and research is absurd. Today it may be fun to laugh at crude reconstructions of Neanderthal life, but to imply that present-day researchers have in some way been brainwashed by these reconstructions into believing that Neanderthals were limited in their mental capabilities is a calumny. Researchers who believe that Neanderthals were 'mentally challenged' do so because they believe the archaeological evidence points to this conclusion.

The implication that researchers are duped by cartoonists is encapsulated in the broader view that *all* accounts of the past are necessarily and entirely 'constructs' moulded by the present. It has become politically *de rigueur* to claim that the social milieu in which archaeologists work shapes their explanations of the past. Taken at face value this assertion is not really controversial, nor is it as new as we are sometimes led to believe. What is controversial is the implication that the present is ineluctable. This is not the place to enter into a discussion of present-day relativism and epistemology. So I shall simply make a couple of brief points.

It has long been known that history can be a tool in the hands of a dominant minority – what was known as 'biased history', now reinvented as 'constructs'. The interests of the present may well colour the past – no one doubts that – but it is nevertheless possible to find out certain truths. Those who successfully challenge tendentious illustrations and cartoons show that constructs can be exposed: some accounts of the past are demonstrably closer than others to what actually happened. Constructs can be exposed by facts.

So it is with the Neanderthal question. Some younger researchers today claim that their youth spent during the 1960s when segregation was at last seriously challenged in the United States has shown them that it is racist to believe that Neanderthals were mentally inferior to anatomically modern humans and that older researchers who do think this are still enmeshed in the trammels of colonial racism. This position is even more absurd than to say that those older (and not so old) researchers are the victims of cartoons. By impugning the morality of their academic opponents, the 'free the Neanderthals' school of thought is able to dismiss without argument evidence and logic that it finds uncomfortable. The upshot of these unfortunately prominent components of present-day debate is the implication that the palm must go to the morally pure and that any evidence contrary to their position is somehow tainted.

Part of the problem that we face in debating the nature of the Neanderthal mind may (it is impossible to be certain about such matters) derive from those turbulent 1960s. Since then, Western society seems to have placed an increasing value on 'spirituality'. It is therefore the denial of Neanderthal spirituality (evidenced, it is said, largely by Neanderthal burials that indicate a belief in life after death) that seems to elicit the most vehement response from Neanderthal supporters (see debate on Neanderthal burials in Gargett 1989, 1999; Riel-Salvatore & Clark 2001; Stringer & Gamble 1993). Whether or not the Neanderthals had the ability to conceive of a life after death is a matter that I discuss in a later part of this chapter; for the moment all I need say is that, in my view, spirituality (closely associated as it is with beliefs in supernatural realms and influences) is a part of human existence best left behind. In a later section I describe the neurological foundation of spirituality. Certainly, the notion that spirituality is a fine and defining trait of *Homo sapiens* should not cloud the issue of the evolutionary status of the Neanderthals.

This mix of fact and morality in the Neanderthal debate is inimical to the advance of knowledge. The problems that it has generated therefore need to be confronted head-on, not side-stepped, if we are to get to a position in which debates about the nature of the past do not have to be couched in the politically correct language of the present – even if they touch on such inflammatory issues as belief in the supernatural and spirituality. It is here that archaeology can supply crucial data relevant to discussions between religionists and scientists.

## Neanderthal evolutionary status

In this debate, there are certain facts (I use the word unashamedly) that I believe we cannot avoid. I state them briefly:

- There was a time ($\pm 40,000$–33,000 BP) when in France, Spain and Portugal Neanderthals lived side by side with *Homo sapiens* communities who had moved in to western Europe from the east. Just how closely 'side by side' is sometimes debated, but the available dates show that, whether the two groups alternately occupied the same caves or not, they were contemporary in the geographic region that matters for the issues that we are addressing. They could not have avoided knowing about each other, even if the population was sparse at that time.
- The Neanderthals developed their tool kits and social structure very slowly (if at all in some places) prior to the arrival of the *Homo sapiens* groups. Where some changes in stone tool technology can be

discerned in late Neanderthal sites they can, by their temporal closeness to the physical arrival of *Homo sapiens* groups, be explained by what Paul Mellars calls the 'bow-wave effect'. Ideas can spread swiftly and far through hunter-gatherer populations.

- Immediately after the arrival of the *Homo sapiens* groups in western Europe Neanderthal life became more similar to *Homo sapiens* life-ways – but not entirely so and with highly significant exceptions. In short, they borrowed some things from their new neighbours but not others (see below). If Neanderthals were mental equals of *Homo sapiens*, why did they not borrow*everything* and so confront their new neighbours on their own terms?

- Neanderthals seem to have begun to bury some of their dead, perhaps by the bow-wave effect or by imitating their new neighbours. But they did not place elaborate grave goods in their graves, an omission that suggests that their notions of death and burial were different from those of *Homo sapiens* (although see also J. Renfrew, *this volume*).

- When the Neanderthals borrowed stone tool technologies, they used the tools for the same purposes as did *Homo sapiens* people. (For instance, Neanderthals used scrapers for scraping skins and so forth.) By contrast, when Neanderthals used (rarely) body ornaments (e.g., pendants) which they themselves made or obtained from *Homo sapiens* groups, those ornaments must have had different social meanings in the Neanderthal context from what they signified in *Homo sapiens* communities. Body ornaments signify social distinctions. Neanderthal society was differently structured from that of *Homo sapiens*, and their ornaments must therefore have signified differently.

- After a few thousand years of side-by-side living, the Neanderthals died out without contributing to the *Homo sapiens* genepool. It seems that, although inter-species copulation may have taken place, there was no successful, long-term interbreeding. The Neanderthals and *Homo sapiens* were two species.

- It was at this time of west European cohabitation that *Homo sapiens* communities began to make two- and three-dimensional imagery. Neanderthals did not make imagery.

These seven points stand independently of any moral objections. And, moreover, independently of any discussion of whether Neanderthals were capable of 'symbolic thought' – in any event a very slippery, ill-defined concept that inhabits the literature on this topic. Because of the definitional difficulties with such phrases, it is better to seek a more empirical way of finding out about differences between Neanderthals and *Homo sapiens.*

What we need to explain now is: Why did *Homo sapiens* begin to make abundant imagery of astonishing sophistication, often in deep caves, while the Neanderthals did not and eventually died out? One way of answering this question is to propose a hypothesis and then to see (a) if any evidence contradicts it, (b) if it explains the available evidence, (c) if, in doing so, it co-ordinates what may otherwise seem disparate types of behaviour.

## Intelligence and consciousness

Accounts of human evolution almost invariably emphasise intelligence and ignore human consciousness. But a difference in intelligence alone does not sufficiently explain the distinctions between what the Neanderthals borrowed and what they ignored. I therefore propose that it was differences in consciousness, rather than in intelligence, that are the key to the questions that I ask in this chapter about the origins of image-making. To support this hypothesis, I outline the nature of modern human consciousness and then distinguish between types of consciousness.

Human consciousness is not a unitary mental state. It is not a case of simply being conscious or unconscious. Rather, consciousness is better thought of as a spectrum that grades from alert states through more meditative conditions, to day-dreaming, to deep reverie, to dreaming, and on to 'unconsciousness' (e.g., Martindale 1981). The spectrum thus has alert and introverted ends. Daily, all people move back and forth along this spectrum.

The shifting nature of consciousness is a fact (again that word) that many archaeologists ignore. They assume that, in decision-making contexts, both early and recent *Homo sapiens* always experienced only the alert end of the spectrum. Behaviour and actions that are explained as adaptation to the environment are therefore (usually tacitly) accepted as the result of ancient rational decisions.

What are some of the consequences of the shifting character of human consciousness for archaeologists?

In the very nature of communal life, all communities are obliged to divide up the spectrum of consciousness into recognized and, importantly, evaluated sections. In modern Western life it is the alert end of the spectrum that is most valued, for it is in alert states that scientific and technological advances are believed to be generated. Day-dreaming and fantasising are treated with scepticism. Dreams are generally regarded as amusing, or, in some instances, terrifying, but no great significance is accorded them (except by a couple of schools of psychology). If an answer to a problem comes to a researcher in a dream, its origin is no argument for its value: the answer has to be tested under rigorous conditions.

This pattern of evaluation of the spectrum of consciousness was not always embraced in the West, nor is it universally accepted today. In mediaeval times dreams were believed to be one of the ways in which God spoke to his chosen, or one of the routes by which the Devil infiltrated himself into human souls. Other cultures place different value on dreams. People may believe them to be the voices of ancestors or intimations of hidden witchcraft. Apart from dreams, Westerners cannot agree, even today, on how to evaluate the introverted, meditative end of the consciousness spectrum. New Age and associated movements employ various techniques to shut out the immediate environment and to cultivate states that they call 'spiritual', a word that automatically bestows high value. These examples show that we cannot assume that Upper Palaeolithic people evaluated the spectrum of consciousness in the same way that highly rational Westerners do today. In all probability, they did not.

For whatever reasons (a study in itself), people in all times and cultures go further than valuing the introverted end of the consciousness spectrum. They interfere with consciousness and launch it on what may be called an intensified trajectory. This trajectory leads through stages of what we call altered consciousness to a 'deep' state in which subjects experience visual, somatic, aural, gustatory and olfactory hallucinations (Lewis-Williams 2002). In this stage people 'see' animals, monsters, bizarre transformations and so forth. The intensified trajectory may be entered upon by the ingestion of psychotropic substances or by audio and rhythmic driving, intense concentration and meditation, sensory deprivation, prolonged pain, or pathological conditions such as temporal lobe epilepsy and schizophrenia. Recent criticisms (Bahn & Helvenston

2002) that suggest that all three of the stages are induced only by certain psychotropic substances are incorrect (Lewis-Williams 2004).

People evaluate the intensified trajectory, as they do the ordinary spectrum of consciousness. It is socialized and people in a given community agree on what it signifies, though there are often those who contest the generally accepted evaluation. The process of socialization often entails parts of the trajectory being marked off as the preserve of special people, the 'seers', those who 'see' and thereby have access to realms that ordinary people can only glimpse in their dreams. The seers (others words may be used: priests, shamans, prophets, psychopomps) often control other people's access to the intensified trajectory, and becoming a seer involves learning to experience and understand the stages of altered consciousness. The intensified spectrum of consciousness thus becomes a powerful foundation for social discrimination that cross-cuts stratifications based on sex, age and brute strength.

How did human beings come to have this distinctive way of underwriting social distinctions?

## Two types of consciousness

Adopting an evolutionary perspective, Gerald Edelman (1992, 2004; Edelman & Tononi 2000) distinguishes two kinds of consciousness, primary and higher-order.

*Primary consciousness* is not a single, unitary condition. Animals other than human beings experience it to varying degrees; early hominids had it, also in different degrees. It entails an awareness of the environment and the entertaining of mental images in the present. Edelman likens it to being in a dark room with a flashlight. As the beam moves around, it illuminates parts of the room and then lets them slip back into darkness. Primary consciousness thus permits the construction of an integrated mental scene in the present that does not require language or a true sense of self. This is what Edelman calls 'a remembered present'. As a result of its essential restriction to the present, animals with primary consciousness do not have a sense of a person with a past and a future. They have some long-term memory, but they are unable to plan an extended future based on memory. Some animals may have what may be called a protolanguage, but one without past and future tenses. In short, they can have no socially constructed self. A consequence of primary consciousness is that animals with it dream (sleep is a condition that leads to the manufacture of proteins in the brain; Greenfield 1997, 2001; Rock 2004) but are unable to remember and socialize their dreams. Altered states of consciousness of the intensified trajectory may be induced in them, but they do not remember and later act upon socially constructed understandings of those experiences.

*Higher-order consciousness* is the kind of consciousness experienced today by all human beings and, in a restricted sense, by some primates (Edelman 2004). According to Edelman, it evolved out of primary consciousness not just by gross changes in brain morphology but, more importantly, by the establishment of what he calls 'reentry' circuitry. This new 'wiring' within the brain contributed substantially to a new order of complexity (he uses the phrase 'meshwork of the thalamocortical system') and to the integration of conscious experience (Edelman & Tononi 2000: 216). Because Upper Palaeolithic *H. sapiens* communities were anatomically fully modern, we can assume that their neurological wiring was the same as it is today. We therefore have a neurological bridge to the Upper Palaeolithic.

Higher-order consciousness is characterized by recognition of one's own acts and emotions, concepts of a deep past, a future model of the world, a socially constructed self, and long-term storage of socially constructed symbolic relations. This kind of consciousness is founded on complex language that embraces past, present and future tenses and the utterance of never-before articulated sentences that can be understood by members of the language community. It makes possible long-term planning and strategizing, the maintenance of complex kinship systems, and the manipulation of symbols to express and impact upon complex social relations. In addition, higher-order consciousness permits people to remember and to socialize dreams and visions.

This kind of consciousness probably evolved in Africa, so that by the time *Homo sapiens* communities reached western Europe they had the potential to experience all of its functions. Discussions of 'modern human behaviour', a concept difficult to define, usually omit any mention of consciousness. Yet it is higher-order consciousness that makes modernity possible. Modern human behaviour came together piecemeal and spasmodically in Africa (McBrearty & Brooks 2000) on, I argue, a foundation of higher-order consciousness. It cannot be understood without an appreciation of that sort of consciousness.

The differences between the two types of consciousness that Edelman distinguishes are empirical issues: they are not open to moral evaluation.

## The consciousness hypothesis

The hypothesis that *Homo sapiens* communities had higher-order consciousness and that the Neanderthals had *a form of* primary consciousness is a hypothesis that explains why Neanderthals were able to borrow certain things but not others, and why *Homo sapiens* supplanted the Neanderthals in western Europe. I focus on burials and image-making.

Without higher-order consciousness Neanderthals would have been unable to conceive of a spirit realm or an afterlife – a state of being far removed in the future or, rather, outside of time. They would therefore have been incapable of understanding the placing of valuable items in *Homo sapiens* graves; grave goods could have had no meaning for them. Nor could they have had any clear idea of why some *Homo sapiens* people were given elaborate burials and others were not. Without any notion of social distinctions based on criteria other than age, sex and strength they would have been baffled as to why someone who seemed to have so little going for him or her would be accorded such treatment. They may have been able to see some purpose in placing bodies beneath the ground, if only to emulate *Homo sapiens* behaviour or to perform an act of concern, but they could not have entertained any religious concepts about death and burial. Neanderthals were congenital atheists.

Upper Palaeolithic image-making poses more complex problems than burials. First, we need to ask how people came to believe that small, static marks on a two-dimensional surface could represent a huge, live, moving, three-dimensional bison or horse. (For a discussion of three-dimensional image-making, see Lewis-Williams 2002). The conventions of two-dimensional representations are not inherited; they have to be learned. This is what the anthropologist Anthony Forge (1970) found in New Guinea. The Abelam, among whom he worked, did not understand photographs. When he explained the conventions to them, they readily learned to 'see' photographs, but the ability was not in-built. It is this point that exposes the inadequacy of some of the old explanations of image-making. People could not have fortuitously discerned the outline of, say, a bison in natural or random human-made marks on cave walls without *first* having a concept of two-dimensional pictures.

The popular notion that an especially intelligent individual noticed such an outline and then told others about it, or simply invented image-making, is therefore flawed. If the origin of image-making was idiosyncratic in this way, we cannot explain why, right from the beginning of image-making over the whole of Western Europe, the makers confined themselves to a fairly restricted set of animals: bison, horses, felines, aurochs. Other creatures, such as birds, mammoths and reindeer, were less frequently depicted; still other motifs, such as human beings, are extremely rare. Proportions between depicted species varied through the Upper Palaeolithic, but the fundamental set of motifs remained the same. There was never a time when people made pictures of anything that caught their fancy. The most plausible explanation is that the vocabulary of motifs existed *before* people started making images of them. There was a widely shared, socialized bestiary of animals with symbolic associations, and this bestiary (not some 'aesthetic sense') in some way triggered and informed the beginnings of image-making. Along with stone tool technologies, the incoming Aurignacians brought an established religion and symbology, although not highly developed and subterranean image-making. That came later, when they were living near Neanderthals in Western Europe.

## Seeing and making images

The answer to the question of how people came to understand and make two-dimensional images of this bestiary lies in features of higher-order consciousness and the intensified trajectory (Lewis-Williams & Dowson 1988; Lewis-Williams 2002). Neuropsychological research has shown that hallucinations experienced on the intensified trajectory are projected onto plane surfaces, such as walls or ceilings. Subjects liken this experience to a slide or film show (Klüver 1926: 505, 506; Siegel & Jarvik 1975: 109; Siegel 1977: 134). Nonveridical mental imagery can thus come to be associated with a surface in front of the subject. Four implications flow from this observation.

First, Upper Palaeolithic people did not have to invent two-dimensional imagery. If *some* of them experienced projected imagery under certain circumstances, as they had the neurological potential to do, two-dimensional 'pictures' would already have been part of their world *under certain mental and emotional conditions.* Those conditions would almost certainly have been associated with religious or spiritual experiences.

Secondly, if the vocabulary of motifs was established before image-making started, as the archaeological evidence shows it was, the projected images of those selected animals must have had symbolic significance beyond being 'pictures' of creatures seen in daily life. They were not staple food animals. The projected images must have had some value or 'power' beyond being sources of food.

Thirdly, it would then have been a short step for people in a 'light' altered state to reach out to touch their projected images and thus to fix them on the walls with a finger in soft surfaces or with pigment. Or, after having returned to the alert end of the spectrum, they may have made images in an attempt to call back and recreate mental images on the surfaces on which they had been projected while they were in a deeper state. The first images were therefore not 'pictures of real life' but rather fixed, projected mental images of important animals that were part of an established symbolic bestiary.

Fourthly, as Forge was easily able to teach the Abelam the conventions of two-dimensional imagery, so too would Upper Palaeolithic seers have been able to teach others to comprehend projected imagery that they had fixed on rock walls. Once those people were able to understand the conventions involved in two-dimensional imagery, they would have been able to make their own pictures without having experienced an altered state and projected mental images. The fact that they did not then start making pictures of a wide range of subjects shows that they, like the seers, were bound by the religious, symbolic bestiary. Image-making remained within the sphere of religion.

This explanation for the origin of two-dimensional image-making is supported by characteristics of the painted and engraved images in the caves of south-west Europe.

- Researchers have long noticed that they appear to float on the walls without any suggestion of a ground line or other context – there are no trees, grass or hills. Often, animals have 'hanging' hoofs that are not oriented to a ground surface.
- The images are often integrated with the convolutions of the surface; it is as though the projected mental image locked into features of the rock wall. As a result, some images are in vertical positions, not as animals would have been seen outside the cave.

- In some instances, it is necessary to hold one's lamp in a given position so that the shadows cast across the wall form, say, the dorsal line of a bison. The image-fixer then added legs and perhaps horns to complete the figure. If the viewer moves the lamp back and forth, the image disappears and re-appears.
- An impression of 'appearing' is also created by images that are positioned so that they seem to be coming out of cracks or fissures in the rock walls.

The consciousness hypothesis thus coordinates and explains empirically observed features of Upper Palaeolithic images. Further, the intimacy of the relation between images and surfaces, and the highly selective vocabulary of the motifs are two points that lead to inferences about the caves and their topography.

## Subterranean realms

Perhaps the most striking feature of Upper Palaeolithic cave images is their location in deep underground chambers, passages and small niches. In some instances, people walked, waded, crawled and squeezed through narrow openings for more than a kilometre underground before they made images. These were not 'art galleries' for leisurely contemplation of *objets d'art*. Some of the remote images may never have been seen by anyone apart from their makers; others, by contrast, are in large chambers that could have accommodated a number of people. What did 'viewing images' mean to Upper Palaeolithic people?

The answer to this question lies again in the spectrum of human consciousness and its intensified trajectory. Two hallucinatory experiences that are wired into the brain are of importance (Lewis-Williams & Dowson 1988; Lewis-Williams 2002).

First, as subjects move along the intensified trajectory, they may experience a sensation of rising up, attenuation and flying. Secondly, they may experience a vortex, a constricting tunnel, through which they pass and emerge on the other side into a realm of hallucinations where they 'see' monsters, people and bizarre events.

These two hard-wired experiences, I argue, give rise to worldwide beliefs in spirit realms above and below the level of daily life. There is, of course, no empirical evidence in everyday life for the existence of such spheres of supernatural, or spiritual, existence, yet people everywhere believe in them. The only persuasive explanation for this universality is that the experiences of rising up and sinking down into the ground are hard-wired in the *Homo sapiens* brain and lead to beliefs in the existence, though not the details, of realms above and below. The Christian concept of Heaven above and Hell below is but one example. In some instances, the upper and nether realms are subdivided into multiple levels.

Belief in a tiered cosmos explains why Upper Palaeolithic people went underground to make images of a set of symbolic animals and why those images are intimately integrated with the walls of the caves. Physical entry into the caves paralleled, was perhaps indistinguishable from, mental entry into the neurologically generated vortex that leads to deeply altered states and hallucinations. The caves *were* the nether world, a realm inhabited by powerful animals and, probably, beings. These animals and beings lived in the chambers or behind cave walls. They were sought by sight, touch, the interplay of light and shadow, echoing sound, and probably by responding to aural hallucinations of animal sounds. It was the aim of the deeply penetrating subterranean quester to 'see' these powerful animals, sometimes to draw them through the 'membrane' of the walls and to 'fix' them there. They were *fixed visions* of special, powerful animals whose supernatural, empowering essence image-seekers and image-makers desired. The context of the images was not 'Nature' but rather the nether realm and the membrane of the cave wall. The image-makers went into the cave to seek visions of animals; they did not consciously take recollections of real animals and incidents with them so that they could paint or engrave them.

What, then, was the relationship between the 'fixed' spirit animals and their look-alikes that roamed outside the cave? Worldwide hunter-gatherer ethnography offers some clues. For instance, the nineteenth-century /Xam San of southern Africa believed that some of their !gi:ten (ritual specialists, shamans; sing. !gi:xa) possessed spirit animals that could be caused to go among a herd of springbok and lead them in the direction of the hunters' ambush. One !gi:xa described such an animal as her 'heart's springbok' (Bleek MS L.V.10.4729 rev.). Unless they behaved in some peculiar way, spirit animals were indistinguishable from real animals, and an informant told how one was accidentally shot, with unfortunate consequences (Bleek 1935: 44–47). A !Kung (Ju/'hoan) person said that her husband had hunted a giraffe that unexpectedly turned out to be a spirit animal; the man then acquired supernatural potency from it (Biesele 1993: 68–69). Such beliefs are a reflection of the immanence and simultaneous transcendence of the spirit world. Generated in a person's head, the spirit world is both 'with' one and 'beyond' one.

Further hints come from the South American Desana, who speak of Vaí-mashë, Lord of the Animals, a being who has control of animals that he keeps in spiritual form in his maloca, or house (Reichel-Dolmatoff 1971:80–86). He is associated with isolated rock formations that rise out of the Amazonian forest 'like dark islands on the horizon'. In their 'caverns and dark recesses' there are painted images made by shamans, who alone are strong enough to visit such dread places. They do so in reality and in trance (induced by inhaling the narcotic powder of *vihó*, the plant *Piptadenia*). Once in the presence of Vaí-mashë, they negotiate with him to release animals for the benefit of hunters. In addition to being the place where supernatural animals and beings reside, the rock formations are said to contain illness

> and their dark and inhospitable aspect indicates danger. The cracks, caverns, and tunnels are the entrances to the interior of the hills, to the great malocas of the animals. There, within their dark interior, the gigantic prototypes of each species exist and thousands of animals are kept. (Reichel-Dolmatoff 1971: 81)

In some west European caves, such as Enlène, people pushed small pieces of bone into cracks in the walls. In the small Chamber of the Lions, in the adjacent cave Les Trois Frères, a cave bear tooth was placed in a small niche. The pieces of bone in Enlène are so small and the cracks so narrow that intense concentration and close scrutiny of the cave wall must have been necessary. In the total darkness of the chambers the person's flickering tallow lamp must have sharply focused his or her attention. People were carefully passing pieces of animals back through the membrane, perhaps propitiating the spirits behind the rock wall, perhaps hoping that the pieces would reconstitute themselves into spirit animals which some guiding being, perhaps a Lord of the Animals, would later release into the outside world as real animals that could be hunted.

Whilst direct, one-to-one parallels with ethnographically recorded practices, such as the San and Desana reports I have cited, are naive and potentially misleading, they do give us something of the flavour of the relationship that Upper Palaeolithic people may have perceived between real animals, spirit animals and the caves. Upper Palaeolithic society and belief almost certainly have no present-day ethnographic analogues. But, given the hard-wired experiences of human consciousness, we can formulate generalities that provide a multi-component context for tentative interpretation of Upper Palaeolithic image-making.

In some instances, ethnography records the hallucinogen that people used to access the spirit world, but in others, such as the San, no psychotropic substances are used today. In the West European Upper Palaeolithic the altered state of consciousness necessary to induce projected mental imagery could have been generated by any of the mechanisms I listed earlier. But it is worth noting that sensory deprivation of the kind experienced in the totally dark, silent caves induces altered states of consciousness. To expectant minds, isolated for long enough in the bowels of the earth, images would have appeared.

Some images are, however, so large that they could have been made only by cooperating people. Those in the Hall of the Bulls in Lascaux are examples. Elaborate images such as these are usually in large chambers and are often fairly close to the cave entrance or easily accessed. These images, I suggest, were communally produced rather than the result of the sort of individual experiences that led to the limning of the more briefly made images in the spatially constricted depths.

## Social differentiation

There were thus what I call 'activity areas'. These were selected places in the labyrinthine caves where images of different kinds and executed by means of different techniques (some by a few solitary, deft strokes, others by pooled labour) or where other kinds of ritual, such as chanting and dancing, took place. An implication of this conclusion is that the caves were templates for social discriminations (Lewis-Williams 1997, 2002). Religion is always socially divisive, both within religious communities and between those communities and other people (as a reading of the Bible or a newspaper exemplifies) and those discriminations are often reproduced by movement in defined spaces. Temples are always social templates.

How may these divisions of space have functioned in the Upper Palaeolithic? It seems likely that the entire community was associated in multiple ways with the land immediately beyond the entrance to a cave.

Perhaps ordinary people gathered outside caves while seers penetrated the depths. They were unseeing witnesses to subterranean rituals.

Then, as at, for instance, Lascaux, a large entrance chamber near or relatively easily accessible from the entrance contained communally made, striking images that prepared novices, or even experienced seers, for what they would 'see' in the isolated depths. These large images were probably dramatically revealed, perhaps enveloped in a nimbus of chanting. Animated by flickering lamps and torches, they would have informed the mental imagery of subsequent altered states. People hallucinate what they expect to hallucinate. There is, however, always the potential for unexpected hallucinations. If this happens, the seer must decide whether to ignore the novelty or to seize on it as a unique revelation. Communally made images may not have originated in a single vision; they were probably composite, socially stabilized recreations of powerful animals, the cooperative manufacture of which expressed and constructed their significance not just for individuals but for society as a whole. Certainly, they could not have been made by people in deeply altered states of consciousness. But, importantly, they none the less derived from the symbolic bestiary and contributed to the reproduction of that bestiary.

A select group that exercised control of the embellishment of the subterranean world was probably associated with the large chamber. Beyond that, the narrow passages and small niches ensured that only a few people could penetrate far underground – far into the nether spirit realm. These were the vision questers or initiates who were seeking personal revelations.

The intensified consciousness trajectory thus paralleled the topography of the caves: different states of consciousness were associated with different activity areas. Outside the cave everyone could experience dreams, euphoria, awe, or fear; deeper altered consciousness was experienced by a group in front of impressive images; in the remote parts of the cave a few experienced deeply altered consciousness and its vivid visions. The cave was a map of the mind.

Moreover, the consciousness trajectory and the topography of the caves combined to reinforce social structure. A powerful group of people could protect both the cave and the parallel intensified trajectory of altered consciousness; they could decide to whom special, subterranean experiences could be made available. Why did people excluded from those experiences accept the authority of the controlling seers? Social pressures must have been significant, but even ordinary people could glimpse the spirit world in their dreams. Those dreams were confirmation of the more elaborate intimations of spirituality of which the seers spoke. Social distinctions were thus expressed and constructed both neurologically and spatially.

Despite mechanisms of this kind, complete consensus is seldom obtained in religious matters. The rather nebulous, neurological origin of spiritual experience guarantees dispute. The intensified trajectory, together with its concomitant social and topographic distinctions, was probably contested from time to time. As a result, the social discriminations associated with those multiple distinctions almost certainly changed during the Upper Palaeolithic. Both the caves and human consciousness were sites of contestation, active social negotiation and change. As Stephen Shennan rightly points out, '[A] key locus for the generation of social inequality in forager societies was the cultural transmission of ritual knowledge, even in the absence of material inequalities' (Shennan 2002: 224). Roy Rappaport adds the foundation for 'ritual knowledge': 'The relationship between alterations of the social condition and alterations of consciousness is not a simple one, but it is safe to say that they augment and abet each other' (Rappaport 1999: 219).

## A nexus of origins

This brief account of a more wide-ranging argument (Lewis-Williams 2002; Clottes & Lewis-Williams 1996/1998, 2001) points to a period in which some of the components of daily life that we today consider to be different were in fact integrated.

As *Homo sapiens* communities became aware of the implications of the differences in consciousness between themselves and Neanderthals, they emphasised those distinctions as a social strategy. They consolidated their own corporate identity by creating social and conceptual distance between themselves and the Neanderthals, whose form of consciousness, though more advanced than that of other animals, prevented them from entertaining mental imagery, remembering their dreams and visions, conceiving of spiritual worlds, and making images. We do not know exactly what the circumstances of contact were. Perhaps the Neanderthals were able to learn a 'pidgin Aurignacian' language and were thus able to establish some linguistic contact with their new neighbours. But they were shut out from mental and fixed imagery and thus from the religion that was the foundation of *Homo sapiens* society.

Simultaneously, the making of religious, two-dimensional imagery to emphasise (at least in part) the distinction between themselves and the 'other', the Neanderthals, had effects within *Homo sapiens* communities. The practice of making images entrenched social distinctions that probably existed inchoately in the in-coming communities and that were linked by different relationships (other than image-making) with the bestiary of mental imagery. The manifestation of the spirit world became more and more socially important not only between themselves and their Neanderthal neighbours but also within their own communities. At the beginning of the Upper Palaeolithic, social and mental mechanisms were thus initiated, together with their ritual and image-making concomitants. Those mechanisms continued to play a social role as the Upper Palaeolithic unfolded, long after the last Neanderthals. People were making their own history in a fashion that the Neanderthals did not – indeed, could not.

In this way, cosmology (a tiered universe), religion, image-making and social discrimination came together. At that time, I argue, it was impossible to distinguish between them:

- A tiered cosmology was fashioned out of, principally, hard-wired flying and vortex experiences.
- Religion was traversal of the tiered cosmology by means of altered states and with concomitant social and psychological effects.
- Image-making was a religious ritual aimed, at least initially, at fixing and controlling visions of powerful animals and thereby creating social distinctions between those who had direct access to those animals and those who did not.
- Social differences were thus more and more founded on criteria that went beyond age, sex, and strength and that derived from differential access to mental and subterranean experiences.

Society as we know it in all its complexity, cross-cutting discriminations, situational identities, rituals and imagery was burgeoning, an extended, complex process begun long before among *Homo sapiens* populations in Africa.

## Beyond both cave and laboratory

The consciousness hypothesis holds implications not only for the way in which we understand the period during which *Homo sapiens* communities began to make images, but also for the way in which we today confront the enigma of religion. I say 'enigma' because the word 'religion' is notoriously difficult to define; many definitions are actually diffuse pleonasm. We cannot now enter into a protracted discussion of all the various attempts to define religion. Instead, I note what I take to be the fundamental characteristic of religion, one that many writers shy away from because of its anomalous implications in a modern, essentially 'scientific', world: all religions are based on some idea of a supernatural realm, dimension or influence that is immune to scientific investigation.

Theology and the history of religion are disciplines that deal with the supernatural and the impact of supernatural beliefs on human affairs. Routinely, they distinguish between animism, ancestor worship, polytheism, monotheism, and some sort of impersonal 'Something' that is said to underlie all creation. All these distinctions are in fact negligible. It does not really matter if Upper Palaeolithic people were polytheists or monotheists – unless one wishes to place them in an evolutionary sequence that ends with monotheistic 'higher' religions. There is something much more important than those categories.

As I have pointed out, all religions claim the existence, in one way or another, of a supernatural realm. All the culturally and historically specific refinements of this broad claim are, in practice, socially discriminatory formulations: the history of the Christian Church is the history of schism and doctrinal disputes that had serious political and economic implications. Doctrinal dicta were (and still are) tools for the exclusion of groups of people from economic and political power, whatever individuals may have thought about their truth. The Nicene Council, for instance, convened in the fourth century to settle doctrinal disputes, actually ensured their longevity by the convoluted circumlocutions of the creed that it produced. Today, the niceties of trinitarian doctrine (and their political implications) with which the bishops of that time wrestled under the watchful eye of the emperor Constantine seem less and less important because the social consequences of believing one or other formulation have largely (but not entirely) disappeared.

Doctrine is always more than religious experience: it is formulated in social and economic contexts.

What remains today is the greatest hurdle that the Church (and all religion) has had to face, greater by far than the robust challenge of nineteenth-century evolutionism. Neurology is now uncovering not just what happened at the beginning of the Upper Palaeolithic, but the fundamental, continuing generation of religious experience in the human brain (e.g., Pinker 1997; Ramachandran & Blakeslee 1998; d'Aquili & Newberg 1999; Newberg, d'Aquili, & Rause 2002). There is no place left for the supernatural and the divisive impact that beliefs about it have on human communities. Instead of atavistically yearning for some indefinable spirituality that is bound up with supernaturalism and that we are said to have 'lost', we should rejoice that a way out of the entangling undergrowth of supernatural beliefs has opened up.

Curiously, this is an issue on which most archaeologists decline to comment. Some judge the moral standing of researchers who think that Neanderthals were 'less advanced' than *Homo sapiens* people, but cannot bring themselves to face and discuss openly the larger issue of the role of belief in the supernatural, not just vestigially in the West but throughout the world and deep human history. Today archaeologists accept that their work is conducted within, and has a political impact on, the community in which they live (e.g., Shanks & Tilley 1987a, 1987b); they speak out on controversial political issues, such as nationalism, gender relations, colonialism and landrights. But they shy away from saying anything about present-day religion and supernaturalism. Yet there is no reason why those topics should be no-go areas. Archaeology provides a uniquely valuable time-breadth and inter-disciplinary complexity for discussions between religionists and scientists.

## Acknowledgements

I thank the Templeton Foundation for the invitation to participate in the 2004 Les Eyzies symposium. I am also grateful to colleagues who read and commented on this chapter: Geoff Blundell, Jeremy Hollmann, David Pearce and Ben Smith. The chapter is based on research funded by the National Research Foundation (grant numbers: 2053693 and 2053470) and the University of the Witwatersrand.

## REFERENCES

Bahn, P. G. & P. A. Helvenston, 2002. *Desperately Seeking Trance Plants: Testing The 'Three Stages Of Trance' Model.* New York: R. J. Communications LLC.

Biesele, M., 1993. *Women Like Meat: The Folklore and Foraging Ideology of the Kalahari Ju/'hoan.* Johannesburg: Witwatersrand University Press.

Bleek, D. F., 1935. Beliefs and customs of the /Xam Bushmen. Part VII: Sorcerers. *Bantu Studies* **9**, 1–47.

Caramelli, D., C. Lalueza-Fox, C. Vernesi., M. Lari, A. Casoli, F. Mallegni, B. Chiarelli, I. Dupanloup, J. Bertranpetit, G. Barbujani & G. Bertorelle, 2003. Evidence for a genetic discontinuity between Neanderthals and 24,000-year-old anatomically modern Europeans. *Proceedings of the National Academy of Sciences of the United States of America* **100**, 6593–7.

Clottes, J. & J. D. Lewis-Williams, 1996. *Les Chamanes de la Préhistoire: Trans et Magie dans les Grottes Ornées.* Paris: Le Seuil. English edition: (1998) *The Shamans of Prehistory: Trance and Magic in the Painted Caves.* New York: Harry Abrams.

Clottes, J. & J. D. Lewis-Williams, 2001. *Les Chamanes de la Préhistoire: Texte Intégral, Polémique et Réponses.* Paris: La Maison des Roches.

d'Aquili, E. & A. B. Newberg, 1999. *The Mystical Mind: Probing the Biology of Religious Experience.* Minneapolis: Fortress Press.

Edelman, G. M., 1992. *Bright Air, Brilliant Fire: On The Matter Of The Mind.* Harmondsworth: Penguin.

Edelman, G. M., 2004. *Wider Than The Sky: The Phenomenal Gift Of Consciousness.* Harmondsworth: Allen Lane.

Edelman, G. M. & G. Tononi, 2000. *Consciousness: How Matter Becomes Imagination.* Harmondsworth: Penguin.

Forge, A., 1970. *Learning to see in New Guinea, in Socialization: The Approach from Social Anthropology*, ed. P. Mayer. London: Tavistock, 269–90.

Gargett, R. H., 1989. Grave shortcomings: the evidence for Neanderthal burial. *Current Anthropology* **30**, 157–90.

Gargett, R. H., 1999. Middle Palaeolithic burial is not a dead issue: the view from Qafzah, Saint-Césaire, Kebara, Amud and Dederiyeh. *Journal Human Evolution* **37**, 27–90.

Greenfield, S., 1997, *The Human Brain: A Guided Tour.* London: Phœnix.

Greenfield, S., 2001. *The Private Life of the Brain.* Harmondsworth: Penguin.

Hublin, J. J., 2000. Modern-nonmodern hominid interactions: a Mediterranean perspective, in *The Geography of Neanderthals and Modern Humans in Europe and the Greater Mediterranean*, eds. O. Bar-Yosef & D.R. Pilbeam. Cambridge (MA): Peabody Museum of Archaeology and Ethnology, 157–82.

Klüver, H., 1926. Mescal visions and eidetic vision. *American Journal of Psychology* **37**, 502–15.

Krings, M., A. Stone, R.W. Schmitz, H. Krainitzki, M. Stoneking & S. Pääbo, 1997. Neanderthal DNA sequences and the origin of modern humans. *Cell* **90**, 19–28.

Krings, M., H. Geisert, R.W. Schmitz, H. Krainitzki & S. Pääbo, 1999. DNA sequences of mitochondrial hypervariable region II from the Neanderthal type specimen. *Proceedings of the National Academy of Science of the United States of America* **96**:5581–5.

Lewis-Williams, J.D., 1997. Art, agency and altered consciousness: a motif in French (Quercy) Upper Palaeolithic parietal art. *Antiquity* **71**, 810–30.

Lewis-Williams, J.D., 2002. *The Mind in the Cave: Consciousness and the Origins of Art*. London: Thames and Hudson.

Lewis-Williams, J.D., 2004. Neuropsychology and Upper Palaeolithic art: observations on the progress of altered states of consciousness. *Cambridge Archaeological Journal* **14**, 107–11.

Lewis-Williams, J.D. & T.A. Dowson, 1988. The signs of all times: entoptic phenomena in Upper Palaeolithic art. *Current Anthropology* **29**, 201–45.

Martindale, C., 1981. *Cognition and Consciousness*. Homewood (IL): Dorsey Press.

McBrearty, S. & A.S. Brooks, 2000. The revolution that wasn't: a new interpretation of the origin of modern human behaviour. *Journal Human Evolution* **39**, 453–563.

Mellars, P.A., 1990. *The Emergence of Modern Humans: An Archaeological Perspective*. Edinburgh: Edinburgh University Press.

Mellars, P.A., 1996. *The Neanderthal Legacy: An Archaeological Perspective From Western Europe*. Princeton: Princeton University Press.

Mellars, P.A., 2000. The archaeological records of the Neanderthal-modern human transition in France, in *The Geography of Neanderthals and Modern Humans in Europe and the Greater Mediterranean*, eds. O. Bar-Yosef & D.R. Pilbeam. Cambridge (MA): Peabody Museum of Archaeology and Ethnology, 35–47.

Newberg, A., E. d'Aquili & V. Rause, 2002. *Why God Won't Go Away*. New York: Ballantine Books.

Pinker, S., 1997. *How the Mind Works*. New York: Norton.

Ramachandran, V.S., & S. Blakeslee, 1998. *Phantoms in the Brain*. New York: William Morrow.

Rappaport, R.A., 1999. *Ritual and Religion in the Making of Humanity*. Cambridge: Cambridge University Press.

Reichel-Dolmatoff, G., 1971. *Amazonian Cosmos: The Sexual and Religious Symbolism of the Tukano Indians*. Chicago: University of Chicago Press.

Riel-Salvatore, J. & G.A. Clark, 2001. Middle and early Upper Palaeolithic burials and the use of chronotypology in contemporary Palaeolithic research. *Current Anthropology* **42**, 449–79.

Rock, A., 2004. *The Mind at Night: The New Science of How and Why We Dream*. New York: Basic Books.

Shanks, M., & C. Tilley, 1987a. *Social Theory and Archaeology*. Cambridge: Polity Press.

Shanks, M., & C. Tilley, 1987b. *Re-Constructing Archaeology: Theory and Practice*. Cambridge: Cambridge University Press.

Shennan, S., 2002. *Genes, Memes and Human History: Darwinian Archaeology and Cultural Evolution*. London: Thames and Hudson.

Siegel, R. K., 1977. Hallucinations. *Scientific American* **237**, 132–40.

Siegel, R. K. & M.E. Jarvik, 1975. *Drug-induced hallucinations in animals and man, in Hallucinations: Behaviour, Experience and Theory*, eds. R.K. Siegel & L.J. West. New York: Wiley, 81–161.

Stringer, C. & C. Gamble, 1993. *In search of the Neanderthals*. London: Thames and Hudson.

| |

# Ritual and music: parallels and practice, and the Palaeolithic

*Iain Morley*

Considerations of the emergence of symbolic and spiritual culture have understandably often focused principally on the rich record of representational and abstract imagery of the Upper Palaeolithic of Europe. There is, however, at least one other medium of expression relevant to such considerations and which can leave an archaeological trace – musical activity. Although there are some notable discussions of evidence for musical activity in the Upper Palaeolithic (many of which are cited in this chapter), discussions of music in the context of the early manifestation of symbolic and religious activity are surprisingly rare, with early musical artefacts and activities receiving a brief mention in that context, if they are mentioned at all (a particularly notable exception is provided by d'Errico et al. 2003). The archaeological record of reputed sound-producers from the Upper Palaeolithic is, in fact, a relatively rich one, including over 120 objects which have been, at various times (admittedly with variable likelihood), interpreted as flutes and more than ninety objects interpreted (again, with variable likelihood) as whistles (see Morley 2003; also Morley 2005). There is also a number of other objects with sound-producing potential, interpreted as bullroarers (Dams 1985; Alebo 1986; Dauvois 1989, 1999; Scothern 1992) and rasps (Huyge 1990, 1991; Dauvois 1989, 1999). Finally the sound-producing potential of rocks and caves themselves also appears to have been exploited (Glory 1964, 1965; Dams 1984, 1985; Reznikoff & Dauvois 1988; Dauvois 1989, 1999). At present the oldest widely accepted musical instruments are two swan-bone pipes dated to around 36,800 + /– 1000 years BP, found in context with Aurignacian II split bone points at Geissenklösterle, Germany (Hahn & Münzel 1995; Turk & Kavur 1997; Richter et al. 2000), and a remarkable multi-part pipe made from mammoth ivory from the same site, of around the same age (Conard et al. 2004).

Along with language, musical behaviours and religious behaviours are conspicuous in sharing an apparent universality amongst modern humans. As John Blacking (1995) said in a now oft-quoted passage, "every known human society has what trained musicologists would recognise as music" (p. 224), and whilst a precise definition of 'religion' might be no more easily reached than of music (see Henshilwood, this volume, for a discussion), it would probably be true to say that every human culture exhibits behaviours that we would recognise as 'religious'. Very often these two sets of behaviours coincide, with musical activities forming a fundamental part of ritual activities, and spiritual significance being attributed to musical activities.

It is important to remember that in discussing music we are not talking about detached 'autonomous' patterns of sounds. As Begbie (2000) puts it: "To insist that a work of music consists entirely of sound-patterns heard in a certain way, or sound-patterns codified in a score, is artificial and inadequate – for it also consists of actions, and this means actions that can only properly be understood as temporally constituted and situated" (p. 10). This embodied and contextual aspect of musical activity is one that is often overlooked, from the perspective of modern western art-music. The only form in which music might genuinely be said to *lack* embodied and performance-dependent traits is that of sheet music. Nevertheless this concept of music as something which can exist as an entity in its own right, a pattern independent of action and situation, is one that prevails amongst much analytical discussion of it. In contrast, a discussion of music and ritual must rely upon a consideration of its form and role in human action and context.

Equally, it is important to remember that, on the basis of what we know of other societies from around the world, and ours until very recent years, for the vast majority of people for the vast majority of the past there would be no separation between 'religion' and other daily activities. 'Ritual' and belief might be as much a part of (what we would call) a daily practical activity such as making a tool out of stone or metal, or cooking a meal, as they are a part of an activity like making a votive offering in the corner of a room. By the same token, making a votive offering in the corner of a room might be seen as just as 'practical' as making a tool or a meal. Each such activity may equally be viewed as one which has to be carried out in order to ensure that the world is the way that it needs to be in order to ensure survival. A religious belief system can provide ethics, moral guidelines, laws, explanations and understandings of the world, of people, and of illness and mortality. For many, it constitutes philosophy, science, law and medicine – a framework for understanding and interacting with the world which is thus integral to daily life. A 'belief system' is not as in the sense that we often use the term, an *accessory* to *knowledge* and *understanding*, but *is* knowledge and understanding.

## Music and ritual: shared roles, shared traits and shared conceptions

With this in mind it might be expected that religious significance of some form would be attached to almost all activities, and its association with musical activities is thus perhaps unsurprising. However, there is more to it than that. Musical activities and religious, or spiritual, activities have much in common. Both are frequently orchestrated by an 'empowered' individual, or individuals, but are highly communal, social and integrative activities. Both have the potential to elicit powerful emotional responses in participating individuals, and to have significance, both at a very private, personal level and at a social, communal level. Both musical and religious behaviours can thus be simultaneously profoundly personal and at the same time creators of communality through shared experience. These traits are explored further later in this chapter.

Another significant trait that music and ritual have in common is the difficulty of their definition – ontologies of which are apparently at least as numerous as the cultures practicing them. Some cultures famously have no single word for music itself, although they have words for musical activities and instruments of various sorts (e.g. the Hausa people of Nigeria); others have terms for music which encompass activities which we, from the Western tradition, would not consider to be part of music. Delineating the parameters of ritual activity faces similar problems. Nevertheless there are particular combinations of traits of both ritual and musical activities which allow us to recognise them, even if it is difficult to impose parameters on them.

It is not simply that musical and ritual activities have many traits in common, however. One thing which becomes clear upon examination of ontologies of music in other cultures is the frequency with which conceptions of music are inseparable from ritual and religion. In considering the varied ways in which music takes roles in other cultures Bohlman (2002) conspicuously chooses to illustrate this diversity with examples of music's roles within religious practice:

> By the epistemology of music we mean its ability to be a part of culture as a whole and thus to acquire meaning in relation to other activities. Examining music cross-culturally, we recognise that religious meaning accrues to music in many ways. Music may serve as a vehicle for shaping the voice of a deity; it may demarcate time so that it is more meaningful for the performance of ritual; music may provide one of many ornaments that make religious practice more attractive; certain domains of music-making (e.g. instrumental music in many religions) may raise images of magic or immorality, thus causing some religions to prohibit music in worship. (p. 5)

But music is frequently more than just a facilitator of ritual and religion, and in many cases is conceptually inseparable from them. Of thirteen different ontologies of music from around the world given as examples by Bohlman (2002), eight are explicitly associated with religion and/or cosmologies. These vary from concepts such as *qirā'ah* (in Islam) and *ta'ameh ha-mikrah* (in Judaism), the chanting of religious texts, which would be identified as music by external observers but never by practitioners (music being defined by them not by form but by context), to the Afro-Brazilian *candomblé* religion in which music is so ubiquitous that the term is used virtually synonymously for religion and music.

Another example of synonymity of music and ritual is provided by the Maring of Papua New Guinea (Rappaport 1999). At the Kaiko festival Maring groups perform a dance which signifies commitment to come to the martial aid of the group who is hosting the festival, should such aid be required in the future; the dance and the ritual are inseparable. The dance in this sense is indexical, indicating a pledge – it does more than to symbolise the pledge, it is indexical of it because to the Maring to dance *is* to pledge – pledging is intrinsic to the conventionalised act of dancing (Rappaport 1999). A fundamental characteristic of ritual here is its ability to bring about a conventional state of affairs – to affirm, transform, or bring into being a particular natural order – that is, it is meant to affect the world (ibid.).

In this latter sense ritual is separated by Rappaport from 'drama' by its intended causal influence on the world. A participant in a ritual has a part in 'the enduring order that their participation brings into being' (p. 136) unlike an actor whose part and actions last only as long as the performance. Coming from the western musical tradition we tend to be inclined to consider the actions of a musician, the act of performing, and the performance itself, in much the same way as those of the 'actor' and the 'drama' – with no lasting or causal influence on the world. However, as the above example illustrates, such a distinction from 'causally influential' ritual cannot always be made, either for 'drama' or for 'music'.

Indeed, substituting the word 'performance' for 'drama' and 'performer' for 'actor' in the above discussion, it is made equally relevant for both music and drama. As Rappaport himself observes, a particular act may contain both ritual and drama [performance], and 'stand somewhere on a continuum . . . between the two polar forms' (p. 136). Certainly there are numerous examples, one of which cited by Rappaport is the performance of religious music in a church. Others that present them-selves are that an actor or musician (or writer) might hope that their performance would have some transformative effect on the world, through its effect on the audience. Conversely a ritual participant may adopt a persona (of an ancestor or animal for example) for only the duration of the ritual, but this is still nevertheless perceived to have a lasting transformative effect on the order of the world.

So is it possible ever to separate ritual and performance? I would suggest that in fact there is no such thing as *pure* (polar) ritual or *pure* (polar) performance (by Rappaport's criteria) and that the continuum is one only of varying relative proportions of the two, the ends of which are not absolutes. For example, it is impossible to absolutely separate the two on the basis of the intended temporality of effects of the activity on the world, or on the temporality of the personae adopted. It is also impos-sible to separate the two on the basis of the extent to which they effect change through appeal to a supernatural agent rather than through other humans. The Maring pledge dance-ritual alluded to above makes no recourse to a supernatural agent, but still brings into being a new state of affairs. It is also impossible to separate ritual and performance in terms of the extent to which change is effected 'directly' on the world rather than via affecting the actions of others (as in the actor-audience example above), be they natural or supernatural, for the 'direct' effect of a ritual could conceivably only be manifest in terms of a change in human behaviour.

One of the most important traits of ritual activity contributing to the maintaining or changing of established order comes from the sense of unity, *communitas*, that can be created by coparticipation. Once again Rappaport provides an erudite elucidation, and is worth quoting in full here:

> Indeed, the boundary between individuals and their surroundings, especially others participating in ritual with them, may seem to dissolve . . . such a sense of union is encouraged by the coordination of utterance and movement demanded of congregations in many rituals. To sing with others, to move as they move in the performance of a ritual is not merely to symbolize union. It is *in and of itself* to reunite in the reproduction of a larger order. Unison does not merely symbolize that order but *indicates* it and its acceptance. The participants do not simply *communicate* to each other *about* that order but *commune with* each other *within* it. In sum, the state of communitas experienced in ritual is at once social and experiential. Indeed, the distinction between social and experiential is surrendered, or even erased, in a general feeling of oneness with oneself, with the congregation, or with the cosmos. (1999, p. 220, italics in original)

It will be noted that the description of singing and coordination of movement with others is not merely an exemplar in this conception of ritual activity and its role, but is integral to it. These roles are fulfilled *through* singing and dance activity. Music and dance can fulfil this role so effectively within ritual because, in fact, with the substitution of 'music and dance activity' for 'ritual' in the paragraph it constitutes as good a description of the potential effects of participation in musical and dance performance as of ritual performance. The difference is that music and dance are intrinsic to the description of the potential effects of ritual activity, whereas the reverse is not the case; i.e. ritual relies on music to achieve these effects, but music does not rely on ritual to achieve them itself.

## Performance and participation – audience and congregation

These benefits of, and parallels between, ritual and musical activity depend to a great extent upon direct participation. The perception of being an audience-member, or observer, of a ritual activity would likely only be held by individuals who consider themselves detached from the belief system itself; others would consider themselves participants, to one degree or another. Similarly, the category of audience, as opposed to participant, is one that is predominant in modern Western music, but is relatively rare elsewhere. So at what point in the experience of musical activity can one be considered to be a *participant*, in the sense that we use the word? Does the simple act of moving your body in time with the tempo of the music transform you from 'audience' to 'participant'? From 'audience' to 'congregation'? If so, at what point in the scale of magnitude – from tapping your finger on the arm of your chair to full body movement dance – do you cease to be audience and become participant?

What do we really mean by *participant* or *participation* in performance – be it ritual or musical? The fact that we would be reticent to apply the appellation of 'participant' to someone dancing to recorded music would suggest that there is more to participation than magnitude of physical reaction; indeed, this observation can apply in the case of dancing to 'live' music, although in some circumstances this *could* be considered to be participation.

Perhaps, then, it is the extent to which your action is perceived to have an effect on the stimulus to which you are reacting. The extent to which you *contribute*. At what point is response perceived to have an effect on the music (or ritual) itself? For the individual themselves, as soon as they start to react to the music, their reaction itself becomes one of the stimuli; this in itself, then, is not enough to constitute contribution, as this would apply in all cases, recorded or live. So it must be dependent on the perception *by others* that your action contributes to or transforms the stimulus *they* are experiencing. Or, rather, because no one has objective knowledge of others' perception, it is the extent to which each individual [a] conceives that other individuals [n] perceive that they [a] are contributing to the stimulus experienced by those other individuals [n]. It can be seen that to consider oneself a participant, in the sense used here, in a performance (ritual or musical) relies upon a strong sense of the perception of you by others engaged in the activity, that is, it relies on well-developed theory of mind and social awareness.

## Music, meaning and symbolism

In addition to – and possibly because of – music's roles within ritual and religious practice it also features heavily in doctrine and mythology concerning creation, with early beings very often being musicians, and using music in various transformative ways (Bohlman 2002), as a building block of humanity and the world, and as a medium for the transformation of boundaries between the natural and supernatural, the sacred and the profane.

However, musical activities do not *rely* on symbolism or a symbolic capacity for their existence. Whilst many, or even the majority, of musical activities that we experience in the modern world have direct symbolic associations made explicit, the activity itself of music-making need not be predicated upon symbolising.

For example, amongst the Blackfoot and Sioux Plains Indians of North America, music is for the most part considered to have no direct symbolic content. Song has minimal lyrical content, vocalisations instead consisting of *vocables*, which are emotive sounds with no obvious symbolism. It would seem that the main purpose of this type of vocalisation is to contribute to the emotional responses evoked by the music (McAllester 1996), and that it has no (conscious) symbolism behind it. According to Nettl, "native informants are able to say almost nothing on the symbolic aspect of their [nonlexical] music" (Nettl 1956, p. 25). A very similar situation exists amongst the Aka and Mbuti Pygmies of equatorial Africa, also traditional hunter-gatherer societies, in that the majority of the melodic content of their music consists of vocable vocalizations, apparently lacking any direct symbolic content (in terms of lexical meaning or mimicry) (Turino 1992).

This being said, whilst the music itself is said to have no symbolic content, it is clearly often used in close association with activities which do have symbolic content and associations, and a particular song can relate very specifically to a particular activity. It is evident that whilst the creation of music *can* occur without any symbolising, with a symbolising capacity in place music (its performance and perception) provides a perfect medium for carrying symbolic associations, because of its combination of having no fixed meaning ('floating intentionality' to use Cross's 1999 term) whilst having the potential to stimulate powerful emotional reactions.

In a sense, much of what constitutes religious belief systems and practice has the same potential – elements, such as explanations of the world and descriptions of spiritual entities, gain much of their currency from their ambiguity; they can be many things to many people. The combination of enough specificity of meaning to allow an interpretation to be made, with the flexibility to allow that (process of) interpretation to be personal, is a powerful one, and could apply equally to the experience of a trance state, understanding a passage of doctrinal text, or experiencing/participating in musical activity. The fact that one has to decide upon (or accept) an interpretation of these ambiguities is one of the elements that makes a particular belief system (or, indeed, type of music) powerfully personal whilst at the same time profoundly uniting, in the belief that conspecifics share similar personal interpretations and appreciations.

If one can believe that one has come to a particular interpretation of one's own volition, an interpretation that is thus very personal, but can also believe that others have come to the same interpretation of *their* own volition, this can create the sense of a powerful bond of shared thought and emotion between the individuals, that is, a perceived empathy. This is in spite of the fact that in reality both the sense of independent volition (in coming to an interpretation) and the similarity of interpretation of the individuals concerned, are to an extent illusory. This is because the interpretation is often structured by suggestion (what we might term 'bounded ambiguity') and because the *precise* natures of the 'shared' beliefs are often never made explicit.[1]

## Music and ritual in the Palaeolithic

So how do the above observations add to our picture of music in the Palaeolithic? Several things are clear: outside of the recent Western musical tradition, ritual and musical practice are often closely related, and in some cases virtually interdependent (even within the recent Western musical and religious systems the two are powerfully related in a number of ways, and such overlaps are explored in some depth by Begbie 2000). The overlaps are a consequence not just of symbolic relatedness emergent from the contexts in which they are carried out, but upon shared characteristics in their forms, execution and their effects on individuals. It seems likely that where we find music in the Upper Palaeolithic archaeological record, we find ritual too. Also, that these are not solitary meditative activities, but communal and integrative.

As noted in the introduction there are numerous examples of objects from Upper Palaeolithic contexts (Aurignacian, Gravettian, Solutrean, and Magdalenian) which have been interpreted as musical instruments or, less specifically, sound-producers. Unfortunately, in many cases they were excavated before techniques allowed for a fine resolution of spatial and stratigraphic relationships, meaning that palimpsests and the circumstances of deposition are impossible now to detect. As a consequence, with the majority of examples of reputed instruments we cannot be certain as to whether they were used in solitary musical activity or as part of a group activity. In contrast, some of the more recent finds have been subject to far greater scrutiny and thorough contextual recording, including the aforementioned examples from Geissenklösterle, the earliest currently known instruments associated with anatomically modern *Homo sapiens*. The following section describes a few cases of different types of sound-producer where it is possible to say a little more about their contexts of use. Of course, we should bear in mind that musical behaviours and instrumental use are not synonymous, and the former can occur without the latter. It is likely that behaviours we would recognise as musical predated the occurrence of instruments in the archaeological record by many years. Nevertheless, the identification of musical instruments from the Palaeolithic remains the 'acid test' of the existence of musical behaviour, and can tell us something about the contexts in which such activities were carried out.

By far the richest known source of intentionally produced sound-makers is Isturitz, in the French Pyrenees. This cave site was an important focal point for large groups of people throughout the Upper Palaeolithic (Bahn 1983), showing evidence of use from Aurignacian through to Magdalenian contexts. It seems to have been a focus for major gatherings in spring and autumn in particular and has produced a variety of art and bone-working. Seventeen bone flute-like objects have been retrieved, from throughout the period of occupation of the site, and several of these show deliberate signs of working, with truncated ends, holes bored and then smoothed, incised lines, and even some which might have been block-and-duct examples (like a modern recorder) (Scothern 1992). Graeme Lawson and Francesco d'Errico (2002) have carried out extensive analyses of the most complete examples (Lawson and d'Errico 2002; d'Errico et al. 2003), and suggest that at least two of the Aurignacian examples seem to have been designed to be played as end-blown trumpet- or reed-voiced pipes, rather than as flutes. There seems to be a great consistency in their manufacture, and they closely resemble numerous Mayan and mediaeval examples. It is the various Isturitz examples that are most frequently cited and discussed in the literature regarding Palaeolithic instrumentation, and they are particularly significant in appearing to indicate large scale communal musical activity or, at least, musical activity at large scale communal gatherings, and over a very extended period of time.

Similarities in the stone and bone artefacts with those from the Dordogne area, and the transferral of flint over distances over 100km (Gamble 1983) suggest wide social contact (Scothern 1992). Parallels in the bone flute design and engravings are displayed by examples from Mas d'Azil, Le Placard and Marcamps; Mas d'Azil shows similar evidence of large aggregations of people (Scothern 1992), and this may also be represented by the nine examples from the Magdalenian contexts of the site of Le Placard. At least two of these are made from eagle bone, a choice which it is hard to believe did not have significance beyond its sound-producing potential, given the likely difficulty of the acquisition of the material. It is worth remembering that a perfectly functional flute/pipe can be made from much more readily available materials than bird bone, let alone that of an eagle.

The flutes are commonly found inside the decorated caves of these sites, suggesting either that acoustics were particularly important, or their relation to the cave art, or both. Of course, this is not to suggest that all music (or ritual, or artistic) activity was carried out in caves, as evidence of such activities in other locations is less likely to be preserved or to be discovered. It is also difficult to demonstrate whether the production of music in the caves was a group activity indulged by all or an activity performed only by a select few, an issue which also applies to the production of cave art. However, in her analysis of the Solutrean lithophones (natural cave structures such as stalactites, stalagmites and stalactitic flutings which produce clear tones when struck) Dams (1984; 1985) notes that they occur in caves which generally also allow a number of people to congregate in nearby chambers, up to twenty to thirty people at Roucador, for example (Dams 1985). Indeed, the cave of Nerja has been used in recent times as a venue for concerts and dance during the summer months (Dams 1984). It is worth noting, however, that the locations of the lithophones are dictated by natural cave features rather than human agency so their position in relation to other large chambers is not premeditated. What would be particularly valuable as a comparison would be to know of caves in the same regions with the same calcified structures in them that *haven't* been decorated and used percussively. If such examples exist, it might suggest that the ones in the caves described by Dams were chosen selectively because they could accommodate many people.

There are many similarities between the features and decoration of the lithophones at the various widespread sites that Dams describes, which suggests wide social contact between the people responsible and the possibility that large groups of people congregated to experience (and perhaps participate in) the sound produced by them. Whether the activities involved many or few people, it is clear from the work of Glory (1964; 1965), Dams (1984; 1985) and Reznikoff and Dauvois (1988) that the acoustics of the caves were highly significant, and that sound production bore an important relationship with both abstract and representational art.

A set of six mammoth bones from Mezin, Ukraine, dated to twenty thousand years ago, provides another potential example of public percussive sound production. These appear to have been deliberately and repeatedly struck, and were found in context with two beaters and a variety of ivory 'rattles' (Bibikov 1978). Also found in the same settlement were piles of red and yellow ochre, and other mammoth bones which had been incised and painted. The 'orchestra' bones (including a shoulder blade, thigh bone, jaw bones and skull fragments) produce a selection of tones when struck with beaters (Bibikov 1978) and were found in a large, open-fronted, communal hut in the Mezin settlement, rather than a small dwelling. This does suggest, if it is indeed a collection of instruments, that the sound produced was supposed to be heard by the community, and was not performed in solitary private rites.

While the artefacts do show wear from percussion, Scothern (1992) and Lawson et al. (1998) point out that this does not necessarily merit a musicological explanation, as many daily activities involve percussive actions. Hopefully further microscopic and use-wear analysis of the assemblage in the future may help to resolve the issue of whether they were directly struck by the neighbouring 'beaters' or whether they were struck indirectly as part of another process. Their contextual association with the reindeer antler mallet and beaters, as well as what appear to be rattles, counts in favour of the musicological interpretation, though. There is evidence for the trafficking of raw materials and visually related goods between European populations and those of the Russian plains of the Magdalenian (Scothern 1992), so it is quite possible that sound-production traditions were also shared.

## Concluding remarks

Musical and religious activities have much in common with each other, in the ways that they are carried out and their effects on individual participants. In many cultures conceptions of music are to various degrees inseparable from conceptions of ritual and religion. Indeed, 'ritual' and 'performance' are in many ways synonymous. Music is often conceived as a medium for the transformation of boundaries between the sacred and the profane, and the natural and supernatural, probably because of the roles that it fulfils in that respect in many societies' rituals. These roles, in turn, are a product of the commonalities in the potential effects of musical and ritual performance. The generation of a state of *communitas* is an important product (and often goal) of much of both ritual and musical activity, and in the context of ritual frequently dependent on musical activity to be achieved. Because musical activities themselves stimulate some of the same reactions as ritual activities can, and share some of the characteristics of religious stimuli, musical activities are a remarkably effective facilitator of the desired effects of participation in ritual activities.

The performance and perception of music can provide the perfect medium for carrying symbolic (including religious) associations because of its combination of having no fixed meaning ('floating intentionality') whilst having the potential to stimulate powerful emotional reactions. Many elements of ritual and doctrine share the same combination of having no fixed meaning (which in these circumstances might be called 'bounded ambiguity') and of having the potential to stimulate powerful emotions. This combination of traits allows the experience of a particular belief system or type of music to be powerfully personal whilst at the same time profoundly uniting, in the belief that conspecifics share similar personal interpretations and experiences.

The ability to hold such beliefs about others' beliefs and mental states relies on a well-developed theory of mind ability, and this can be argued also to be the case for actual participation in performance activities: to be a *participant* in performance can be argued to rely on the individual conceiving that others perceive them as contributing to the stimuli to which they are all reacting; that is, it is highly social and also relies on a well-developed theory of mind.

Given the above we can reasonably expect that amongst anatomically modern humans, musical activity is likely to have played an important role in the situations where we see evidence for ritual activity, and where there is archaeological evidence for musical activity it will frequently have had associations with concepts that we would think of as religious. It is perhaps, then, unsurprising that where we have contextual evidence for musical finds from the Upper Palaeolithic, they are frequently in association with other evidence of symbolic and communal activities. Much of what we have at present comes from cave contexts; this is due largely to taphonomic and excavation biases, so should not be taken to indicate that this is the main context in which musical (and indeed artistic or ritual) activities took place.

Much of the material that is already known warrants further examination such as that carried out by Scothern (1992) and d'Errico et al. (2003), but there are nevertheless some cases where it seems that musical activity was an important part of large communal activities. Undoubtedly the majority of the music archaeology of the Palaeolithic has been lost; hopefully there is much still to be found and recognised. Increasingly accurate archaeological knowledge of the contexts of deposition of the evidence for musical activity in the Palaeolithic will allow us to flesh out the relationship between ritual and musical activity at that time, but we can reasonably expect that there was a powerful relationship between the two.

In considering the relationship between music and ritual, music can seem on first examination to be a mere condiment, or at best, an optional ingredient in ritual activity, subservient to the requirements of ritual; on closer inspection it is revealed to be a prime mover in determining the nature and genuine effects of ritual, with rhythm, dance and song frequently relied on to confer many of the most important individual and social benefits associated with ritual activity.

This chapter has only scratched the surface of the potential parallels and overlaps between the functional qualities of ritual and music; this is an area with much potential for future investigation. Exploration of the phylogenic and ontogenic relationships between ritual, play, music and performance activities could all bear significant results for models of the emergence of modern social relations, beliefs and symbolism.

## NOTES

[1] Of course, these properties also have the potential to be profoundly divisive, with differing interpretations being seen as personally incompatible, and easily identified with ingroup/outgroup categorisations.

## BIBLIOGRAPHY

Alebo, L., 1986. Manufacturing of drumskins and tendon strings for prehistoric musical instruments, in *The Second Conference Of the ICTM Study Group On Music Archaeology: Volume I, General Studies*, ed. C. S. Lund. Royal Swedish Academy Of Music, Stockholm, 41–8.

Bahn, P., 1983. Late Pleistocene economies in the French Pyrenees, in *Hunter-Gatherer Economy In Prehistory: A European Perspective*, ed. G.N. Bailey. Cambridge University Press, 167–85.

Begbie, J. S., 2000. *Theology, Music and Time*. Cambridge: Cambridge University Press.

Bibikov, S., 1978. A stone age orchestra, in *Readings in Physical Anthropology and Archaeology*, eds. D. E. K. Hunter & P. Whitten. Harper and Row, London.

Blacking, J., 1995. *Music, Culture and Experience*. University of Chicago Press, London.

Bohlman, P. V., 2002. *World Music: A Very Short Introduction*. Oxford: Oxford University Press.

Conard, N. J., M. Malina, S. C. Münzel & F. Seeberger, 2004. Eine Mammutelfenbeinflöte aus dem Aurignacien des Geissenklösterle: Neue Belege für eine Musikalische Tradition im Frühen Jungpaläolithikum auf der Schwäbischen Alb. *Archäologisches Korrespondenzblatt* **34**, 447–62.

Cross, I., 1999. Is music the most important thing we ever did? Music, development and evolution, in *Music, Mind and Science*, ed. Suk Won Yi. Seoul National University Press, Seoul, 10–39.

d'Errico F., C. Henshilwood, G. Lawson, M. Vanhaeren, A.-M. Tillier, M. Soressi, F. Bresson, B. Maureille, A. Nowell, J. Lakarra, L. Backwell & M. Julien, 2003. Archaeological evidence for the emergence of language, symbolism and music – an alternative multidisciplinary perspective, *Journal of World Prehistory* **17**, 1–70.

Dams, L., 1984. Preliminary findings at the "Organ Sanctuary" in the cave of Nerja, Malaga, Spain. *Oxford Journal Of Archaeology* **3**, 1–14.

Dams, L. 1985. Palaeolithic lithophones: descriptions and comparisons. *Oxford Journal Of Archaeology* **4**, 31–46.

Dauvois, M., 1989. Son et musique Paléolithiques, *Les Dossiers D'Archéologie* **142**, 2–11.

Dauvois, M., 1999. Mesures acoustiques et témoins sonores osseux paléolithiques, in *Préhistoire d'os, recueil d'études sur l'industrie osseuse préhistorique, offert à Mme Henriette Camps-Fabrer.* Aix-en-Provence: Publications de l'Université de Provence.

Gamble, C., 1983. Culture and society in the Upper Palaeolithic of Europe, in *Hunter-Gatherer Economy In Prehistory: A European Perspective*, ed. G.N. Bailey. Cambridge: Cambridge University Press, 201–11.

Glory, A., 1964. La Grotte de Roucador, *Bulletin de la Société Préhistorique Française* **61**, clxvi–ix.

Glory, A., 1965. Nouvelles découvertes de dessins rupestres sur le causse de Gramat. *Bulletin de la Société Préhistorique Française* **62**, 528–36.

Hahn, J. & S. Münzel, 1995. Knochenflöten aus den Aurignacien des Geissenklösterle bei Blaubeuren, Alb-Donau-Kreis. *Fundberichte aus Baden-Würtemberg* **20**, 1–12.

Huyge, D., 1990. Mousterian skiffle? Note on a Middle Palaeolithic engraved bone from Schulen, Belgium. *Rock Art Research* 7, 125–32.

Huyge, D., 1991. The "Venus" of Laussel in the light of ethnomusicology. *Archeologie in Vlaanderen* **1**, 11–8.

Lawson, G. & F. d'Errico, 2002. Microscopic, experimental and theoretical re-assessment of Upper Palaeolithic bird-bone pipes from Isturitz, France: ergonomics of design, systems of notation and the origins of musical traditions, in *Studien zur Musikachäologie III*, in eds. E. Hickman, A.D. Kilmer & R. Eichman. Rahden: Verlag Marie Leidorf.

Lawson, G. C. Scarre, I. Cross & C. Hills, 1998. Mounds, megaliths, music and mind: some acoustical properties and purposes of archaeological spaces. *Archaeological Review From Cambridge* **15**, 111–34.

McAllester, D.P., 1996. North America/Native America, in *Worlds of Music: An Introduction to the Music of the World's People* (3rd ed.), ed. J.T. Titon. New York: Schirmer, 17–70.

Morley, I., 2003. *The Evolutionary Origins and Archaeology of Music: An Investigation into the Prehistory of Human Musical Capacities and Behaviours.* Ph.D. thesis, University of Cambridge. Available at http://www.dar.cam.ac.uk/dcrr

Morley, I., 2005. The long-forgotten melody? Music in the Mesolithic, in *Mesolithic Studies at the beginning of the 21st Century*, eds. N. Milner and P. Woodman. Oxford: Oxbow, 212–24.

Nettl, B., 1956. *Music in Primitive Culture.* Cambridge (MA): Harvard University Press.

Rappaport, R., 1999. *Ritual and Religion in the Making of Humanity.* Cambridge: Cambridge University Press.

Reznikoff, I. & M. Dauvois, 1988. La dimension sonore des grottes ornées, *Bulletin de la Société Préhistorique Française* **85**, 238–46.

Richter D., J. Waiblinger, W.J. Rink & G.A. Wagner, 2000. Thermoluminescence, electron spin resonance and C-14-dating of the Late Middle and

Early Upper Palaeolithic site of Geissenklosterle Cave in southern Germany. *Journal Of Archaeological Science* **27**, 71–89.

Scothern, P. M. T., 1992. *The Music-Archaeology of the Palaeolithic Within its Cultural Setting*. Ph.D. thesis, University of Cambridge.

Turino, T., 1992. The music of Sub-Saharan Africa, in *Excursions in World Music*, eds. B. Nettl, C. Capwell, P. Bohlman, I. Wong & T. Turino. Englewood Cliffs (NJ): Prentice Hall, 165–95.

Turk, I. & B. Kavur, 1997. Palaeolithic bone flutes – comparable material, in *Mousterian "Bone Flute" and other finds from Divje babe I cave site in Slovenia*, ed. I. Turk. Ljubljana: Institut za archaeologijo, Znanstvenoraziskovalni Center Sazu, 179–84.

# SECTION III

# THE EUROPEAN EXPERIENCE

# 12

# Materiality and meaning-making in the understanding of the Palaeolithic 'arts'

*Margaret W. Conkey*

we [also] need to carry the mute body of prehistory with us rather than step over its corpse on the road to civilization and texts. (Gamble 1999)

Perhaps we will have to be content with intuiting that they came here [into the caves] to experience, and to carry away with them in memory, special moments of living a perfect balance between danger and survival, fear and a sense of protection. Can one hope for more at any time? (Berger 2002)

## Introduction

Despite the regular and repeated attempts to consider the image-making of the Upper Palaeolithic period as being 'beyond art' (e.g. White 1992; Conkey et al. 1997), certain views persist: that these are images that somehow functioned in Upper Palaeolithic society and culture, and in ways that we can infer; that they may be referable to certain absolutes of human experience (e.g. fertility or magic); and that they can be taken by us as a certain hallmark in the evolution of human cognition and culture. In this chapter, I want to probe somewhat different dimensions in trying to move us 'beyond art'. Specifically, I want to begin to lay out some ideas regarding 'materiality' and also 'meaning-making', as we engage with the visual and material culture(s) of the Upper Palaeolithic of Eurasia – that corpus of archaeological materials that we have labeled 'Palaeolithic art', which includes, of course, many objects, images, forms, and materials.

For some time now, we have thought about the appearance and apparent elaboration of image-making in terms of a symbolic or information 'explosion' (e.g. Pfeiffer 1982; Barton et al. 1994; White 1989). We now have evidence for 'early art' elsewhere in the world (e.g. in White 2003; Henshilwood et al. 2004; Henshilwood, this volume) (see Plate XVI), and it has always been hard to rule out symbolic behaviors and information-processing at various times and places just because there is a lack of empirical (preserved?) archaeological evidence. Given this, I find it more productive to think that what we have throughout the Upper Palaeolithic of Europe (*sensu latu*) is a rich corpus of preserved archaeological materials from which we can surely infer an elaborated engagement with material culture and an engagement that was surely about the making of meanings. Thus, for me, the Upper Palaeolithic is much more productively considered in terms of materiality and meaning-making; both dimensions encourage us to envision the Upper Palaeolithic peoples as active social agents who constructed their worlds in social and political contexts.

Many of us, especially the wider public who are so often fascinated by the riveting images that predominate in the display or telling of Palaeolithic (usually cave) art, have been seduced by both our own notion of art as aesthetic creations and the uncanny resonances that many (and the most often illustrated) Palaeolithic images have with our own aesthetic sensibilities. But as Gell (1998: 1–36) has so powerfully argued, maybe art is not primarily an expression of aesthetics, nor does it necessarily function to express a culturally specific aesthetic system. This view does not deny that such aesthetic systems exist nor does it suggest that they are trivial in our anthropological understandings (e.g. Taylor et al. 1994; Graburn 2005). Rather, the enquiry is re-directed: how might those aesthetic principles that are 'at work' (in the making of images, of 'art') been mobilized in social action? Our starting points for a deeper (or perhaps just a different angle of) understanding rest more on the premise that the objects, images, and forms are linked to concepts of the world through cultural praxis, not just *through* social action but *as* social action.

Many years ago, Geertz also advocated such a turn: "works of art", he noted, are not merely functional, not merely "mechanisms for defining social relationships, sustaining social rules" (Geertz 1976: 1478), as so many of our early social approaches to Palaeolithic art assumed (e.g. Conkey 1978; Gamble 1982; Jochim 1983). To Geertz (1976), the connection between art and collective life lies not on an instrumental plane, but on a semiotic one. Thus, in order to address meaning-making, I have spent a little bit of time considering what the field of 'semiotics' has to offer (e.g. Conkey 2001, 2002) since it is a field explicitly concerned with the signifying process. Indeed, one of my own starting assumptions is that the images are signs, in the semiotic sense; that is, they are vehicles of and for meanings.

However, there are many problematic ways in which semiotics have been drawn upon, even if we just look at this in the study of rock art. Of course, there are many different dimensions and notions of what semiotics 'is' (for archaeology, see, for example, in Preucel & Bauer 2001). Certainly, many object to the often-universalizing tendencies of semiotic approaches (e.g. Lock 1994) and the way that some semiotically-inspired studies remain primarily quantitative and abstracted from any sense of the informing contexts of meaning-making (see, for example, this critique by Lewis-Williams 1990). Nonetheless, there are some interesting questions raised by some of the semiotic premises.

If I take the images of 'Palaeolithic art' as signs, I nonetheless resist the notion that they merely 'refer' to some external meaning(s), and that our job is to 'reveal' those meanings. Rather, the materials and the images themselves are integral to both the production of signs as well as the production and mobilizations of meaning(s). The material culture must be taken on its own terms, not as mere signs in the cultural arena. As interpreters, we are concerned with *how* signs signify, as much as with what they might signify, and this is necessarily social *and* political. The signs and symbols of Palaeolithic image-makers have a place in semiotic (that is, in meaning-making) systems that "extend far beyond the craft that they practiced" (Geertz 1976: 1488). The images, and perhaps everything about them – their colors, shapes, placements, relations to other images, the textures of the walls or of the ivory support, among many possibilities – materialize a way of experiencing. Or, as Geertz said so articulately: ". . . they bring a particular cast of mind into the world of objects, where [men] people can look at it" (Geertz 1976: 1488), *and*, I would add, where social uses can be made of them.

While far too few Palaeolithic archaeologists have really put ourselves into the slippery interpretive terrain of Palaeolithic belief systems (much less Palaeolithic religion),[1] if any of us are really the anthropologists we claim to be, we can not possibly deny that at least some of the signs and symbols of Palaeolithic art-makers surely derived from, fed into, and even constituted spiritual worlds, cosmologies and belief systems. To 'go' there – as interpreters – means we are willing to work with 'the evidence' as material, visual, experiential parameters that can allow us to explore Ice

Age sensibilities. This is why, for example, some of us have been rather insistent on displacing the term 'art' from our vocabularies. Actually, it is not so much that we want to dismiss 'art' as it is that our preferred concern is with the material and social life of objects and images, and the experiential worlds that they produce and constitute. The images and forms were generated within and by *communities of practice*. They are, in that sense then, not art images; rather, they are an 'artful integration' (see Suchman 1999) of many entangled material and social factors.

Given this, I then assume that the images are material practices and performances that are linked to social facts and cultural logics, both as products of such and as ways of constituting them. We have now begun to accumulate an array of studies and analyses, such as on pigments, on the *chaîne opératoire* of making specific images, on 'bead' making (e.g. White 1989; Buisson et al. 1996; Fritz 1999a, 1999b; Dobres 2003; Tosello 2003) that provide us with the necessary forensics that readily sustain the suggestion that the raw materials, the techniques, the forms, the subject matter, the arrangements, the tools used, the surfaces selected (or not), are integral to the making-of-meaning(s) and, in fact, 'materialize a way of experiencing'. These image-makers were not only and quite literally making meanings and producing visual culture; they were *making culture*. Upper Palaeolithic life was, given the evidence at hand, rich with culture-making practices.

For example, we have increasingly documented the circulation of materials – be they flint raw materials (e.g. Lacombe 1998, Gamble 1999: 317–19); shells (Taborin 1993); decorated objects ('mobiliary art'); pigments or pigment components (Clottes 1997). This is, in fact, a circulation of culture-making. Materiality 'goes out' from and even 'comes in' to certain locales, material culture that is integral to the telling, the circulation, and the mobilisation of important stories. Perhaps the so-called super sites (Bahn 1982) or aggregation sites (Conkey 1980) are as much about the foci where materiality both comes in (in the diversity and abundance of portable art, for example) and goes out. Because of their very materiality, the culturally constructed images are 'public representations', even if the audience for them (as perhaps in some of the caves) is small, infrequent, and, in effect, restricted. Sperber (1992: 60–64), shows how absolutely crucial the existence and the making of such 'public representations' are – and in their disseminations and circulations – in the very creation of society.

Of course, one problem about any approaches that are based on the recursive relationships between materiality and social facts/cultural logics is that, for Palaeolithic archaeology, we have yet to do most of the work that would allow us to infer social facts or cultural logics, but that work has begun, to be sure. We are dealing with 'deep time', time that is well off the written record – problematically so, for most archaeologists. Perhaps because of this, much of what we have to say has been mostly about fairly general propositions about the human experience(s), if experiences are even explicitly considered in our archaeological accounts. To give our students a sense of what Palaeolithic experience might have been like, most of us have had to rely on (productively) assigning 'Ice Age Novels', such as *Reindeer Moon* (Thomas 1987), *The Inheritors* (Golding 1955), or *Dance of the Tiger* (Kurtén 1980), among others.

To engage with the Palaeolithic entails a particular epistemic choice of position from which to do archaeology itself, and we find ourselves at risk in the interpretive domain – given the distance from ethnographic parallels or historic connectivities. This is a risk that is compounded by the prevailing interpretive preferences (and associated epistemic privileging) of archaeology to engage with situations and contexts that are 'more knowable' and with so-called better data. Clive Gamble recently exhorted us to not despair (see opening epigraph), even if some hold the idea (e.g. Renfrew 2001) that more recent periods both have 'more data' and 'more going on' in terms of human life.

## Thinking semiotically

While we may not have an ethnography of the Upper Palaeolithic, in the strict (and perhaps all-too-narrow) sense, I do believe we can begin something of an 'ethnography of the vehicles of meaning' (after Geertz 1976), and a history of the signs and symbols made material by the practices of Upper Palaeolithic peoples. What I find particularly exciting about all the image-making at these early times in other parts of the world, or about the increasingly earlier evidence in Africa, for example, for intentional ochre-marking and perhaps bead-making, is that the visual culture of Upper Palaeolithic Eurasia can indeed be approached on its own historical and contextual terms. This visual culture no longer has to 'stand for' the origins of art, or of anything. Our focus must be resolutely more local, more historical, and yet engage with the general processes of meaning-making as culture-making.

There may be one aspect of semiotics that has some salience here; namely, the concept of 'unlimited semiosis' (after C. S. Peirce). Simplistically, the idea here is that images (and other material manifestations of form, representations and symbolic concepts) tend to 'open out', to allow for a multiorder system of signification, a kind of 'unlimited semiosis'. If we accept that there is in 'Palaeolithic art' some aesthetic use of imagery, forms, shapes, marks, spaces, places, and contexts, the signifiers tend to manifest a high degree of plurality, even ambiguity. This may especially be the case with visually realistic images (see Herzfeld 1992: 68–69), such as the animal depictions that have been taken as characteristic of so much Palaeolithic art (See Plates III, XIII, XIV, XV). The images, however, are not haphazard, as we know not only from all sorts of structural studies (Leroi-Gourhan 1965; Sauvet & Wlodarczyk 1995), but also from the many patterns we have been able to infer (Clottes, this volume).

Semiotically speaking, we might say that the so-called art is a way of connecting cultural messages together in order to produce 'texts' in which the rule-breaking roles of ambiguity and self-reference are fostered and organised (after Eco 1976: 262). The effect (whether viewed or experienced by a few or by many) is to generate a kind of continuous transformational process of significances; just as each level of meaning is established, it is broached, and its denotations are transformed into new connotations (as Barthes has discussed for myths, 1972: 109–59). We never arrive at a final decoding or reading – there is no one final and absolute 'meaning' – because each ambiguity generates further rule-breaking and invites us to continuously dismantle and reassemble what the imagery seems to be 'saying' or is 'about' (after Hawkes 1977: 142).

The main point here is to consider the idea that what the *materiality* of Palaeolithic imagery has the potential to do is to not only elicit feelings but also to produce further (new) knowledge and understandings (Eco 1976: 274). The materiality of Palaeolithic images do not merely reflect but mobilise, even galvanize, meanings. Those who engage with the images (images in the widest possible sense) not only begin to 'see the world' differently, but learn how to create a new world. This semiotic perspective reinforces the recognition – and all of its potential implications for social, cognitive, evolutionary, and semantic interpretation –

that Palaeolithic image-making is not the 'mere embroidery' of reality, but a way of knowing it, of coping with it and of (potentially) changing it (Hawkes 1977: 143). Or, as Whitney Davis (1984) has pointed out, "graphic representation is a mode of knowledge" and representation is the "material site of one's thought about one's knowledge of the world", and of one's experiences with the world. Thus, one way to think about the material manifestations of knowledge and experiences – what we call images, art, or artefacts – is that they are both vehicles for and our evidence for semantic displacement and multiorder signification. They can be taken as evidence of a semiotic process that is producing (new) knowledge; they are evidence of the reinscription of a multiplicity of meanings and their further semantic transformation that could potentially expand and ramify into new understandings and elaborated knowledge.

What we see is, semiotically speaking, a breaking of the rules of signification – a painted horse is no longer (just) a horse. On the one hand, this 'rule breaking' tends to produce ambiguous multiple significations that do not 'fix' meaning, but galvanize it. This does not merely record knowledge but produces further knowledge. But, on the other hand, there is now the potential to selectively 'fix' meaning through the social uses of materiality. Perhaps here is where we might consider how materiality 'works' as part of the establishment and enactment of 'the sacred'. Perhaps, as Rappaport suggested long ago in his discussion of the evolution of the sacred (1971, and see again in Rappaport 1999) – as did Wobst (1977) in reference to the emergence of style – it was with the appearance and elaboration of the 'unlimited semioses' of cultural practices that such constraints – like 'the sacred' and 'style' – simultaneously emerged.[2]

While such truncated musings on semiotic aspects might be frustrating until applied to certain images or materialities, they may give another vantage point on considering the effects that 'materializing experience' can have. One question that was placed before those of us who have contributed to this volume was if and how material forms might have served as 'tools' for future ritual practice. I think we can push this question somewhat further. Materializations of experience are integral to what some have considered as the basics, so-to-speak, of what 'religion' is about. What a religion (sensu latu) 'does' is to "establish powerful, pervasive and long-lasting moods and motivations in people by formulating conceptions of a general order of existence, and clothes these conceptions with such an aura of factuality that the moods and motivations seem uniquely realistic" (Geertz 1966). This is brought into existence through a system of symbols and meaning-making practices. While knowledge of all sorts may be 'recorded' in images, which is used to promote new and further knowledge, it is the embodiment of this knowledge at both the level of the individual and the social group that, one might say, mobilised a semiotic – not just an information – elaboration during the Upper Palaeolithic. And, to judge by the apparent increase in materiality – for example, the so-called invasion of bone/antler implements with images and signs, by the Magdalenian period (fifteen thousand years ago) (see Figure 6.6) – this semiotic elaboration engendered further materialisations.

What this might imply for research is to pull together what we know about those socially practiced contexts of meaning-making, of materializing experiences. The corpus of excellent forensic studies has been growing, but they can only really be understood anthropologically within a conceptual framework of materiality and social practice. From the less-discussed world of mobiliary (instead of primarily the cave) art, a number of examples come immediately to mind, and I could envision a study entitled, "Materializing Experience: Portable 'Art' and the Social Construction of Belief in the Upper Palaeolithic World".

Why, for example, do we have such a notably differential distribution of mobiliary art (Conkey 1990) among the known sites of the later Upper Palaeolithic (Magdalenian), the times during which there appears to be the veritable 'explosion' in materiality of representations and objects? Relatively few Magdalenian sites account for most of the objects, including objects bearing striking resemblances to objects found at smaller sites, as with the well-known example of *propulseurs* (spear-throwers) (see Figure 6.6) across the Pyrénées (see in Thiault & Roy 1996). As suggested above, are these loci to which materiality 'travels in' as well as sites from which materiality 'travels out'? This suggests that there are clusters of materiality, and that there may be, with some objects, something akin to craft-specialisation; what is it about animal-ended *propulseurs* that motivated the imaginations and practices of perhaps just one or a few antler-workers?

It clearly cannot be a coincidence that not only do most of the so-called *contours decoupées* ('cut-outs') bear an image of a horse's head, but that they are usually made from the hyoid (throat) bones from horse. Furthermore, these *contours* are made according to highly standardised techniques, even if they 'end up' in a number of different sites (Buisson et al. 1996), although they are concentrated, it seems, along the Pyrenean chain. From some detailed studies of assemblages of engraved bone/antler artefacts, it appears that the geometric designs chosen and even some of the animal images are influenced primarily by the shape of the support, a certain iconic merging of raw materials, form and shape of the support, and 'design' (Conkey 1982).

The project would be to bring together such material practices with the burgeoning number of technical studies (e.g. White 1995, 1997; Crémades 1996; Fritz 1999a, 1999b; Tosello 2003; Dobres 2003) as part of an approach that suggests that it is not just specific objects that are being produced, but also, if you will, what we might consider to be specific (human) subjects. That is, with shared performance of patterns of behavior we might infer not only that a communal appreciation of belonging is produced, but simultaneously particular kinds of subjects are produced who cannot be disassociated from the collective (after Fortier 1999). One might continue then to consider the gnarly, but probably crucial, processes whereby 'the other' – or a certain alterity (Csordas 2004) – is produced with the emergence of language and the development of life-worlds full of objects (or 'thing-ness') (e.g. Bataille 1989: 56–57).[3]

## The power of place and the place as sign?

As archaeologists, we must work from the known to the unknown (and back again). We don't always make the most of what we have, in terms of material evidences. Both animals and caves, as two significant, if not just obvious, aspects of 'Palaeolithic art' could be pushed further, as the work of Clottes and Lewis-Williams (e.g. 1996) has shown so well. For example, this work has reinforced an important rethinking of the semiotic possibilities of caves and rock surfaces, which are the very baseline evidence we have of 'cave' art. Of course, there have always been the observations regarding the 'interiority' of caves, and the many possible associations (with an 'under-world', with what we know of as the womb, etc.). And we have also long held out the possibilities for the caves as liminal (betwixt and between) locales, where one can be neither 'in' the world (of everyday life) or 'in' one's normal state.

More recently, Lewis-Williams and Clottes (e.g. 1998) have persuasively argued for the rock surfaces themselves to have been part of the images and their signification, especially with the notion of the rock surface as a 'veil', as a frontier or membrane between the spirit world and the human world (see also Lewis-Williams, this volume). They point to where certain painted/engraved images appear as if emerging from cracks and crevices. The recent understanding of the red dots at the Grotte Chauvet as having been made with pigment on the palm of the hand, applied – in a set of plausibly performative gestures – up against the rock surface is a compelling example of how a material and tactile (even haptic) connection to and perhaps through the rock wall was enacted (Baffier & Feruglio 1998, 2001). We have long noted the prevalent use of natural shapes by cave image-makers, and how the imagery is often 'in' the material – whether it is the cave wall or the bone/antler from within which images appear to have been 'released'.

Few serious 'Palaeolithic art' scholars today would be able to sustain the idea that the pictures and images are static and separable, separate from the context, surface, and setting. This is yet another reason why one must consider the materiality, and not 'just' the image. This is, however, both a semiotic possibility and a semiotic challenge. This gives us much more, so-to-speak, to work with as interpreters. But, at the same time, as one recent critic of the uses of semiotics by many rock art scholars has pointed out, we must ask whether there is anything at a petroglyph site that is *not* a sign and "how much of the surrounding material *is* the picture?" (Lock 1994: 409) (italics added). Knut Helskog (2000) has presented us with a compelling study of a particular petro-glyph surface in Norway, where the very cracks, fissures, and cupules in the rock surface are as integral to the imagery and 'scene' as are the pecked-out figures, figures that attract our eyes and that we dutifully record.

Lock (1994) noted something similar for petroglyphs in Ontario (Canada), where an underground stream runs torrentially in the winter, which is taken by indigenous peoples as acoustic evidence of the rock 'talking'. The pecked out figures on the rock surface may only be brought into existence when the rock 'talks'. To us, the petroglyphs may appear to 'be' there all the time, but this is not the understanding that the local indigenous peoples have. This, too, is a cautionary tale that our own visual conventions (especially that of 'visual realism', c.f. White 1997) – which tend to hold pictorial signs as static and stable, and tend to unquestioningly assume that they endure independently of their 'maker' – might be sending us down some problematic interpretive paths. How *do* we locate any boundary between the sign and its context/setting?

## Once again, beyond art: charting conceptual connections

This is not a chapter to which there are any conclusions, for it has been primarily and explicitly an attempt to array some concepts and ideas for future study. I have tried here to suggest some concepts through which we might try to connect our understandings of the archaeological evidence, on the one hand, with some semiotically inspired thoughts, on the other hand, about the production (and galvanizing) of meaning through images and forms. In order to 'go there' we have to think more broadly and deeply about several themes, enough of them to constitute a major conceptual project. I have been advocating a semiotic approach that, however, resists the delimited notions of material culture-as-sign, as something else, as referring to another (often more privileged or primal) essence or substance (such as status, identity, magic, fertility, the hunt). At this point, the wider anthropological and art historical landscape has given way to the idea that objects, forms, styles, images, and functions are evolving, more mutable, and multivalent without essential properties.

If we are to move 'beyond art', beyond understanding 'Palaeolithic art' just as information, and if we are to try to engage with questions of experience, which might include 'the spiritual', we might profit from grappling with such questions as:

- how might have these images and forms materialized experience?
- how were they produced by communities of practice and thus, how do they – the images and their makings – constitute culture-making?
- how did all this bring out particular casts of mind?
- how might the images and associated practices have been 'at work' to sanctify cultural premises and beliefs?
- how did they contribute to the establishment of moods and motivations that informed daily and spiritual lives and social relations, and perhaps even formed humans as cultural subjects?

## Acknowledgements

I wish to thank the organisers of the Templeton conference held in Les Eyzies, France for having invited me to join a unique and provocative group of scholars in wrestling with the issues presented in this volume. I was delighted to make some new acquaintances and to renew some collegial connections. I am especially indebted to Jean Clottes who, over the years, has allowed me some unparalleled opportunities to visit Palaeolithic sites and study materials.

### NOTES

[1] Of course, some have perhaps correctly argued (and objected to the fact) that most of the interpretations of Palaeolithic art – ever since the early twentieth century – have been more or less religious interpretations, or derive from a set of religious assumptions: that the caves are sanctuaries, that the image-making practices were derived from an underlying mythogram, or that the images are part of a 'religious mystery' (e.g. Berhmann & Gonzalez 1999). But this appeal to a generally religious nature or motivation has not often led to a genuine engagement with what a 'religion' or belief system would have been like among these mobile foragers, what aspects of the images and their production 'worked' in religious systems or cosmologies, and so forth (for exceptions, see Mithen 1996, 1998; Lewis-Williams 2002). Although drawing primarily on more universalised notions of hunter-gatherer shamanism, the Clottes and Lewis-Williams's (e.g. 1998) interpretations of shamanistic practices that produced much of the imagery do engage explicitly with some of these dimensions.

[2] For Rappaport, it is the evolution and appearance of 'the sacred' that must have happened simultaneously. "The innumerable possibilities inherent in words and their combinations are constrained, reduced, and ordered by the unquestionable Word enunciated in ritual's apparently invariant canon. Sanctity orders a versatility that otherwise might spawn chaos" (Rappaport 1999: 418).

[3] Some of this might also be augmented with the recent ideas about what we see with anatomically modern humans is the "emergence of individuals as creative agents beyond the limits set by the rules of co-presence" (Gamble 1999: 269); the social, technical and cultural "separation of the gesture from the body" or what Gosden (1994: 183) has called the (emergence of) "public time". In some ways, the widespread and patterned variations in what we take to be, broadly, 'body ornamentations', may be some of the most compelling materiality of not just an individuated 'self' of some sort, or of 'social identity', but of an internalisation of 'otherness', of 'alterity', which seems to play a provocative role in understanding 'religion' (Csordas 2004).

### REFERENCES

Baffier, D. & V. Feruglio, 1998. First observations on two panels of dots in the Chauvet Cave (Vallon-Pont-d'Arc, Ardèche). *International Newsletter on Rock Art* 21, 1–4.

Baffier, D. & V. Feruglio 2001. Les points et les mains. In *La Grotte Chauvet: L'art des Origines*, ed. J. Clottes. Paris: Le Seuil, 164–5.

Bahn, P.G., 1982. Inter-site and inter-regional links during the Upper Palaeolithic: the Pyrenean evidence. *Oxford Journal of Archaeology* **1**, 247–68.

Behrmann R.D. & J.J.A. Gonzalez, 1999. Vie quotidienne et Vie religieuse. Les sanctuaires dans l'art Paléolithique. *L'Anthropologie* **103**, 23–49.

Barthes, R., 1972. *Mythologies* (trans. A. Lavers). London: Cape.

Barton, C.M., G.A. Clark & A.E. Cohen, 1994. Art as information: explaining Upper Paleolithic art in western Europe. *World Archaeology* **26**, 185–207.

Bataille, G., 1989. *Theory of Religion*. New York: Zone Books.

Berger, J., 2002. Past present. *Guardian Review* December 10, 18–19.

Buisson, D., C. Fritz, D. Kandel, G. Pinçon, G. Sauvet, & G. Tosello, 1996. Analyse formelle des contours découpées de têtes de chevaux: Implications archéologiques. *Pyrénées Préhistoriques: Arts et Societies. Actes du 188e Congrès National des Sociétés Historiques et Sciéntifiques (Pau, France, 1993)*. Paris: Editions du Comité des Travaux Historiques et Scientifiques, 327–40.

Clottes, J. 1997. New laboratory techniques and their impact on Paleolithic cave art, in *Beyond Art: Pleistocene Image and Symbol*, eds. M. Conkey, O. Soffer, D. Stratmann & N. Jablonksi. Berkeley: University of California Press, 37–52.

Clottes, J., & J.D. Lewis-Williams, 1996. *Les Chamanes de Préhistoire*. Paris: Le Seuil.

Clottes, J. & J.D. Lewis-Williams, 1998. The mind in the cave – the cave in the mind: altered consciousness in the Upper Paleolithic. *Anthropology of Consciousness* **9**, 13–21.

Conkey, M., 1978. Style and information in cultural evolution: toward a predictive model for the Paleolithic, in *Social Archaeology: Beyond Subsistence and Dating*, eds. C. Redman, M.J. Berman, E.V. Curtin, W.T. Langhorne Jr., N.M. Versaggi & J.C. Wanser. New York: Academic Press, 61–85.

Conkey, M. 1980. The identification of prehistoric hunter-gatherer aggregation sites: the case of Altamira. *Current Anthropology* **21**, 609–30.

Conkey, M. 1982. Boundedness in art and society, *Symbolic and Structural Archaeology*, ed. I. Hodder. Cambridge: Cambridge University Press, 115–128.

Conkey, M. 1989. Art mobilier et l' établissement de geographies sociales, in *L'Art des Objets au Paléolithique 2*, ed. J. Clottes. Paris: Ministre de la Culture, 163–72.

Conkey, M., O. Soffer, D. Stratmann & N. Jablonski, 1997. *Beyond Art. Pleistocene Image and Symbol*. Berkeley: University of California Press.

Crémades, M., 1996. L'art mobilier Pyrénéen: analogies technologiques et relations inter-sites. *Pyrénées Préhistoriques: Arts et Societies*. Paris: Editions du Comité des Travaux Historiques et Scientifiques, 367–380.

Csordas, T., 2004. Asymptote of the ineffable: embodiment, alterity, and the theory of religion. *Current Anthropology* **45**, 163–86.

Davis, W., 1984. Representation and knowledge in the prehistoric rock art of Africa. *African Archaeological Review* **2**, 7–35.

Dobres, M.-A., 2003. Meaning in the making: agency and the social embodiment of technology and art, in *Explorations in the Anthropology of Technology*, ed. M. B. Schiffer. Albuquerque: University of New Mexico Press, 47–76.

Eco, U., 1976. *A Theory of Semiotics*. Bloomington: Indiana University Press.

Fortier, A.-M., 1999. Remembering places and the performance of belonging(s), in *Theory, Culture & Society* 16, 41–64.

Fritz, C., 1999a. *Les gravures dans l'art mobilier Magdalénien. Du geste á la representation*. Paris: Editions de la Maison des Sciences de l'Homme.

Fritz, C. 1999b. Towards the reconstruction of Magdalenian artistic techniques: the contribution of microscopic analysis of mobiliary art. *Cambridge Archaeological Journal* **9**, 189–208.

Gamble, C., 1982. Interaction and alliance in Paleolithic society. *Man (n.s.)* 17, 92–107.

1998. *The Paleolithic Societies of Europe*. Cambridge: Cambridge University Press.

Geertz, C., 1966. Religion as a cultural system, in *Anthropological Approaches to the Study of Religion*, ed. M. Banton. London: Tavistock, 1–46.

1976. Art as a cultural system. *Modern Language Notes* **91**, 1473–99.

Gell, A., 1997. *Art and Agency: An Anthropological Theory*. Oxford: Oxford University Press.

Golding, W., 1955. *The Inheritors*. New York: Harcourt, Brace and Co.

Graburn, N., 2004. From aesthetics to prosethetics and back. Materials, performance, and consumers in Canadian Inuit sculptural arts; or, Alfred Gell in the Arctic. *Les Cultures á l'oeuvre. Rencontres en art*, eds. M. Coquet, B. Derlin, M. Jeudy-Ballini. Paris: Editions de la Maison des Sciences de l'Homme, 47–62.

Gosden, C., 1984. *Social Being and Time*. Oxford: Blackwell Publishers.

Hawkes, T., 1977. *Structuralism and Semiotics*. Berkeley: University of California Press.

Helskog, K., 2000. The Alta rock carvings. *International Newsletter of Rock Art* 27, 24–8.

Henshilwood, C. S., F. d'Errico, M. Vanhaeren, K. Van Niekerk & Z. Jacobs, 2004. Middle Stone Age shell beads from South Africa. *Science* **304**, 404.

Herzfeld, M., 1992. Meta-patterns: archaeology and the uses of evidential scarcity, in *Representations in Archaeology*, eds. J. Gardin & C. Peebles, Bloomington: Indiana University Press, 66–86.

Jochim, M., 1982. Paleolithic cave art in ecological perspective, in *Hunter-Gatherer Economy in Prehistory*, ed. G. Bailey. Cambridge: Cambridge University Press, 212–19.

Kurtén, B., 1980. *Dance of the Tiger. A Novel of the Ice Age.* New York: Random House.

Lacombe, S., 1998. Stratégies d'approvisionement en silex au Tardiglaciaire. L'exemple des Pyrénées centrales Françaises. *Préhistoire Ariégeoise* LIII, 223–66.

Leroi-Gourhan, A., 1965. *Treasures of Prehistoric Art.* New York: Abrams.

Lewis-Williams, J. D., 1990. Documentation, analysis and interpretation: dilemmas in rock art research: a review of 'The Rock Paintings of the Upper Brandberg, Part I: Amis Gorge' by H. Pager. *South African Archaeological Bulletin* 45, 126–36.

Lewis-Williams, J. D., 2002. *The Mind in the Cave.* London: Thames and Hudson.

Lock, C., 1994. Petroglyphs in and out of perspective. *Semiotica* **100**: 405–20.

Mithen, S., 1996. *Prehistory of the Mind: A Search for the Origins of Art, Religion and Science.* London: Thames and Hudson.

Mithen, S. 1998. The supernatural beings of prehistory and the external storage of religious ideas, in *Cognition and Material Culture:The Archaeology of Symbolic Storage*, eds. C. Renfrew & C. Scarre. Cambridge: McDonald Institute for Archaeological Research, 97–106.

Pfeiffer J., 1982. *The Creative Explosion: An Inquiry into the Origins of Art and Religion.* New York, Harper and Row.

Preucel, R. & A. Bauer, 2000. Archaeological pragmatics. *Norwegian Archaeological Review* **34**, 85–96.

Rappaport, R. A., 1971. The sacred in human evolution. *Annual Review of Ecology and Systematics* 2: 23–44.

  1999. *Ritual and Religion in the Making of Humanity.* Cambridge: Cambridge University Press.

Renfrew, C., 2000. Symbol before concept: Material engagement and the early development of society, in *Archaeological Theory Today*, ed. I. Hodder, 122–40.

Sauvet, G. & A. Wlodarczyk, 1994. Eléments d'une grammaire formelle de l'art pariétal Paléolithique. *L'Anthropologie* **99**, 193–211.

Sperber, D., 1992. Culture and matter, in *Representations in Archaeology*, eds. J. Gardin & C. Peebles. Bloomington: Indiana University Press, 56–65.

Suchman, L., 1999. The working relations of technology production and use, in *The Social Shaping of Technology* (2nd ed.), eds. D. MacKenzie & J. Wajcman. Buckingham: Open University, 258–68.

Taborin, Y., 1992. *La Parure en Coquillage au Paléolithique* (Gallia Préhistoire Supplement, No. 29). Paris: Centre National de la Recherche Scientifique.

Taylor, T., M. Vickers, H. Morphy, R. R. R. Smith & C. Renfrew, 1994. Is there a place for aesthetics in archaeology? *Cambridge Archaeological Journal* 4, 249–69.

Thiault, M.-H. & J.-B. Roy, 1994. *Art Préhistorique des Pyrénées*. Paris: Editions de la Réunion des Musées Nationaux.

Thomas, E. M., 1987. *Reindeer Moon*. Boston: Houghton-Mifflin.

Tosello, G., 2000. *Pierres gravées du Périgord magdalénien. Art, symbols, territories*. (Gallia Préhistoire Supplement No. 36). Paris: Centre National de la Recherche Scientifique.

White, R., 1989. Visual thinking in the Ice Age. *Scientific American* **261**, 92–9.

    1992. Beyond art: towards an understanding of the origins of material representation in Europe. *Annual Review of Anthropology* **21**, 537–64.

    1992. Ivory personal adornments of Aurignacian age: technological, social and symbolic perspectives, in *Le Travail et l'Usage de l'Ivoire au Paléolithique Superieur*, eds. J. Hahn, M. Menu, Y. Taborin, P. Walter & F. Widemann. Ravello: Centre Universitaire Euopéen pour les Biens Culturels, 29–62.

    1992. Structure, signification, and culture: different logics of representation and their archaeological implications. *Diogenes* 180, 97–113.

    2003. *Prehistoric Art: The Symbolic Journey of Humankind*. Abrams: New York.

Wobst, H. M., 1977. Stylistic behaviour and information exchange, in *Papers for the Director: Research Essays in Honor of James B. Griffin* (*University of Michigan Anthropological Papers*), ed. C. E. Cleland. Ann Arbor: University of Michigan, 317–42.

13

# Sticking bones into cracks in the Upper Palaeolithic

*Jean Clottes*

One of the most appropriate ways in which to approach meaning for Palaeolithic cave art is to study its archaeological context, that is, the traces and remains left by the people who visited the caves. After sketching various aspects relevant to the archaeological context, one particular example will be examined more in detail in this paper.

In twenty-two Palaeolithic painted caves (including thirteen in the French Pyrenees), various objects have been either deposited or stuck into cracks of the walls, or even stuck into the ground. Those apparently non-utilitarian gestures have been noticed from Asturias in Spain to Burgundy in France, from at least the Gravettian to the end of the Magdalenian, that is, for a period which lasted for thirteen thousand to fourteen thousand years. This phenomenon wide-ranging in time and in space enables us to have some inklings about the motives of its authors.

One of the major clues to Palaeolithic religious thinking is the art in the caves. To access some of its meaning(s) three main lines of research are available. The most obvious one is studying the art itself, its themes, its placement, the interrelations between the themes themselves and with the morphology of the cave. A second line of research, which has been gaining more and more acceptance these days, is studying cave art in the light of what is directly known of the beliefs and practices of hunter-gatherers elsewhere in the world. Finally, the context of the art, wherever it is well-preserved, can bring information on the activities of those who frequented the caves in the Pleistocene, all the more so as valuable clues about the actions of those visitors are better preserved in them than in any other environment.

The internal context of a cave can be defined as the remains and traces – other than works of art – left by humans and also by animals on the ground and on the walls. In the twentieth century, this was neglected for decades. Specialists studied the paintings as if they had been hanging on the walls of a gallery: what was important then was to investigate themes, techniques, styles and their cultural and chronological attributions. Artefacts in a cave were only considered of interest when they could yield information about the dating of the art. Gradually the attitude of researchers changed, particularly with the discovery of well-preserved caves in the seventies (Fontanet, Le Réseau Clastres in the Ariège) and with the in-depth study of what could be salvaged from long-discovered caverns, such as Lascaux (Leroi-Gourhan and Allain (ed.) 1979). Then one became aware of the wealth of information to be found in the archaeological context. Nowadays research on the context is considered as an integral part of cave art studies (see the work being carried out at Chauvet in Clottes (ed.) 2003a, 2003b).

## The archaeological context of cave art

The context of cave art also includes the traces and remains of animal activities, because animals occasionally wandered into the deeper galleries, and some animals, particularly cave bears, hibernated in them. When there were soft sediments bears dug lairs to sleep in. They left their footprints on the ground and thousands of scratches on the walls. Some died and their skulls and bones were strewn on the ground. All this was seen by Palaeolithic people in the dim light of their burning torches when they groped their way through the dark passages. For them some caves must have been perceived as filled with the presence and the power of the Bear. The very noticeable scratchings may sometimes have spurred people to make finger tracings (Chauvet) or engravings (Le Portel) next to or on top of them (Figure 13.1). At times cave bear bones were picked up, displaced and used: in Le Tuc d'Audoubert (Ariège) they were strung along the way and their impressive canines were removed from the bear skulls and taken away. In Chauvet, a skull was deposited on a big rock in the middle of a chamber and two humeri were forcibly stuck into the ground not far from the entrance (Figures 13.9 and 13.10).

When the ground was soft (sand, wet clay), naked human footprints remained printed in it (Niaux (Figure 13.2), Le Réseau Clastres, Le Tuc d'Audoubert, Montespan, Labastide, Fontanet, Pech-Merle, L'Aldène, Chauvet). This enables us to know that children, at times very young ones, accompanied adults when they went underground, and also that

**13.1.** Finger tracings (horizontal) superimposed on cave bear scratches (vertical). Chauvet Cave (Ardèche). Belvédère Gallery. (Photo J. Clottes & Y. Le Guillou)

the visitors of those deep caves were not very numerous because footprints and more general human traces and remains are so few, even when the conditions were favourable. Footprints became a special field of research called 'ichnology' whose specialist in Europe is Michel Garcia (Clottes 1993). Such traces provide invaluable information about the prehistoric visitors to the caves (their numbers and their ages) and they are the only testimony to living dynamic activities. For example, we can tell that three children in Le Réseau Clastres (Ariège) walked slowly and carefully along a wall in a vast chamber and that they stopped cautiously in front of an obstacle before running, as children will do, after they had crossed it (Clottes & Simonnet 1990) (Figure 13.3). A careful examination of those traces and of others in the cave could determine that the three children were accompanied by two adults, probably a male and a female (Garcia, Duday, & Courtaud 1990).

That deep caves have consistently been considered as numinous places is a fact common to people on all continents and at all times (see later in this chapter). Therefore, the most likely explanation for the type of behaviour we find in the French and Spanish caves is that children and even babies – in Gargas there is a stencil of a baby's hand held at the wrist by an adult – were brought into them for ceremonies in order to take

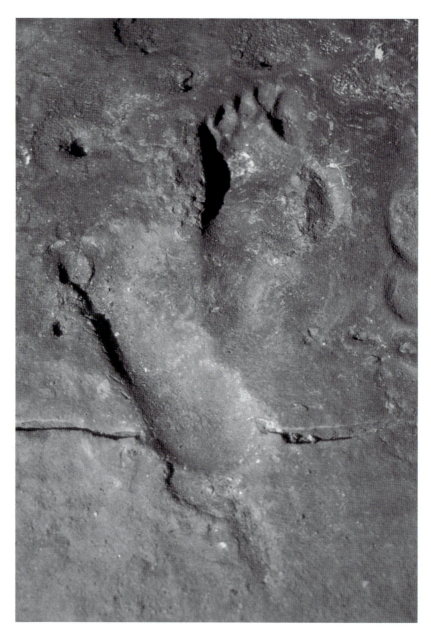

**13.2.** Children's footprints in a side gallery of the Niaux Cave (Ariège). (Photo J. Clottes)

advantage of the power to be found there. Drawing meanders with one's fingers on the wet clay of the walls (Cosquer, Gargas, Trois Frères, Pech-Merle, Rouffignac) or again engraving or painting indeterminate lines in so many caves might be a means to access the potency immanent in the rock. In their case, the aim was not to recreate a reality as was done with the animal images but to trail one's fingers and to leave their traces on the wall, wherever this was possible, in order to establish a direct contact with the powers underlying the wall. This might be done by non-initiates who participated in the ritual in their own way and with their own means. In Rouffignac, children were raised up by adults to make finger flutings on the high ceiling of a chamber, which proves how deliberate such actions were (Sharpe & Van Gelder 2004).

Humans left various sorts of traces, whether deliberately or involuntarily. The charcoal fallen from their torches, their fires, a few objects, bones and flint tools left on the ground may be the remains of meals or of sundry activities. They are part of the documentation unintentionally left by prehistoric people in the caves. From their study, one can say that in most cases painted or engraved caves were not inhabited, at least for long periods. Fires were temporary and remains are relatively scarce. Naturally, there are exceptions (Lascaux, Enlène, Labastide, Le Mas d'Azil, Bédeilhac, Tito Bustillo). In their case, it is often difficult to make out whether those settlements are in relation – as seems likely – or not with

**13.3.** Heaps of charcoal abound in the Megaloceros Gallery of the Chauvet Cave (Ardèche). (Photo J. Clottes)

the art on the walls. The presence of portable art – as in the caves mentioned – may be a valuable clue to establish such a relationship.

In Chauvet, many fires were made in a relatively narrow gallery leading to the End Chamber. Great quantities of charcoal were well preserved and most were not trampled. The study of the area led to the following conclusions: the fires were made in order to get charcoal with which to make the drawings (lots of big charcoal and not much ash or cinders) (Figure 13.4); the place where they are located is much higher than the End Chamber and the percentage of carbon dioxide is, as a consequence, far less important there, thus allowing fires to be made far more easily; finally, the near absence of prehistoric trampling testifies to that part of the cave – where the most spectacular images are – to have been rarely frequented.

As to the extraordinary seven or so Gravettian burials recently dis-covered in the Cussac cave (Aujoulat et al. 2001), they pose a huge problem. It is the first time that human skeletons have been found inside a deep cave with Palaeolithic art. Until they have been excavated and studied properly it will be impossible to know whether those people died there by accident (a most unlikely hypothesis), whether they were related to those who did the engravings, whether they enjoyed a special status, and so on. Their presence just stresses the magic/religious character of art in the deep caves.

The main problem regarding wall art in a cave or shelter with an archaeological context is *proving* a relationship between the two. Owing to their attention to detail, modern excavations give us a wealth of information and sometimes, even, a direct proof of the relationship we are looking for. For instance, Combier (1984: 597) found some drops of red paint in the midst of a very thin layer right under a painted wall in the cave of Bidon (Ardèche), thus establishing a direct link between the art and the remains on the ground. The latter could be dated to 21,650 bp ± 800 (Ly 847), a date which also applies to the painted panel.

The localisation of the paintings relative to the level of an archaeo-logical layer can also give some credible idea, if not actual proof, as to which interpretations are possible and which are not. For example, in Le Placard (Charente), only Upper Solutrean strata are situated at such a distance from the paintings and engravings as would allow it to be physically possible to draw them on the walls (Clottes, Duport, & Feruglio 1990).

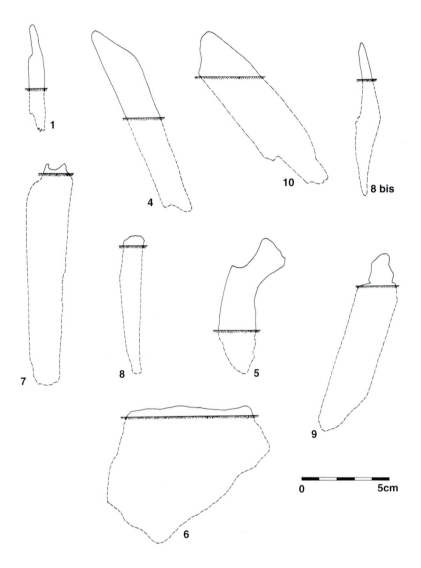

**13.4.** In the Enlène End Chamber, many fragments of bones and other objects were stuck into the ground at the beginning of the occupation of that deep chamber. The examples shown here include one stone plaquette (no. 6). The others are bones. The horizontal lines indicate the level of the ground in relation to them at the time of discovery. (Drawing S. Lacombe)

Another well-grounded assumption about the contemporaneity of the works of art with their archaeological context exists when the conditions in a painted cave are such that the remains on the ground are very few and cannot be explained as resulting from habitation, for example when the cave is very deep and the art is localised in remote galleries.

We can then safely infer a relationship because we know from numerous well-documented examples that Palaeolithic humans did not live far underground and that each time they stayed several hundred meters from the entrance for any length of time it was in caves with wall art (e.g. at Labastide, Bédeilhac, Trois Frères). Thus, the remains found in the upper gallery of Tuc d'Audoubert, and probably also those in the middle gallery of the same cave, can safely be ascribed to the Magdalenians who made the works of art or who went to the ends of the cave because of them for ceremonies or other related activities (Bégouën & Clottes 1983).

## A Palaeolithic gesture in painted caves

A number of years ago, we drew our colleagues' attention to the results of some very peculiar actions of Magdalenian visitors to the Volp Caves in the Ariège (Enlène, Le Tuc d'Audoubert, Les Trois Frères), as well as in some other Pyrenean caves (Le Portel, Bédeilhac, Fontanet, Montespan) (Bégouën & Clottes 1981). In particular, bones, flint and other objects had been stuck or deposited into cracks and fissures of the walls (also see Clottes 1984: 365) and occasionally implanted in the ground (Bégouën et al. 1995) (Figure 13.5).

Nowadays this phenomenon has been evidenced in 22 painted or engraved Upper Palaeolithic caves in France and in Spain. They are:

> *In the French Pyrenees*: Enlène (Figures 13.6 and 13.7), Les Trois Frères and Le Tuc d'Audoubert (Montesquieu-Avantès), Le Portel (Loubens), Bédeilhac (Bédeilhac-et-Aynat) and Fontanet (Ornolac-Ussat-les-Bains) (Figure 13.8) in the Ariège; Montespan (Ganties-Montespan) in the Haute-Garonne; Grotte du Moulin (Troubat), Grotte des Chevaux (Labastide) and Gargas (Aventignan) in the Hautes-Pyrénées; Etxeberri (Camou-Cihigue) and Erberua (Isturitz) in the Pyrénées-Atlantiques; Grotte du Pape (Brassempouy) in the Landes.
>
> *In Spain*: Altxerri (Aia) in the Pais Vasco and Llonín (Peñamellera Alta) in Asturias.
>
> *In Quercy*: Sainte-Eulalie (Espagnac) and Les Fieux (Miers) in the Lot.
>
> *In Périgord*: Le Pigeonnier (Domme), Bernifal (Meyrals) and Lascaux (Montignac) in the Dordogne.

**13.5.** Many pieces of bones have been forcibly stuck into the cracks of the walls in the cave of Enlène (Ariège). (Photo J. Clottes)

*In Burgundy:* Le Cheval (Arcy-sur-Cure, Yonne).
*In the south-east of France:* Chauvet (Vallon-Pont-d'Arc, Ardèche).

Putting into cracks objects which apparently do not present any particular interest is a mostly Pyrenean phenomenon, as it has been evidenced in thirteen Pyrenean Paleolithic painted caves, from the Ariège in the east to the Basque country in the west. Most of those objects are undistinguished fragments of animal bones. Identical examples have been found in Spanish caves as far as Asturias and also, in France, in the Lot. This was thus a fairly widespread custom. In the Dordogne, it is rarer (Lascaux) and flint was more often used for deposits (Lascaux, Bernifal, Le Pigeonnier), as it was too, in far away Burgundy. Nothing of the sort, however, was found in the painted caves of south-eastern France, even in caves with lots of cracks like Chauvet or Cosquer where in-depth research has been carried out.

Implanting bones into the ground can be construed as being a related gesture. It was done less often, most times in the center of the Pyrenees (Enlène (Figure 13.5), Le Portel, Montespan, Fontanet, Labastide), except for Chauvet where two cave bear humeri were half-way stuck

**13.6.** Many pieces of bones have been forcibly stuck into the cracks of the walls in the cave of Enlène (Ariège). (Photo J. Clottes)

into the ground not far from the original entrance to the cave (Figures 13.9 and 13.10).

The phenomenon under study lasted for a very long time, thirteen thousand to fourteen thousand years at least. In Gargas, the bits of bones are closely associated with the famous hand stencils (Figure 13.10). A date of $26,800 \pm 460$ bp was obtained for one of the splinters, which tallies with the Gravettian age generally attributed to stencilled hands in Southern France (Clottes et al. 1992). Another bone splinter was also found next to some other hand stencils in the Gravettian cave of Les Fieux (Miers, Lot), which corroborates the Gargas find (Lorblanchet 1999). The one in Brassempouy could also be quite old, if we consider the archaeological context of that site (Aurignacian and Gravettian) (Buisson 1995). On the other hand, Magdalenian dates are certain for most of the Pyrenean caves (Enlène, Le Tuc d'Audoubert, Trois Frères, Labastide, Montespan, Fontanet), as well as for Sainte-Eulalie in the Lot. The recent discoveries at Troubat stress the long duration of the phenomenon, as late as the end of the Magdalenian (Barbaza 1997).

For a great many millenia, Palaeolithic people have thus behaved in exactly the same way in a fair number of painted or engraved caves both in France and in Spain. Other discoveries of the same kind will no doubt be made in the years to come. That a custom should be so widespread, both in time and in space, should not be surprising within the context of cave art. After all, the art itself lasted between twenty thousand to twenty-five thousand years at least and it is to be found all over Europe, from the southern tip of Spain to the Urals. In addition, in the Parpalló cave, near Valencia (Spain), thousands of painted or engraved plaquettes were excavated from archaeological layers covering more than thirteen thousand years (Villaverde Bonilla 1994), which testifies to the same sort of deposits being made again and again in the same place over uncounted centuries.

The deposition in the caves of the objects mentioned cannot be explained away either by natural processes or by so-called functional purposes and activities. They are too numerous and the conditions they were found in are such that it is impossible to contemplate their being

**13.7.** In the cave of Fontanet (Ariège), part of a reindeer antler has been stuck into the soft soil of a high recess next to eleven slits made in the clay. (Photo J. Clottes)

**13.8.** A cave bear humerus was stuck halfway into the ground in the Chauvet Cave in the Entrance Chamber. (Photo J. Clottes)

lost or forgotten, or brought there by running water or by animals, or that they were the result of casual gestures, or could have been used to bear anything or even to delineate a particular space. The caves where they were discovered, moreover, are always caves with rock art and not mere habitation sites, and the bones, flint, and other objects deposited or stuck into fissures are mostly close to some of the works of art. All this means that we are dealing with a very special gesture performed in very special places.

### How to interpret those facts

An interpretive hypothesis can only be based upon two series of observations: on the one hand the hard facts observed, such as have just been mentioned briefly. On the other hand, on commonalities in the beliefs and behavior of people that may not only support the hypothesis but make it more plausible than any other. Two such observations can be made: they relate first to the way the subterranean world is generally

**13.9.** Another cave bear humerus was stuck halfway into the ground about thirty feet from the other one. (Photo P. Morel)

**13.10.** In the cave of Gargas (Hautes-Pyrénées), one of the pieces of bone found in cracks next to stencilled hands was dated to 26,800 ± 460 bp. (Photo J. Clottes)

perceived and second to well-documented gestures of depositing and sticking objects into rock hollows.

Everywhere in the world caves have been considered as being the place of spirits, of gods, of fairies or of the dead. This was the case for the ancient Greek (see the River Styx) as well as for the Kalash of Pakistan (Lièvre and Loude 1990: 42). Sometimes the rocks themselves are the places where the spirits dwell (see Whitley 2000: 78, for examples in California; Lewis-Williams 2003: 56, for examples in South Africa; Flood 1997: 244, for Australian Quinkan spirits). The ubiquity of this sort of belief makes it possible to extrapolate it to the Upper Palaeolithic. Deliberately venturing into the depths of the rocks and of the earth – where people did not live – was not a casual sort of activity. The few who did so knew that they would have to face supernatural dangers in those awesome power-laden places. The spirits of the other-world were there within reach and this might well explain why objects were deposited as they were.

The obvious reason for doing so was a desire to reach beyond the ordinary world, that of the living, to pierce the veil (Lewis-Williams & Dowson 1990) barely separating it from the supernatural forces literally at hand and to touch them either directly or by means of an offering – however symbolic it might be. Innumerable examples are available. Only a few will be mentioned, from very different social and geographical contexts. The most famous one is what occurs everyday at the Wailing Wall, in Jerusalem, where some of the faithful squeeze scraps of paper bearing their prayers into the insterstices of the monumental stones. The gesture is of course meant to approach the Divinity in a place perceived as being sacred.

In the eighties, in my capacity as director of Prehistoric Antiquities for the Midi-Pyrénées region in southern France, I had to deal with an urgent archaeological excavation to be carried out not far from the sacred Massabielle cave in Lourdes, where millions of Roman Catholic pilgrims congregate each year. In the woods next to it, there was another small cave, a few hundred yards away, that is, well away from the sanctuary, in a remote place where pilgrims have no reason – and most certainly are not incited or invited – to go. Now, on one of the sides of the cave, a natural cavity in the rock, about half a cubic meter, was nearly filled with offerings and deposits of all sorts: spectacles, wallets, coins, messages, etc. In this case, it was the subterranean milieu, sanctified by its vicinity with the historical holy cave, which even in our days had been spontaneously considered by many people as a passage to the other world.

In 1991, before visiting a rock art site in central California, our Yokuts guide carried out a propitiatory ceremony after which he asked us to deposit bits of native tobacco into the cracks of the wall right below rock paintings (Clottes 1999: 140–1). Ten years later, in Montana, I saw coins, small pearls, cigarettes and other small objects (Plate XXIV) deposited in the fissures of a cliff called Arrow Rock inside which the spirits, called the Little People, are believed to dwell.

Depositing various objects into the hollows of the walls deep inside painted caves is akin to the examples cited above. About the bones thus stuck into cracks, the hypothesis was made that it could have been "a restitution ritual", that is, that the people were both drawing the spirits under an animal form from inside the rock and sending back fragments of animals in a kind of "two-way traffic" (Lewis-Williams 2002: 253). This hypothesis, however, could not apply to shells nor to the lithic material.

If the basic idea motivating those acts – i.e. contacting the other-world – is beyond reasonable doubt, it can still be put into effect in two different ways: either by depositing or by sticking objects into the walls or into the ground. When depositing offerings – however modest and symbolic (Plate XXIV) – one establishes a one-way link from our world to the other-world without expecting an immediate result, except perhaps some protection, largesse or immunity during the time one happens to be there or later. It is a gesture of allegiance.

Sticking objects into cracks or into the ground could be a related but slightly different action. In this case, one perhaps wanted to pierce the veil separating the world of the living from that of the spirits. It was not the object itself that was important – and this might explain why the splinters of bones are so commonplace – but rather the gesture, the will to bridge the gap and to contact the power hidden within the rock or the ground in that supernatural world of the dark and to bring away some of it in order to help with the eternal problems of everyday life, such as illnesses, luck, and the provision of food.

**REFERENCES**

Aujoulat, N., J.-M. Geneste, C. Archambeau, C. Delluc, H. Duday & D. Henry-Gambier, 2002. La Grotte ornée de Cussac – Le Buisson-de-Cadouin (Dordogne): premières observations. *Bulletin de la Société Préhistorique Française* **99**, 129–37.

Barbaza, M., 1997. Troubat: Grotte du Moulin. *Bilan Scientifique 1996, S. R. A. Midi-Pyrénées*, 154–5.

Bégouën, R. & J. Clottes, 1981. Apports mobiliers dans les Cavernes du Volp (Enlène, les Trois-Frères, le Tuc d'Audoubert). *Altamira Symposium*, Madrid-Asturias-Santander, 15–21 Octobre 1979, 157–88.

    1982. Des Ex-votos Magdaléniens? *La Recherche* **132**, 518–20.

    1983. À Propos d'une datation radiocarbone de l'habitat magdalénien du Tuc d'Audoubert. *Bulletin de la Société Préhistorique Ariège-Pyrénées* **XXXVIII**, 119–22.

Bégouën, R., J. Clottes, J.-P. Giraud & F. Rouzaud, 1996. Os plantés et peintures rupestres dans la caverne d'Enlène, in H. Delporte & J. Clottes (eds.) *Pyrénées Préhistoriques: Arts et Sociétés* (Actes du Congrès du 118ᵉ Congrès National des Sociétés Savantes, Pau, 1993), 283–306.

Buisson, D., 1995. Brassempouy: présentation du site et problèmes posés par les fouilles récentes, in H. Delporte & J. Clottes (eds.) *Pyrénées Préhistoriques: Arts et Sociétés* (Actes du Congrès du 118ᵉ Congrès National des Sociétés Savantes, Pau, 1993), 423–437.

Clottes, J., 1984. Midi-Pyrénées, in *L'Art des Cavernes: Atlas des Grottes Ornées Paléolithiques Françaises*. Paris: Ministère de la Culture, Imprimerie Nationale, 358–68.

    1993. Ichnologie, in *L'Art pariétal paléolithique: Techniques et méthodes d' étude*, ed. Groupe de Réflexion sur l'Art Pariétal Paléolithique (GRAPP), 59–66.

    1999. *Grandes Girafes et Fourmis vertes: Petites Histoires de Préhistoire*. Paris: La Maison des Roches.

    2003a. *Return to Chauvet Cave*. London: Thames & Hudson.

    2003b. *Chauvet Cave: The Art of Earliest Times*. Salt Lake City: The University of Utah Press.

Clottes, J., L. Duport & V. Feruglio, 1990. Les signes du Placard. *Bulletin de la Société Préhistorique Ariège-Pyrénées* **XLV**, 15–49.

Clottes, J. & R. Simonnet, 1990. Retour au Réseau Clastres. *Préhistoire Ariégeoise, Bulletin de la société préhistorique Ariège-Pyrénées* **XLV**, 51–139.

Clottes, J., H. Valladas, H. Cachier & M. Arnold, 1992. Des dates pour Niaux et Gargas. *Bulletin de la Société Préhistorique Française* **89**, 270–4.

Combier, J., 1984. Grotte de la Tête-du-Lion. *L'Art des Cavernes: Atlas des Grottes Ornées Paléolithiques Françaises*. Paris: Ministère de la Culture, Imprimerie Nationale, 595–9.

Flood, J., 1997. *Rock Art of the Dreamtime*. Sydney: Angus & Robertson.

Garcia, M., H. Duday & P. Courtaud, 1990. Les Empreintes du Réseau Clastres. *Bulletin de la Société Préhistorique Ariège-Pyrénées* **45**, 167–87.

Leroi-Gourhan, Ar. & J. Allain, 1979. *Lascaux Inconnu*. Paris: C.N.R.S.

Lewis-Williams, J. D., 2002. *The Mind in the Cave*. London: Thames & Hudson.

Lewis-Williams, J. D. & T. Dowson, 1990. Through the veil: sand rock paintings and the rock face. *South African Archaeological Bulletin* **45**, 5–16.

Lièvre, V. & J. Y. Loude, 1990. *Le Chamanisme des Kalash du Pakistan.* Paris: C.N.R.S.

Lorblanchet, M., 1999. Grottes ornées paléolithiques du Quercy: analyse des pigments. *Bilan Scientifique 1998, S. R. A. Midi-Pyrénées,* 188–9.

Sharpe, K. & L. van Gelder, 2004. Children and Paleolithic 'art': indications from Rouffignac Cave, France. *International Newsletter on Rock Art* **38**, 9–17.

Villaverde Bonilla, V., 1994. *Arte paleolítico de la cova del Parpalló: estudio de la colección de plaquetas y cantos grabados y pintados.* Valencia: Diputació.

Whitley, D. S., 2000. *The Art of the Shaman: Native American Rock Art of California.* Salt Lake City: University of Utah Press.

# 14

## Cognition and climate: why is Upper Palaeolithic cave art almost confined to the Franco-Cantabrian region?

*Paul Mellars*

Les Hommes du Paléolithique supérieur restent pourtant les premiers à nous laisser le message d'une humanité parvenue sur notre sol au dépassement spirituel qui conduit á la création artistique. (Denise de Sonneville-Bordes 1960: 500)

Unquestionably the most dramatic – if enigmatic – expression of human spirituality in the course of early human development is provided by the extraordinary concentration of cave art hidden deep inside the interiors of over a hundred separate caves in southern France and northern Spain. The social, symbolic, and spiritual 'meaning' of this art has occupied a large part of the archaeological literature over the past century (Leroi-Gourhan 1968; Ucko & Rosenfeld 1967; Lewis-Williams 2002). To say that the cognitive meanings of this art remain highly controversial is no doubt an understatement, as several of the papers in the present volume show. Even so, few would dispute that the art must reflect some kind of deeply 'spiritual' belief systems, presumably reflecting beliefs in some forms of spiritual entities, gods, or other 'supernatural' forces, which can fairly be described as early forms of 'religious' expression.

In many ways the most remarkable aspect of this art however is its geographical concentration (with a few notable exceptions) within one very restricted area of western Europe, extending from the Loire valley of central France to the Cantabrian mountains of northwestern Spain (see Figure 14.1). The present paper focuses specifically on this aspect. What, in short, were the underlying social, demographic or other factors which led to this extraordinary eruption of cave art over such a comparatively restricted geographical zone of Upper Palaeolithic Europe?

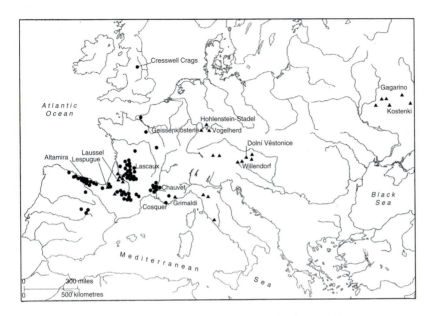

**14.1.** Distribution of Upper Palaeolithic cave art in Europe (black circles) showing the massive concentration in the Franco-Cantabrian region. Occurrences of Upper Palaeolithic portable art are indicated by triangular symbols. (Adapted from Stringer & Andrews 2003)

Part of the answer to this question of course lies in geology. The extensive limestone formations of southwestern France, the Pyrenees and Cantabrian Spain evidently provided ideal conditions for the formation of underground cave systems, which in turn provided the essential pre-requisite (in a sense the essential artistic canvases) for the production of the art. But the occurrence of similar geological formations in many other parts of Europe demonstrate beyond any doubt that geology alone can never provide more than a small part of the explanation for the remarkable concentration of cave art within the so-called Franco-Cantabrian region.

Even if geology alone cannot provide the answer, I would argue that the ultimate causes for the concentration of cave art within these regions must be sought in some form of broadly environmental factors. In brief, I will suggest that the explosion of this art within this particular region can be seen as a reflection of various demographic mechanisms directly related to the special nature of climatic and associated ecological conditions within the region throughout the time span of the Upper Palaeolithic period – that is, during the later part of the last ice age, between ca. thirty-two thousand and thirteen thousand years ago in 'raw' (i.e. uncalibrated) radiocarbon terms, or between ca. 36,000 and 14,000 BP (before present) in actual calendrical years (Hughen et al. 2004, Fairbanks et al. 2005). In the first section below I will look at the special ecological features of this region under ice-age conditions, while in the second part I will look at the apparent impact of these features on particular aspects of the demographic and social dimensions of the contemporaneous Upper Palaeolithic societies. In the third section I will attempt to suggest – more speculatively – some of the potential cultural mechanisms whereby these social and demographic patterns could have led to the extraordinary florescence of the Franco-Cantabrian cave art. Throughout the paper the emphasis will be primarily on the classic southwest French region, though it can be argued that closely similar factors can be extended to both the Pyrenean region and the adjacent, ecologically similar areas of Cantabrian Spain. The discussion draws on a number of my own earlier papers (Mellars 1973, 1985, 1996) together with other important studies by Jochim (1983), Hayden et al. (1987), Mithen (1990) and others.

## Environmental factors

I would suggest that there were three particular features of climatic and environmental patterns within the southwest French region during the Upper Palaeolithic period which directly underlay the remarkable con-centration of both Upper Palaeolithic occupation and the florescence of cave art. Briefly, these can be summarized as follows.

### CLIMATIC PATTERNS

In climatic terms the critical features of the southwest French region derive from its extreme oceanic position along the western Atlantic coastline of Europe. At the present day this is reflected in summer-season temperatures which are much cooler than those in the more central, continental regions of Europe and – equally if not more significantly – substantially warmer winter temperatures. At present, summer temperatures in this region are around 5°C cooler than in the more continental regions, with winter temperatures up to 8°C warmer. The extrapolation of these temperature contrasts into the Upper Palaeolithic time range is inevitably more hypo-thetical, and of course varied with some of the rapid climatic oscillations which have now been documented from the deep-sea core and ice-core oxygen-isotope records and associated pollen sequences over this time range (see Figure 14.2) (Dansgaard et al. 1993, Shackleton et al. 2000, Sanchez-Goni et al. 2002, van Andel & Davies 2003). Nevertheless, the combined evidence from these climatic records suggest that the overall temperature range within the oceanic, southwest French region varied between ca. −2°C in winter and 12°C in summer, compared to ranges between −10°C and 18°C in the interior areas of central and eastern Europe (van Andel & Davies 2003).

**VEGETATION PATTERNS**

The most direct impact of these temperature regimes was on the character of the vegetation within southwestern France – and in particular on the density of tree cover. Tree growth in general is dependent much more on summer than on winter temperatures, and it is now clear that

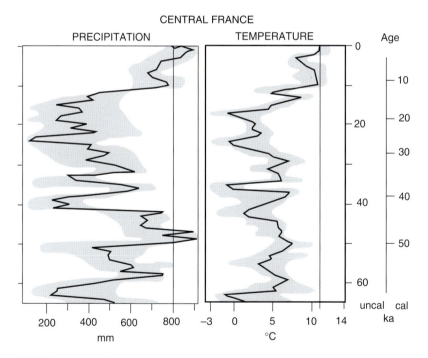

**14.2.** Reconstructed climatic fluctuations in central France over the past 60,000 years, based on a long pollen sequence from the Massif Central. Note the occurrence of significant oscillations during the course of the Upper Palaeolithic period (ca. 40,000–12,500 BP) and the sudden onset of much warmer conditions at the time of the Magdalenian to Azilian transition around 12,500 (radiocarbon years) BP. (Reproduced from Van Andel & Davies 2003)

the relatively low summer temperatures experienced throughout southwestern France during at least the greater part of the last glaciation would have led to the virtual elimination of significant tree growth in all except the most sheltered, south- or west-facing valleys (Huntley et al. 2003, Leroi-Gourhan 1977). What this means in geographical terms is that these southwestern areas of France and the adjacent regions of Cantabrian Spain would have supported the most southerly areas of essentially open, tundra or steppe/tundra-like vegetation encountered anywhere in Europe during the last glaciation (Figure 14.3) (Butzer 1971; Iversen 1973; Van Andel & Tzedakis 1996). At the same time, however, these very southerly areas of steppe/tundra would also have benefited from significantly greater sunlight than those in the more northerly regions of Europe, and accordingly a much richer and more productive growth of all forms of low-growing vegetation – together with a correspondingly longer period of growth into the late autumn, winter and early spring months. As Karl Butzer (1971: 463) pointed out over thirty years ago, combined with abundant rainfall, these southwesterly areas of Europe are likely to have

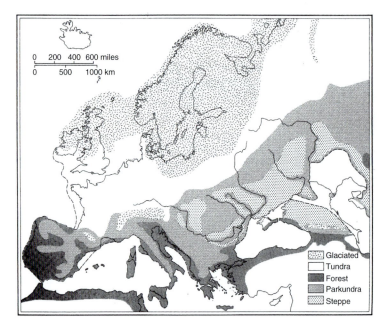

**14.3.** Reconstructed distribution of vegetation zones in Europe at the time of the maximum of the last glaciation, around 20,000 BP. Note how the distribution of open, tundra-like vegetation extends much further to the south in southwestern France than in other regions of Europe. (Adapted from Iversen 1973)

experienced some of the richest conditions (i.e. the highest productivities) for the growth of herbaceous tundra and steppe vegetation available anywhere within the European landmass during glacial times.

## ANIMAL COMMUNITIES

From the standpoint of the contemporaneous human communities, the most significant impact of these combined climatic and vegetational conditions would have been to provide almost ideal conditions to support rich and dense populations of various herbivorous animal species, on which the subsistence and survival of the Upper Palaeolithic populations clearly depended. To visualize southwestern France as a kind of last-glacial Serengeti game reserve would no doubt be an exaggeration, but not necessarily on an overdramatic scale. We know from the actual faunal assemblages recovered from many southwest French Upper Palaeolithic sites that the faunal communities included not only vast herds of reindeer (supported by the rich tundra vegetation, with growths of mosses, lichens, etc.) but also a range of other open-country species including the wild horse, wild oxen (aurochs), steppe bison and red deer (Figure 14.4), together with more sporadic species such as ibex, chamois, mammoth, rhinoceros and (at least during the milder, interstadial episodes) wild pig, roe deer and giant elk – all species well represented in the Palaeolithic cave art itself (Delpech 1983; Boyle 1990; Leroi-Gourhan 1968).

Perhaps the most significant feature which evidently played a crucial role in the Upper Palaeolithic occupation of southwestern France however was the presence of exceptionally rich and migratory populations of reindeer. In almost half of the documented Upper Palaeolithic sites in this region reindeer accounts for over 90 percent of the total faunal remains, and in several sites reaches frequencies of between 95 and 100 percent (see Figure 14.5) (Boyle 1990; Mellars 1973, 2004). The migration patterns of reindeer in this region have stimulated some debate, but there is now increasing evidence from direct seasonality studies of growth-ring patterns in reindeer teeth that these herds must have been present within the major river valleys of the Perigord and adjacent regions throughout most of the winter months, with a probable migration up into the higher elevations of the Massif Central (or conceivably onto the plateaux regions between the main river valleys) during the mid-summer months (Bouchud 1966; Spiess 1979; Gordon 1988; Pike-Tay 1991; Burke & Pike-Tay 1997). It was clearly this particular food resource

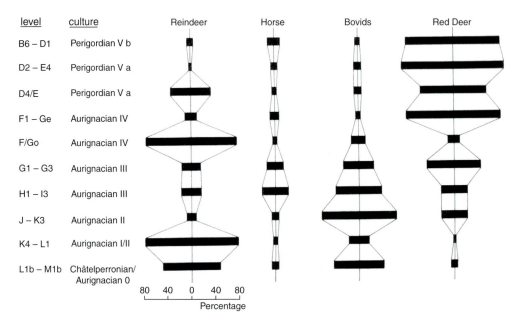

| level | culture | Reindeer | Horse | Bovids | Red Deer |
|---|---|---|---|---|---|
| B6 – D1 | Perigordian V b | | | | |
| D2 – E4 | Perigordian V a | | | | |
| D4/E | Perigordian V a | | | | |
| F1 – Ge | Aurignacian IV | | | | |
| F/Go | Aurignacian IV | | | | |
| G1 – G3 | Aurignacian III | | | | |
| H1 – I3 | Aurignacian III | | | | |
| J – K3 | Aurignacian II | | | | |
| K4 – L1 | Aurignacian I/II | | | | |
| L1b – M1b | Châtelperronian/ Aurignacian 0 | | | | |

80  40  0  40  80
Percentage

**14.4.** Frequencies of different species of animals (reindeer, horse, red deer and either bison or oxen) recorded through the different levels of Upper Palaeolithic occupation at the site of La Ferrassie (Dordogne) between ca. 40,000 and 25,000 BP. This demonstrates that all of these species were clearly present in the southwest French region throughout most if not all of the Upper Palaeolithic sequence. (From Mellars 1985)

that provided the mainstay of the diet of Upper Palaeolithic groups throughout at least the autumn, winter and spring months of the year.

## Demographic and social patterns

### POPULATION DENSITY

The most obvious and direct effect of the various climatic and ecological factors outlined earlier would have been to support the concentration of unusually/exceptionally high densities of human populations within the southwest French region throughout most if not all of the last-glacial period – as the sheer wealth and density of the archaeological record in this region clearly reveals (de Sonneville-Bordes 1960; Mellars 1973; Laville et al. 1981; Demars 1996; Boquet-Appel & Demars 2000). I am assuming here of course that in the final analysis it is primarily Malthusian demographic mechanisms which provide the primary determinant for the varying levels of hunter-gatherer populations in different regions – an assumption which many different analyses of recent hunter-gatherer populations would appear to bear out (Birdsell 1968; Kelly 1995; Pennington 2001; Binford 2001; Read & LeBlanc 2003). The important caveat in this context is what is sometimes referred to as the ecological law of the minimum (or 'Leibig's law'), which asserts that the critical control exerted by environmental factors on biological populations is not so much the *overall* productivity of the ecosystem on a long-term basis, but rather the densities of population that can be supported during periods of maximum scarcity – whether these occur on a regular seasonal or more occasional and unpredictable long-term basis (Read & LeBlanc 2003). In other words, there is little to be gained by populations expanding dramatically during periods of economic 'abundance', if the populations are subsequently cut back by intervening episodes of resource scarcity. In this context therefore the main point to be stressed is not simply the exceptional 'wealth' of animal food resources available within the southwest French region as a whole, but the relative *diversity* of these resources in ecological and economic terms (Delpech 1983; Mellars 1985; Boyle 1990). It is this factor which must have provided the essential safety net for population survival during the occasional periods when the regular migration of large reindeer herds through the valleys of the Dordogne, Vézère and elsewhere failed, as a result of the notorious tendency of reindeer and carribou populations to 'crash' as a result of factors

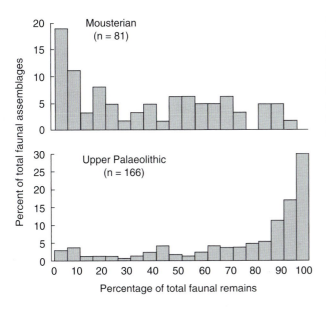

**14.5.** Percentages of reindeer remains recovered from Upper Palaeolithic sites in southwestern France (upper diagram) compared with those from preceding Mousterian (Neanderthal) sites. Over half of the documented Upper Palaeolithic occupation levels show overall frequencies of reindeer greater than 90 percent of the total animal bone assemblages. (From Mellars 1996)

such as the sporadic icing-over of tundra vegetation during the winter months, the effects of vegetation fires in the summer, or indeed the over-exploitation of the reindeer herds by the human groups themselves (Burch 1972; Spiess 1979; Jackson & Thacker 1997). The devastating effects of icing-over of reindeer food supplies experienced a few years ago over large areas of northern Siberia provides a graphic illustration of this. As noted above, the archaeological record clearly reveals that although reindeer provided the overwhelming bulk of winter-season food supplies throughout the greater part of the Upper Palaeolithic, there were always several other animal species present (horse, bison, aurochs, red deer, etc.) which could be exploited during occasional seasons when the reindeer populations failed (Figure 14.3). Unless all these animal species were affected simultaneously by climatic or other factors, the human popula-tions would almost certainly still have been able to survive on these other species, until the reindeer populations recovered. It is this factor, I would suggest – rather than the occasional exploitation of salmon or other fish resources, as suggested by Johim (1983), though as yet with little archaeological support (Mellars 1985; Hayden et al. 1987) – which accounts for the impressive densities of human populations which could be supported within the southwest French region throughout most if not all of the Upper Palaeolithic time range.

### GROUP SIZES

A second probable consequence of the unusual wealth and concentration of animal populations within the southwest French region would be in the formation – for at least part of the annual cycle – of relatively large social and residential groupings, possibly (though more debatably) ori-ented towards the large-scale communal hunting of the migrating rein-deer herds (Kelly 1995; Binford 2001; Lee & DeVore 1968; Demars 1996). Here, of course, it must be acknowledged that incontrovertible evidence for these large social aggregates remains much more difficult to demonstrate from the archaeological data alone, since it is clear that in some cases apparently large, extensive occupation areas in cave and rock shelter sites could conceivably be the products of many repeated visits to the sites by comparatively small groups, as opposed to simultaneous occupation of the entire settlement areas by much larger groups (Mellars 1973). Even so it is difficult to visualize that the very large occupation areas documented at sites such as Laugerie Haute, the Abri Pataud,

Laussel, La Madeleine and elsewhere in the Vézère valley – in some cases extending between seventy and two hundred metres along the adjacent cliff face (Mellars 1973; Laville et al. 1981) – can be attributed entirely to the activities of very small human groups. This is especially the case when (as at the Abri Pataud) several of the occupations seem to have been characterized by large, more or less evenly spaced hearths (Movius 1966). There are also cases (as in the rich, early Aurignacian levels in the closely adjacent sites of Abri Blanchard, Abri Castanet, and La Souquette in the Castelmerle valley) where there are stong suggestions that a number of adjacent rock shelters may have been occupied simultaneously (de Sonneville-Bordes 1960: 41, 146; White 1989). As noted above, the question of how far these sites may reflect the use of large-scale communal hunting strategies for the exploitation of the migrating reindeer herds remains more controversial (Spiess 1979; Enloe 1993; Demars 1998). But even so it is hard to escape the impression that at least some of the social aggregations in these large reindeer-hunting sites must reflect something more than the activities of just three or four nuclear family groups.

**SEDENTISM**

Thirdly, it is equally difficult to escape the impression that at least some of these large reindeer-hunting settlements reflect occupation over substantial parts of the annual cycle, probably representing periods of at least several weeks, if not several months. Tooth-sectioning and other seasonality studies can rarely achieve a very fine level of chronological resolution, but there are at least strong hints from these studies that sites such as the Abri Castanet, Abri Pataud and La Madeleine were occupied over a substantial part of each winter season, probably extending from around December or January to March or April (Spiess 1979; Gordon 1988; Pike-Tay 1991; Burke & Pike Tay 1997). In support of this one could also note the evidence for the excavation of sunken, pit-like living structures at sites such as the Abri Pataud and Fourneau du Diable, and the tendency (noted earlier) to arrange hearths in a fairly regular, evenly spaced way (Mellars 1973; Movius 1966). The sheer wealth, density and concentration of all kinds of occupation debris (lithic artefacts, animal bones, hearth deposits, etc.) documented in many of the sites (Laville et al. 1981) could also argue in the same direction. It is as yet difficult to cite evidence for any equally dense and intensive patterns of Upper Palaeolithic occupation in other regions of Europe, with the notable exception of some of the open-air Gravettian and Pavlovian settlements in central Europe (Dolní Věstonice, Pavlov, etc.) or perhaps some of the broadly similar sites at Kostenki and elsewhere on the South Russian plain (Gamble 1999; Soffer 1985).

### TERRITORIALITY AND ETHNICITY

Finally, one could advance a number of arguments that all of the demographic and social patterns discussed above would have acted as a strong incentive towards the emergence of some fairly sharply defined territorial and ethnic divisions between the different Upper Palaeolithic communities in southwestern France (David 1973, 1985; Mellars 1985, 1996). In the anthropological literature, this point has been argued in several different ways. Dyson-Hudson and Smith (1978) argued that any situation of potential or actual competition or conflict for essential economic resources would lead almost inevitably to more sharply defined territorial boundaries, if only as a means of minimizing infringements and potential conflict between adjacent groups over the exploitation of scarce resources (see also Keeley 1988; Read & LeBlanc 2003). The point has also been made that only groups who *were* living in relatively high population densities would in fact be capable of exercising any kind of effective control or 'policing' over the adherence to territorial boundaries. However these social and economic mechanisms operated, there is a large amount of direct ethnographic evidence that language and kinship-based 'tribal' groupings among hunter gatherers tend to occupy smaller and more tightly defined areas in regions of relatively high population densities than among more sparsely distributed groups – best reflected perhaps in Birdsell's (1968) correlation between dialectical tribal group areas and annual rainfall values in different regions of Australia, and by the supposedly 'magic number' of ca. five hundred individuals for the modal size of many hunter-gatherer tribes (Lee & DeVore 1968; Wobst 1974; Peterson 1978; Kelly 1995).

In archaeological terms, some attempts to define a number of potential dialectical or tribal groupings of this kind were provided in Nicholas David's study of the Noaillian (i.e. later Gravettian) industries within different areas of western and central France, and in similar studies by Philip Smith of the later Solutrian industries (David 1973, 1985; Smith 1966). Nevertheless it should be noted that in all these cases there was substantial evidence for the apparent exchange of various items of material culture (such as high-quality varieties of flint, or decorative prestige items such as sea shells) between these separate regional populations (Taborin 1993; Demars 1998). Arguably these could be seen as a further way of mitigating potential sources of conflict over territorial boundaries and shared resources between the adjacent groups, and perhaps creating what Clive Gamble (1983, 1999) has aptly described as 'alliance networks' to allow some potential sharing of either resources, information or even economic territories, during occasional episodes of seasonal or more long-term resource scarcity (see also Shennan 2002; Read & LeBlanc 2003).

## The social foundations of Upper Palaeolithic art

The final, and most central question, of course, is what relevance all of these social and demographic patterns may have as a potential explanation for the dramatic proliferation of elaborate cave art within the Upper Palaeolithic communities of the Franco-Cantabrian region. Here of course the arguments inevitably become more speculative, and open to a variety of different theoretical perspectives. Briefly, at least three different theoretical scenarios can be visualized in this context.

First, one could see the cave art at least partly as a reflection of the ethnic or territorial divisions within the Upper Palaeolithic groups. As discussed above, the tight packing of Upper Palaeolithic populations within relatively small geographical areas in southwestern France could be argued as promoting more tightly defined territorial and social divisions between the different groups, with a corresponding emphasis on various forms of ethnic symbolism to reflect and reinforce these social and territorial divisions (Wiessner 1983, 1984). Seen in broadly 'phenomenological' terms, one could see the location of the principal cave art sites as an attempt to legitimate and perpetuate these socio-territorial divisions – perhaps representing territorial markers in broadly the same way as is often envisaged for, say, the megalithic tombs and round barrows in later prehistory – although clearly in this case with not such an immediate visual impact on the surrounding landscape. In certain ways perhaps this perspective would recall some of the earlier notions of tribal 'totemic' symbolism (Ucko & Rosenfeld 1967; Lewis-Williams 2002), as a factor underlying the distribution and expression of different forms of cave art.

A second perspective would be to see the art as a particularly graphic reflection of the power of religion and ritual as a means of integrating and consolidating social groups, particularly under the impact of potential competition for territories and resources from adjacent groups, and perhaps even more so under the threat of periodic economic crises resulting from seasonal or more long-term fluctuations in the availability of reindeer or other critical resources – for the various climatic and ecological reasons discussed earlier. Religion and associated ritual in this context could be seen as a powerful psychological force, not only for integrating the social groups and reinforcing adherence to group social norms and values (as it clearly does in the case of present-day religious groups) but also as a psychological force to reduce personal anxiety in the face of various unpredictable risks and dangers to the survival of the society as a whole. At times of personal danger, human groups do perhaps tend to resort to religion and appeals to other 'supernatural' forces more often than in times of social and economic security.

Thirdly, we could see the art much more directly as a reflection of the power and authority of particular individuals within the Upper Palaeolithic communities, and acting as a powerful ritualistic means of reinforcing the status and authority of these individuals among other members of the groups. The individiuals in question could presumably have been either shamans (as David Lewis-Williams and Jean Clottes have argued very effectively in their papers elsewhere and in this volume) or more general 'big men' who were able to emerge within the relatively large and perhaps semipermanent residential groupings postulated for many of the larger Upper Palaeolithic settlements within the southwestern French region. Whichever way the situation is envisaged, there can be little doubt that much of the cave art can be attributed to the activities of specialists, either working directly to support their own status and prestige within society, or as an ancillary part of the power structure of other individuals (Lewis-Williams 2002). Once again, one is reminded of the importance of ritual, art and impressive symbolic centres (such as cathedrals or mosques) in reinforcing the power-base of religious and political leaders within historic and modern societies. As argued earlier, powerful individuals of this kind would seem far more likely to emerge within the context of relatively large and semi-permanent residential units than in the context of very small, dispersed and highly mobile hunter-gatherer groups (Johnson 1982; Keeley 1988; Kelly 1995; Shennan 2002).

No doubt all these speculations could be pursued much further. And of course we should beware of falling into the simplistic assumption that a single explanatory principle can account for the total spectrum of the art, as opposed to a range of more complex (and probably more realistic) multicausal explanations. My purpose here has simply been to show how a variety of what could be termed largely 'functionalist' explanations could be invoked to account for the extraordinary proliferation and diversity of cave art within one small region of Western Europe, and to argue that the most critical single factor underlying this proliferation is likely to have been the exceptional density and concentration of human populations within this region, which were dependent ultimately on the special combination of climatic and environmental conditions within these oceanic regions of Western Europe.

If one is looking for a final demonstration of the powerful role of ecological factors in promoting the extraordinary eruption of cave art within the Franco-Cantabrian region, then this is provided most graphically by the remarkably sudden and abrupt disappearance of the cave art at almost precisely the time when the special combination of climatic and associated environmental features discussed above disappeared at the end of the last-glacial period, at around 12,500 BP in radiocarbon years, or ca. 14,000 BP in 'absolute' calendrical years. This is the period of the transition from the classically 'Upper Palaeolithic' culture of the late Magdalenian to the essentially 'Mesolithic' culture of the immediately succeeding Azilian – now dated closely to around 12,500 BP in radiocarbon terms (Mellars 1994; Housley et al. 1997; Mithen 2003). At this time we know that temperatures in western Europe rose sharply by at least 8–10°C (see Figure 14.2) (van Andel & Davies 2003), followed by the rapid invasion of fully forest vegetation into southwestern France, and the equally rapid extinction of the typically open-country, 'glacial' animal communities on which the subsistence of the whole of the Upper Palaeolithic cultures had depended. Reindeer disappears totally from the faunal assemblages of the Azilian sites, to be replaced by a range of typically woodland, or mixed woodland/open species such as red deer, roe deer, aurochs and wild boar (de Sonneville-Bordes 1960; Delpech 1983; Boyle 1990). From present-day ecological studies we know that these animals would have been living under very much lower overall densities than were the preceding open country species (due to the much lower productivity of low-growing plant communities in the closed-canopy forests: Butzer 1971) while the large migratory herd movements of the reindeer – which had formed the mainstay of the economy and associated demographic and social structures of the Upper Palaeolithic groups – suddenly disappeared (de Sonneville-Bordes 1960: 498–500).

The impact of this change can be seen in all aspects of the archaeological transition from the late Magdalenian to the Azilian: the occurrence of much fewer (and above all much smaller and more ephemeral) occupation sites; a sharp reduction in the size and complexity of both stone tool and bone/antler technology; and the virtual disappearance of all forms of art – with the exception of the enigmatic painted pebbles and a few geometric or simple animal engravings on bone or stone (Figure 14.6) (de Sonneville-Bordes 1960; Mellars 1994; Mithen 2003). The small sizes of the Azilian groups would arguably have allowed little scope for the role of specialists craftsmen or artists. The effectively one-to-one correlation of all these striking social, technological and artistic

**14.6.** Characteristic stone and bone tools of the Azilian period in southwest France (ca. 12,000 BP) showing much simpler forms than those of the immediately preceding Magdalenian period. (From Mellars 1992)

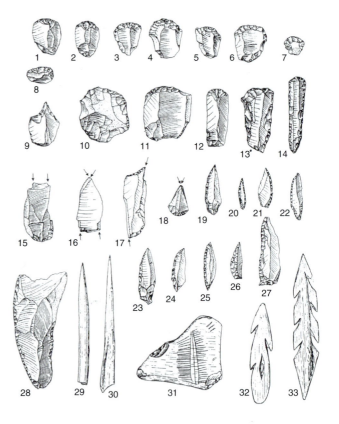

changes with the simultaneous changes in climatic and ecological conditions is beyond dispute. Overall we could see this as perhaps the most graphic illustration in prehistory of a rapid 'degeneration' in technology and the complexity of material culture in the face of environmental change. Stated bluntly, studies of the symbolic and cognitive dimensions of human culture – even in the twenty-first century – will ignore the critical role of strongly environmentally controlled factors at its peril!

What environmental factors cannot explain of course are the specific *forms* taken by the Palaeolithic cave art, and the deeper symbolic and perceptual meanings which lay behind the conception and production of the art. But this is the focus of the discussions of other contributors to this volume.

## REFERENCES

Binford, L. R., 2001. *Constructing Frames of Reference: An Analytical Method for Archaeological Theory Building using Hunter-Gatherer and Environmental Data Sets.* Berkeley: University of California Press.

Birdsell, J. B., 1968. Some predictions for the Pleistocene based on equilibrium systems among recent hunter-gatherers, in *Man the Hunter*, eds. R. B. Lee and I. DeVore. Chicago: Aldine, 229–49.

Boquet-Appel, J.-R. & P.-Y. Demars, 2000. Population kinetics in the Upper Paleolithic in western Europe. *Journal of Archaeological Science* **27**, 551–70.

Bouchud, J., 1966. *Essai sur le Renne et Climatologie du Paléolithique Moyen et Supérieur.* Magne: Périgueux.

Boyle, K. V., 1990. *Upper Palaeolithic Faunas from South-West France: A Zoogeographic Perspective.* Oxford: British Archaeological Reports International Series S557.

Burch, E. S., 1972. The caribou/wild reindeer as a human food resource. *American Antiquity* **37**, 339–68.

Burke, A. & A. Pike-Tay, 1997. Reconstructing "L'Age du Renne", in *Caribou and Reindeer Hunters of the Northern Hemisphere*, eds. L. J. Jackson & P. T. Thacker. Aldershot: Avebury.

Butzer, K. W., 1971. *Environment and Archeology.* Chicago: Aldine.

Cohen, M. N., 1985. Prehistoric hunter-gatherers: The meaning of social complexity, in *Prehistoric Hunter-Gatherers: The Emergence of Cultural Complexity*, eds. T. D. Price & J. A. Brown. Orlando: Academic Press, 99–119.

Dansgaard, W., S. J. Johnsen H. B. Clausen, D. Dahljensen, N. S. Gundestrup, C. U. Hammer, C. S. Hvidberg, J. P. Steffensen, A. E. Sveinbjornsdottir,

J. Jouzel & G. Bond, 1993. Evidence for general instability of past climate from a 250-kyr ice-core record. *Nature* **364**, 218–20.

David, N.C., 1973. On Upper Palaeolithic society, ecology and technological change: the Noaillian case, in *The Explanation of Culture Change: Models in Prehistory*, ed. C. Renfrew. London: Duckworth, 277–303.

David, N.C. 1985. *Excavation of the Abri Pataud, Les Eyzies (Dordogne): The Noaillian (Level 4) Assemblage and the Noaillian Culture in Western Europe*. Cambridge (MA): Peabody Museum, Harvard University.

Delpech, F., 1983. *Les Faunes du Paléolithique Supérieur dans le Sud-ouest de la France*. Paris: Centre Nationale de la Recherche Scientifique.

Demars, P.-Y., 1996. Demographie et occupation de l'espace au Paléolithique supérieur at au Mésolithique in France. *Préhistoire Européenne* **8**, 3–26.

1998. Circulation des silex dans le nord de l'Aquitaine au Paléolithique supérieur. *Gallia Préhistoire* **40**, 1–28.

d'Errico, F. & M.F. Sánchez Goñi, 2003. Neandertal extinction and the millennial scale climatic variability of OIS 3. *Quaternary Science Reviews* **22**, 769–88.

de Sonneville-Bordes, D., 1960. *Le Paléolithique Supérieur en Périgord*. Bordeaux: Delmas.

Dyson-Hudson, R. & E.A. Smith, 1978. Human territoriality: an ecological reassessment. *American Anthropologist* **80**, 21–41.

Enloe, J., 1993. Subsistence organization in the early Upper Paleolithic: reindeer hunters of the Abri du Flageolet, couche V, in *Before Lascaux: The Complex Record of the Early Upper Paleolithic*, eds. H. Knecht, A. Pike-Tay & R. White. Boca Raton: CRC Press, 101–15.

Fairbanks, R.G., R.A. Mortlock, T.C. Chiu, L. Cao, A. Kaplan, T.P. Guilderson, T.W. Fairbanks, A.L. Bloom, P.M. Grootes & M.J. Nadeau, 2005. Radiocarbon calibration curve spanning 0 to 50,000 years BP based on paired 230Th/234U/238U and 14C dates on pristine corals. *Quaternary Science Reviews* **24**, 1781–96.

Gamble, C., 1983. Culture and society in the Upper Palaeolithic in Europe, in *Hunter-Gatherer Economy in Prehistory*, ed. G.N. Bailey. Cambridge: Cambridge University Press, 201–11.

1999. *The Palaeolithic Societies of Europe*. Cambridge: Cambridge University Press.

Gordan, B., 1988. *Of Men and Reindeer Herds in French Magdalenian Prehistory*. Oxford: British Archaeological Reports, International series 390.

Hayden, B., B. Chisholm & H. Schwarcz, 1987. Fishing and foraging: marine resources in the Upper Paleolithic of France, in *The Pleistocene Old World*, ed. O. Soffer. New York: Plenum, 279–91.

Hughen, K., S. Lehman, J. Southon, J. Overpeck, O. Marchal, C. Herring & J. Turnbull., 2004. 14C activity and global carbon cycle changes over the past 50,000 years. *Science* **303**, 204–7.

Huntley, B. & J.R.M. Allen, 2003. Glacial environments III: palaeo-vegetation patterns in Last Glacial Europe, in *Neanderthals and Modern Humans in the European Landscape during the Last Glaciation*, eds. T. van Andel & W. Davies. Cambridge: McDonald Institute for Archaeological Research, 79–102.

Housley, R.A., C.S. Gamble, M. Street & P. Pettitt, 1997. Radiocarbon evidence for the last-glacial human recolonisation of northern Europe. *Proceedings of the Prehistoric Society* **63**, 25–54.

Iversen, J., 1973. *The Development of Denmark's Nature since the Last Glacial*. Copenhagen: Reitzels Forlag.

Jackson, L.J. & P.T. Thacker, 1997. *Caribou and Reindeer Hunters of the Northern Hemisphere*. Aldershot: Avebury.

Jochim, M., 1983. Cave art in ecological perspective, in *Hunter-gatherer Economy in Prehistory*, ed. G.N. Bailey. Cambridge: Cambridge University Press, 212–9.

Johnson, G.A., 1982. Organization structure and scalar stress, in *Theory and Explanation in Archaeology: The Southampton Conference*, eds. C. Renfrew, M.J. Rowlands & B.A. Segraves. New York: Academic Press, 389–421.

Keeley, L., 1988. Hunter-gatherer economic complexity and 'population pressure': a cross-cultural analysis. *Journal of Anthropological Archaeology* **7**, 373–411.

1996. *War Before Civilization: The Myth of the Peaceful Savage*. Oxford: Oxford University Press.

Kelly, R., 1995. *The Foraging Spectrum: Diversity in Hunter-Gatherer Lifeways*. Washington, DC: Smithsonian Institution Press.

Laville, H., J.-P. Rigaud & J. Sackett, 1981. *Rock Shelters of the Perigord*. New York: Academic Press.

Lee, R.B. & I. DeVore, 1968. Problems in the study of hunters and gatherers, in *Man the Hunter*, eds. R.B. Lee & I. DeVore. Chicago: Aldine, 3–12.

Leroi-Gourhan, A., 1968. *The Art of Prehistoric Man in Western Europe*. London: Thames & Hudson.

Leroi-Gourhan, Ar., 1977. Les climats, les plantes et les hommes: Quaternaire supérieur d'Europe occidentale. *Studia Geologica Polonica* **52**, 249–61.

Lewis-Williams, J.D., 2002. *The Mind in the Cave*. London: Thames & Hudson.

Mellars, P.A., 1973. The character of the Middle-Upper Palaeolithic transition in south-west France, in *The Explanation of Culture Change: Models in Prehistory*, ed. C. Renfrew. London: Duckworth, 255–76.

1985. The ecological basis of cultural complexity in the Upper Paleolithic of southwestern France, in *Prehistoric Hunter-Gatherers: The Emergence of Cultural Complexity*, eds. T.D. Price & J.A. Brown. Orlando: Academic Press, 271–97.

1989. Major issues in the emergence of modern humans. *Current Anthropology* **30**, 349–85.

1994. The Upper Palaeolithic Revolution, in *The Oxford Illustrated Prehistory of Europe*, ed. B. Cunliffe. Oxford: Oxford University Press, 42–78.

1996. The emergence of biologically modern populations in Europe: a social and cognitive 'revolution'?, in *Evolution of Social Behaviour Patterns in Primates and Man* (Proceedings of the British Academy vol. 88), eds. W. G. Runciman, J. Maynard-Smith & R. I. M. Dunbar. London: The British Academy, 179–202.

2004. Reindeer specialization in the early Upper Palaeolithic: the evidence from southwest France. *Journal of Archaeological Science* **31**, 613–7.

Mithen, S., 1990. *Thoughtful Foragers*. Cambridge: Cambridge University Press.

Movius, H. L. 1966. The hearths of the Upper Perigordian and Aurignacian horizons at the Abri Pataud, Les Eyzies (Dordogne) and their possible significance. *American Anthropologist* **68**, 296–325.

Pennington, R., 2001. Hunter-gatherer demography, in *Hunter-Gatherers: An Interdisciplinary Perspective*, eds. C. Panter-Brick, R. H. Layton & P. Rowley-Conwy. Cambridge, Cambridge University Press, 170–204.

Peterson, N., 1976. *Tribes and Boundaries in Australia*. Canberra: Australian Institute of Aboriginal Studies.

Pike-Tay, A., 1991. *Red Deer Hunting in the Upper Paleolithic of South-West France: A Study in Seasonality*. Oxford: Tempus Reparatum (British Archaeological Reports, International series 569).

Read, D. W. & S. A. LeBlanc, 2003. Population growth, carrying capacity and conflict. *Current Anthropology* **44**, 59–85.

Sánchez-Goñi, M. F., I Cacho, J.-L. Turon, J. Guiot, F. J. Sierro, J.-P. Peypouquet, J. O. Grimalt & N. J. Shackleton, 2002. Synchroneity between marine and terrestrial responses to millennial-scale climatic variability during the last glacial period in the Mediterranean region. *Climate Dynamics* **19**, 95–105.

Shackleton, N. J., M. A. Hall & E. Vincent, 2000. Phase relationships between millennial scale events 64,000–24,000 years ago. *Paleoceanography* **15**, 565–9.

Shennan, S., 2002. *Genes, Memes and Human History: Darwinian Archaeology and Cultural Evolution*. London: Thames & Hudson.

Smith, P. E.L., 1966. *Le Solutréen en France*. Bordeaux: Delmas.

Soffer, O., 1985. *The Upper Paleolithic of the Central Russian Plain*. Orlando: Academic Press.

Speiss, A. E., 1979. *Reindeer and Caribou Hunters: An Archeological Study*. New York: Academic Press.

Stringer, C. & P. Andrews, 2003. *The Complete World of Human Evolution*. London: Thames & Hudson.

Ucko, P. J. & A. Rosenfeld, 1967. *Palaeolithic Cave Art*. London: Weidenfeld & Nicolson

van Andel, T. H. & W. Davies, 2003. *Neanderthals and Modern Humans in the European Landscape during the Last Glaciation, 60,000 to 20,000 Years Ago*. Cambridge: McDonald Institute Monographs.

van Andel, T. H. & P. C. Tzedakis, 1996. Palaeolithic landscapes of Europe and environs, 150,000–25,000 years ago. *Quaternary Science Reviews* **15**, 481–500.

White, R., 1989. Production complexity and standardization in early Aurignacian bead and pendant manufacture: evolutionary implications, in *The Human Revolution*, eds. P. Mellars & C. Stringer. Edinburgh: Edinburgh University Press, 366–90.

Wiessner, P., 1983. Style and information in Kalahari San projectile points. *American Antiquity* **48**, 253–76.

1984. Reconsidering the behavioral basis for style: A case study among the Kalahari San. *Journal of Anthropological Archaeology* **3**, 190–234.

Wobst, H. M., 1974. Boundary conditions for Palaeolithic social systems: a simulation approach. *American Antiquity* **39**, 1547–78.

Woillard, G. M. & W. G. Mook, 1982. Carbon-14 dates at Grande Pile: correlation of land and sea chronologies. *Science* **215**, 159–61.

# REFLECTIONS ON THE ORIGINS OF SPIRITUALITY

# 15

# Interdisciplinary perspectives on human origins and religious awareness

*J. Wentzel van Huyssteen*

As a Christian theologian interested in human origins and the controversial issue of human 'uniqueness', I have been increasingly drawn to the contributions of palaeoanthropologists and archaeologists to this challenging problem. In my own recent work I have been deeply involved in trying to construct plausible ways for theology to enter into this important interdisciplinary conversation. As a way of facilitating this kind of cross-disciplinary dialogue I have argued for a *postfoundationalist* approach to interdisciplinary dialogue, which implies three important moves for theological reflection. *First*, as theologians we should acknowledge the radical contextuality of all our intellectual work, the epistemically crucial role of interpreted experience, and the way that disciplinary traditions shape the values that inform our reflection about God and what we believe to be God's presence in the world. *Second*, a postfoundationalist notion of rationality should open our eyes to an epistemic obligation that points beyond the boundaries of our own discipline, our local communities, groups, or cultures, toward plausible forms of *interdisciplinary dialogue* (cf. van Huyssteen 1999). Against this background I have argued for distinct and important differences between reasoning strategies used by theologians and scientists. I have also argued, however, that some important shared rational resources may actually be identified for these very different cognitive domains of our mental lives (cf. van Huyssteen 2006). *Thirdly*, it is precisely these shared rational resources that enable interdisciplinary dialogue, and are expressed most clearly by the notion of *transversal rationality*. In the dialogue between theology and other disciplines, transversal reasoning promotes different but equally legitimate ways of viewing specific topics, problems, traditions, or disciplines, and creates the kind of space where different voices need not always be in contradiction, or in danger of assimilating one another, but are in fact dynamically interactive with one another. This notion of transversality thus provides a philosophical window to our wider world of communication through thought and action (cf. Schrag 1992: 148ff; Welsch 1996: 764ff), and teaches us to respect the disciplinary integrity of reasoning strategies as different as theology and the sciences.

This way of thinking is always concrete, local, and contextual, but at the same time reaches beyond local contexts to transdisciplinary concerns. The overriding concern here is as follows: while we always come to our interpersonal and cross-disciplinary conversations with strong personal beliefs, commitments and even prejudices, a postfoundationalist approach enables us to realize that, in spite of our radically different reasoning strategies, there is also much that we share in terms of our rational resources. An interdisciplinary approach, carefully thought through, can help us to identify these shared resources in different modes of knowledge so as to reach beyond the boundaries of our own traditional disciplines in cross-contextual, cross-disciplinary conversation. It can also enable us to identify possible shared conceptual problems as we negotiate the porous boundaries of our different disciplines.

One such shared interdisciplinary problem is the concern for human uniqueness, and how that may, or may not, relate to human origins and the evolution of religious awareness. It is, therefore, precisely in the problem of 'human uniqueness' that theology and the sciences may find a shared research trajectory. Our very human capacity (or mania?) for self-definition can most probably be seen as one of the 'crowning achievements' of our species. As we all know today, however, no one trait or accomplishment should ever be taken as the single defining characteristic of what it means to be human. Moreover, what we see as our humanness, or even our distinct human 'uniqueness', ultimately implies a deeply moral choice: we are not just biological creatures, but as cultural creatures we have the remarkable but dangerous ability to determine whom we are going to include, or not, as part of 'us' (cf. Proctor 2003: 228f). Talking about human uniqueness in reasoning strategies as different as theology and the sciences, therefore, will always have a crucially important moral dimension. We do seem to have a profound moral responsibility when defining ourselves, for naming ourselves always assumes a specific kind of reality that gives shape to the worlds we create and experience. It is also important to ask, however, how reasonable (or not) it might be for a theologian, after immersing him/herself in the challenging contemporary debates in palaeoanthropology and archaeology, to expect scientists to provide a starting point, or important links, for an interdisciplinary discussion of issues like human origins, human nature, human uniqueness, and even human destiny. Last but not least: how realistic is it for a Christian theologian to expect scientists to take theological contributions to these crucially important topics seriously?

An interesting part of our self-perception is that it is often the less material aspects of the history of our species that fascinates us most in the evolution of modern humans. We seem to grasp at an intuitive level that issues like language, self-awareness, consciousness, moral awareness, symbolic behaviour and mythology are probably the defining elements that really make us human (cf. Lewin 1993: 4). Yet exactly these elements that most suggest humanness are often the least visible in the prehistoric record. For this reason palaeoanthropologists have correctly focused on more indirect, but equally plausible material pointers to the presence of the symbolic human mind in early human prehistory. Arguably the most spectacular of the earliest evidences of symbolic behaviour in humans are the Palaeolithic cave paintings in South-West France and the Basque Country, painted toward the end of the last Ice Age. The haunting beauty of these prehistoric images, and the creative cultural explosion that they represent, should indeed fascinate any theologian interested in human origins.

At first blush there does in fact seem to be a rather remarkable convergence between the evolutionary emergence of *Homo sapiens*, and Christian beliefs in the origins of the human creature (cf. García-Rivera 2003: 9). In a sense the famous cultural explosion of the Upper Palaeolithic marks the beginning of a new species much as the creation myths of the Abrahamic religions refer to the arrival of a new species, created in the 'image of God'.[1] But easy comparisons stop here, for in the classic texts of the ancient Near East the primal human being is seen as the significant forerunner of humanity, and as such defines the emerging relationship between humanity and the deity. The theologian, therefore, needs to be aware that the Genesis 1 texts are meant as clear expressions of the uniqueness of the primal human being, who occupies a position between the deity and humanity, and who is the only one who can lay claim to this distinction (cf. Callender 2000: 206f). Theologically, then, being created 'in the image of God' highlights the extraordinary importance of human beings: human beings are in fact walking representations of God, and as such of exquisite value and importance (cf. Towner 2001: 26), a tradition that has been augmented centuries later by a very specific focus on the rational abilities and moral awareness of humans.

Against over two thousand years of complex conceptual evolution in the history of ideas of theological thought, the prehistoric treasures from the Upper Palaeolithic today seem to have become almost impossible to interpret, their 'true meaning' so elusive that it is virtually impossible to recreate any 'original' context of meaning in which they were first created. Yet we join palaeoanthropologists in sensing that these products of ancient imagery may hold the key to what it means to be human, which for theology may significantly broaden and enrich what is meant today by 'human uniqueness', especially if we shift our focus of inquiry to accommodate more contextual and particularist interpretations.

For a theologian like myself, interested in interdisciplinary dialogue, precisely arguments for more local and contextual interpretations of Palaeolithic art are especially intriguing, and it is these more contextual approaches that will resonate with my own postfoundationalist approach to interdisciplinary discourse. A more contextual, local approach would imply that, rather than asking what the enduring *meaning* of these images may be, we should rather try to understand what made them *meaningful* for our early modern ancestors (cf. Conkey 1997: 343ff). What is undoubtedly clear is that a full century of the study of Palaeolithic art has not produced any definite or final theory about this 'art', but rather has brought forth a number of truly conflicting claims. As a serious advocate of a radically contextual approach to interpreting Palaeolithic imagery, Margaret W. Conkey has warned against too glibly calling Upper Palaeolithic image-making 'art', since this superimposes a contemporary Western aesthetic perspective onto our evaluation of these mysterious images. For this reason Conkey and Soffer have recently suggested that our understanding of prehistoric imagery will be greatly advanced if we can manage to decouple this body of archaeological evidence about past lifeways from its categorization as 'art' (cf. Soffer and Conkey 1997: 1ff; see also Conkey, this volume). These scientists believe that precisely the understanding of this material as 'art,' based on unwarranted Western aesthetic assumptions, has greatly constrained our subsequent understanding of the subject matter. For this reason they propose to term this corpus of Palaeolithic data as *prehistoric imagery* and, when using the term, put 'art' in quotation marks.

This growing, and typically postfoundationalist, dissatisfaction with past approaches to prehistoric imagery should be seen as a direct result of prior insufficient attention to the concrete time and places when the images were actually produced and used, and Soffer and Conkey's views, therefore, embody a strong reaction against unwarranted uniformitarian assumptions and broad ahistoric, abstract, and often decontexualized frames of reference (cf. Soffer and Conkey 1997: 1f). For Soffer and Conkey there are various problematic assumptions at work behind the generally used term 'art' for prehistoric images. As defined in the past century, art is a cultural phenomenon that is assumed to function in what we recognize, and even carve off separately, as the aesthetic sphere. It is exactly this aesthetic function that we cannot assume to have existed or functioned similarly in prehistory, and so we cannot assume that the so-called 'artists' of thirty thousand years ago discovered something that is enduring and true for all humans at all times in all places (cf. Soffer and Conkey 1997: 2). The deeper and more abstract assumption, then, that somehow a trans-historic level of the meaning of this prehistoric 'art' may exist, and that this may be 'true for all humans at all times and at all places' does seem to be troublesome and highly a-contextual in its own right. Soffer and Conkey's more particularist and pro-mosaic, contextual approach with its clear transversal intent does seem to resonate well with my own postfoundationalist approach for discerning meaning through interdisciplinary dialogue. Exactly for this reason I have found the notion of *transversal reasoning* helpful to bring the shifting mosaic of current interpretations in palaeoanthropology into direct dialogue with the equally chequered and fragmented history of notions of 'human uniqueness' in Christian theology (cf. van Huyssteen 2006).

In the interdisciplinary conversation between theology and the sciences the boundaries between our disciplines and reasoning strategies are indeed shifting and porous, and deep theological convictions cannot be easily transferred to philosophy, or to science, to function as 'data' in foreign disciplinary systems. In the same manner, transversal reasoning does not imply that scientific data, paradigms, or worldviews, can be transported into theology to there set the agenda for theological reasoning. Transversal reasoning does mean that theology and science can share concerns and converge on commonly identified conceptual problems such as the problem of human uniqueness. By also recognizing the limitations of interdisciplinarity, however, the disciplinary integrity of both theology and the sciences will be protected (cf. van Huyssteen 2003: 161ff). On this view, for instance, the theologian can caution the scientist to recognize the danger of materialist reductionism in scientific worldviews, even as the scientist can caution the theologian against constructing esoteric and imperialistic worldviews, totally disconnected from the reality of the results of scientific research.

These mutually critical tasks presuppose, however, the richness of the transversal moment in which theology and palaeoanthropology may indeed find amazing transversal connections on issues of human origins and uniqueness. Furthermore, I believe that the most responsible Christian theological way to look at human uniqueness requires, first of all, a move away from esoteric and baroquely abstract notions of human uniqueness, and second, a return to embodied notions of humanness, where our sexuality and embodied moral awareness are tied directly to our embodied self-transcendence as creatures who are predisposed to religious belief. I would further argue that, also from a palaeoanthropological point of view, human uniqueness has emerged as a highly contextualized, embodied notion and is directly tied to the embodied, symbolizing minds of our prehistoric ancestors as physically manifested in the spectacularly painted cave walls of the Upper Palaeolithic. This not only opens up the possibility for converging arguments, from both theology and palaeoanthropology, for the presence of religious awareness in our earliest European modern human ancestors, but also for the plausibility of the larger argument: since the very beginning of the emergence of *Homo sapiens*, the evolution of those characteristics that made humans uniquely different from even their closest sister species, that is, characteristics like consciousness, language, imagination, symbolic minds and symbolic behavior, has always included religious awareness and religious behavior.

Ian Tattersall has recently argued exactly this point: because every human society, at one stage or another, has possessed religion of some sort, complete with origin myths that purportedly explain the relationship of humans to the world around them, religion cannot be discounted from any discussion of typically human behaviors (1998: 201). More importantly, in a very specific sense religious belief may be one of the earliest special propensities or dispositions that we are able to detect in the archaeological record of modern humans. It is in this sense, then, that neither history, nor anthropology knows of societies from which religion has been totally absent (cf. Rappaport 1971: 23ff). There is indeed a naturalness to religious imagination that challenges any viewpoint that would want to see religion or religious imagination as an arbitrary or esoteric faculty of the human mind. Therefore, even if we are not certain what exactly the spectacular prehistoric imagery of the European Palaeolithic modern humans represented to the people who made them, it is nonetheless clear that this early 'art' reflected a view held by these people of their place in the world and a body of narrative mythology that explained that place. One of the major functions of religious belief has indeed always been to provide explanations for the deep desire to deny the finality of death, and the curious reluctance of our species to accept the inevitable limitations of human experience. This is exactly the reason why it is possible for us to identify so closely with European Palaeolithic rock 'art', and to recognize that it goes beyond mere representation and as such often also embodies a broadly religious, if elusive, symbolism (cf. Tattersall 1998: 201).[2]

Against this background it is already clear that certain themes naturally emerge as seminal for the interdisciplinary dialogue between palaeoanthropology and theology. It is in these scientific discussions that theologians need to find transversal connections to their own discipline(s). Scholars like Steven Mithen (1996), Ian Tattersall (1998), Merlin Donald (1991, 2001), and Paul Mellars (1990) have all argued that knowing the prehistory of the human mind will provide us with a more profound understanding of what it means to be uniquely human. It certainly helps us to understand a little better the origins of art, technology, and of religion, and how these cultural domains are inescapably linked to the ability of the cognitively fluid human mind to develop creatively powerful metaphors by crossing the boundaries of different domains of knowledge. Iain Davidson has argued that early humans worked out their relationship with their environment and with each other precisely through Palaeolithic 'art', and he sees the burst of image making after 40,000 BP as reflecting the way that these ancestors of ours explored the limits and possibilities of the power of their recently discovered symbolically based communication. Because of this, most scholars in the field would take the Upper Palaeolithic as the standard for recognizing symbolism (cf. Davidson 1997: 125; cf. also Diamond 1998), although powerful and convincing arguments have now been made by Christopher Henshilwood and his team for a more gradual emergence of modern human behavior in Africa, most notably by the discovery of personal ornaments from around seventy-five thousand years ago at the Blombos Cave in South Africa (cf. Henshilwood et al. 2004: 404f). For Iain Davidson any kind of symboling power is tied directly to the origins of language: it would have been impossible for creatures without language to create symbolic artefacts, or to hold opinions about the making or marking of surfaces that would eventually turn them into imagery or 'art'. For this reason Davidson argues that it is precisely the exceptional artistic artefacts from the Upper Palaeolithic that give us unique insights into evolutionary processes, into the evolution of human behavior, and into the very nature of what it might have meant to become a modern human.

The important question now is, what does the origin of language mean for our understanding of prehistoric imagery? For Davidson one of the most distinctive features of language is the arbitrariness of symbols, and how that necessarily results in inherent ambiguity, especially when compared to prelinguistic communication systems (cf. the complex calls of Vervet monkeys) which have no possibility of ambiguity because they have been honed by natural selection. One way to cope with the proliferation of this kind of ambiguous creativity was to produce emblems or signs which we, even today, can recognize as in some sense *iconic* (cf. Davidson 1997: 126f). I believe that successful communication, therefore, requires means of identification that the utterances or images are trustworthy, and in some sense represent a recognizable continuity. We should, therefore, not be surprised to find these kinds of emblems among early language users. We should also not be surprised, I think, that we too are still fascinated by the enigmatic character of these symbolic images and signs, especially since they still appeal to our own aesthetic and symbolic capacities.

This argument that Palaeolithic imagery or 'art' is symbolic, and not just decorative, is considerably strengthened by Margaret Conkey's persuasive arguments *against* trying to capture the generic 'meaning' of Palaeolithic art as a single, inclusive metatheory, and *for* a more contextual understanding of the 'meaning' of this art as enmeshed in the social context of its time. On this view, the original meaning can only be said to have existed through the contexts in which it was first produced as individual paintings or parts of paintings (cf. Davidson 1997: 128). 'Meaning', therefore, is not a timeless property of Palaeolithic imagery in itself, but, as in the case of religious texts, is the result of the *interaction*, then and now, between the human agents and the material. We also, in our own relational, interactive interpretations of this imagery, discover and produce meaning. Therefore, the symbolism or 'meaning' we find in the earliest 'art' produced by people like us clearly is a product of our own interpretative interaction with this stunning imagery. What emerges here is an important convergence between theological and palaeoanthropological methodology, a postfoundationalist argument for the fact that we relate to our world(s) through highly contextualized, interpreted experience only.

For theology, the most important lesson learnt is that, from a palaeoanthropological point of view, all talk of symbolism should be seen as part and parcel of turning communication into language, *but the use of symbols separate from language could only have been a product of language* (cf. Davidson 1997: 153). What this implies is that the prehistoric cave paintings in southwestern France and in the Basque Country of Northern Spain could only have had whatever symbolic, expressive quality they did because of the linguistic, symbolic context in which they must have been created. Hence the imagination, productivity and creativity we associate with humans are very much a product of language, which, in both theology and the sciences, make language and expressive symbolic abilities central to a definition of embodied human uniqueness.

Throughout the history of palaeoanthropological research, one of the primary questions has always been, when did humans begin to think, feel, and act like humans? Central to this question has always been the issue of cognition or creative self-awareness, and how it might be recognized in its initial stages (cf. Donald 1991, 2001). Steven Mithen's answer to this question is an evolutionary approach to the origins of the human mind, and the development of a three stage typology of cognition that follows the evolution of domains of intelligence from the earliest members of the genus *Homo* through to their final integration in modern humans. Only in the final phase, in *Homo sapiens*, do we find a dramatic behavioral break, a 'big bang' of cognitive, technical and social innovation with the rise of cognitive fluidity as the final phase of mind development (cf. Mithen 1996). William Noble and Iain Davidson, in a slightly different approach, see one development, namely language, as pivotal in the evolution of human cognition. Here social context is seen as a primary selective force, and language, symbolization and mind are integrated into an explanatory framework for the evolution of human cognition, centered on the human ability to give meaning to perceptions in a variety of ways. Ultimately Noble and Davidson see language as emerging out of socially defined contexts of communication, encouraged as a more efficient form of gesture, with the selection of language occurring because of its efficiency and flexibility (cf. Noble & Davidson 1996; also Simek 1998: 444f).

For Terence Deacon, early symbolic communication would not have been just a simpler form of language; it would have been different in many respects as a result of the state of vocal abilities. Deacon argues that our prehistoric ancestors used languages that we will never hear and communicated with symbols that have not survived the selective sieve of fossilization. And as far as specific Upper Palaeolithic imagery goes, Deacon seems to be in complete agreement with Iain Davidson: it is almost certainly a reliable expectation that a society which constructed complex tools and spectacular artistic imagery also had a correspondingly sophisticated symbolic infrastructure (cf. Deacon 1997: 365). Deacon's argument confirms the transversal impact of palaeoanthropology on the interdisciplinary dialogue with theology: a society that leaves behind evidence of permanent external symbolization in the form of paintings, carvings, and sculpture, most likely also included a social, iconic function for this activity. As far as Palaeolithic imagery goes, then, the first cave paintings and carvings that emerged from this period do give us the very first direct expression of a symbolizing mind.

What has emerged from the work of Mithen, Noble and Davidson, Donald, Tattersall and Deacon, and should be of primary interest to theologians working on anthropology, is that human mental life includes biologically unprecedented ways of experiencing and understanding the world, from aesthetic experiences to spiritual contemplation. In a recent article, Terence Deacon makes the important point that the spectacular Palaeolithic imagery and the burial of the dead, though not final guarantees of shamanistic or religious activities, do suggest strongly the existence of sophisticated symbolic reasoning and a religious disposition of the human mind (cf. Deacon 2003: 504ff). The symbolic nature of *Homo sapiens* also explains why mystical or religious inclinations can even be regarded as an essentially universal attribute of human culture (cf. Deacon 1997: 436), and opens up an important space for Jean Clottes and David Lewis-William's argument for a shamanistic interpretation of some of the most famous of the Palaeolithic imagery (cf. Lewis-Williams 1997; 2002; Clottes & Lewis-Williams 1996). There is in fact no culture that lacks a rich mythical, mystical, and religious tradition. The coevolution of language and brain not only implies, however, that human brains could have been reorganized in response to language, but also alerts us to the fact that the consequences of this unprecedented evolutionary transition for human religious and spiritual development must be understood on many levels as well. Deacon argues that the way language can symbolically refer to things provides the crucial catalyst that initiated the transition from a species with no inkling of the meaning of life into a species where questions of ultimate meaning have become core organizers of culture and consciousness. It is these symbolic capacities that are ubiquitous for humans, and largely taken for granted when it comes to spiritual and ethical realms. In this sense one can say that the capacity for spiritual experience itself can be understood as an emergent consequence of the symbolic transfiguration of cognition and emotions (cf. Deacon 2003: 504ff). Along similar lines Antonio Damasio has made a powerful argument for the emergence of religious awareness and religious narratives as a result of the strong pressures of basic emotions like joy and sorrow (cf. Damasio 2003: 158f, 284ff). In this sense there is a naturalness to religious awareness: spiritual experiences, religious or otherwise, are embodied mental processes, and should be recognized as biological processes of the highest level of complexity.

The idea that religious imagination might not be an isolated faculty of human rationality, and that mystical or religious inclinations can indeed be regarded as an essentially universal attribute of the human mind, has recently also been taken up in interdisciplinary discussion by some theologians. In a recent paper Niels Gregersen argues that imagination, and therefore also religious imagination, is not an isolated faculty of human rationality, but can be found at the very heart of human rationality. On this view, then, the same 'naturalness' of imagination also applies to religious imagination, and religious imagination should not be seen as something extra or esoteric that can be added, or subtracted, from other mental states (cf. Gregersen 2003: 1f, 23). More importantly, though, a theory about the emergence of religious imagination and religious concepts does not at all answer the philosophical question about the validity of religion, or the even more complex theological question whether, and in what form, religious imagination refers to some form of reality or not. As an *interdisciplinary* problem, however, the reasons that may undergird the unreasonable effectiveness of religious belief and thought may transcend the scope of any one discipline when it comes to evaluating the integrity of religious belief. In this specific conversation we can hopefully reach an interdisciplinary agreement that religious imagination and religious concepts should be treated equally with all other sorts of human reflection. Religious imagination should, therefore, be treated as an integral part of human cognition, not separable from our other cognitive endeavours. Moreover, I also believe that religious imagination should not just be treated as a generic given, but at some point can only be discussed and evaluated contextually within the very specific contexts of specific religions. On this view the crucial role of human imagination in modern human behavior can in fact be an important interdisciplinary link in the dialogue on human uniqueness.

In my recent work I have concluded that, if we have inherited from the coevolution of nature and culture a dependable framework of mind by which to recognize credibly the intentions of others, why would this cognitive and emotive ability let us down when we try to relate to the iconic signals and messages communicated by our own Palaeolithic ancestors through paintings, carvings, and ritual practices? In fact, in the case of our modern human ancestors in Palaeolithic Europe, we are of exactly the same species, with the same symbolic minds, and the same religious propensities. No wonder, then, that we might feel compelled to interpret the cave paintings of the Upper Palaeolithic as embodied expressions of the religious and aesthetic imagination of our direct, but distant, ancestors (cf. van Huyssteen 2006). If being human implies the unique ability to create symbolic meaning, and if our Palaeolithic ancestors were indeed fully human, then we can also assume the following about these ancestors and their life-world: the dimension of meaning that is so irrevocably indigenous to being human, was also a crucial component of these distant, enigmatic people and their world. Our Palaeolithic modern human ancestors could not have been fully human without having the symbolic capacity to imagine, to create, and thus to exist in a dimension of meaning. And even if we may never know what these prehistoric images meant in those distant times and places, our only access to those elusive levels of narrative, symbolic meaning are the images themselves.

While respecting the integrity of science and the boundaries of the scientific approach, we theologians may now discover how asymmetrical reasoning strategies like theology and palaeoanthropology can actually intersect transversally on carefully identified issues like human uniqueness and human symbolic propensities. Here a dimension of prehistoric symbolic existence is revealed in which all contemporary religious belief and behavior is deeply and richly embedded. Beyond sharing these transversal moments on religious imagination, however, a contextual approach calls upon Christian theology to offer its own comprehensive, complementary perspective on the deeper philosophical/theological meaning of what it means to be human. For such a concrete proposal from theology, there is no blueprint for how science should or could respond on religious issues of ultimate meaning. On a postfoundationalist view, the acceptance of the theological perspective as meaningful and enriching, or as irrelevant and speculative, will in the end depend on the specific scientist and his or her worldview.

## In Conclusion

In the prehistoric imagery of the Upper Palaeolithic we are clearly dealing with the unprecedented manifestation of something that is so quintessentially human that it sets us apart from other animals and even from our closest prehuman ancestors. Palaeoanthropologists, like evolutionary epistemologists (cf. Wuketits 1990: 117ff), have linked this full emergence of consciousness and symbolic behavior directly to the emergence of religious behavior. This obviously is not an argument for the truth of any specific religion, nor for the existence of God. It is, however, an argument for the integrity of the earliest forms of religious awareness and behavior, and points to evolutionary reasons for the naturalness and the integrity of religious faith, as well as the possibility of ritual behavior in our earliest human ancestors.

As far as Christian theology specifically is concerned, I have recently argued that Christian theology traditionally always assumed a radical split between human beings, created 'in the image of God', and the rest of creation. This split was mostly justified by cognitive traits like human rationality or intelligence, or by more abstract notions of relationality which served to define what was meant by 'human uniqueness,' even as it floated free above nature and the human body (cf. van Huyssteen 2006).

Within the transversal space of interdisciplinary conversation, however, theology quickly learns that, crucial to the prehistory of the human mind, is the amazing emergence of what Steven Mithen has called 'cognitive fluidity'. Science, art, and religion are all indeed deeply embedded in the cognitive fluidity of the human mind/brain. As such these rich cultural expressions rely on psychological processes which originally evolved in specialized cognitive domains and only emerged when these processes could actually work together. Of perhaps even greater significance, the cognitive fluidity of our minds allowed for the possibility of powerful metaphors and analogy, without which science, religion, and art could not exist (Mithen 1996). What became clear, then, is that *the potential arose in the mind* to undertake science, create art, and to discover the need and ability for religious belief. Clearly early human behavior is not understood if we do not take this religious dimension into account.

I suggest that a theological appropriation of these rich and complex results of science at the very least should inspire the theologian carefully to trace and rethink the complex evolution of the notion of human uniqueness, or the *imago Dei*, in theology. Interpretations of the doctrine of the *imago Dei* have indeed varied dramatically throughout the long history of Christianity. Theologians are now challenged to rethink what human uniqueness might mean for the human person, a being that has emerged biologically as a center of self-awareness, identity, and moral responsibility. Personhood, when reconceived in terms of embodied imagination, symbolic propensities, and cognitive fluidity, may enable theology to revise its notion of the *imago Dei* as an idea that does not imply superiority or a greater value than animals or earlier hominids, but which might express a specific task and purpose to set forth the presence of God in this world (cf. Hefner 1998: 88). I would therefore call for a revising of the notion of the *imago Dei* in ways that would not be overly abstract and exotically baroque, that instead acknowledges our embodied existence, our close ties to the animal world and *its* uniqueness, and to those hominid ancestors that came before us, while at the same time focusing on what our symbolic and cognitively fluid minds might tell us about the emergence of an embodied human uniqueness, consciousness, and personhood, and the propensity for religious awareness and experience.

The most challenging aspect of an interdisciplinary dialogue between theology and palaeoanthropology, however, may be for theology to lift up the specific limitations of this conversation. This implies a quite specific appeal from theology to the sciences: an appeal for a sensitivity to that which is particular to the broader, non-empirical or philosophical dimensions of theological discourse. This kind of disciplinary integrity means that Christian theology has an obligation to explore other issues that are crucial for understanding human uniqueness, issues that may not be empirically accessible. My argument for interdisciplinarity has been precisely about the fact that Christian theology is answerable to canons of inquiry defensible within the various domains of our common discourse (cf. Brown 1994: 4ff). In this open, interdisciplinary dialogue we can learn that criteria for human uniqueness, whether in theology or the sciences, should never be the sole possession of a single perspective or discipline. Because of the transversal rationality of interdisciplinary discourse, not only shared interests and common concerns, but also criteria from other reasoning strategies can be appropriated. This certainly is one way in which a multidisciplinary approach to the problem of human uniqueness can lead to interdisciplinary results when we discover that criteria not only overlap, but can ultimately be shared in reasoning strategies as diverse as theology and science.

In this kind of interdisciplinary conversation theology can actually help to significantly broaden the scope of what is meant by 'human uniqueness.' *Homo sapiens* is not only distinguished by its remarkable embodied brain, by a stunning mental cognitive fluidity expressed in imagination, creativity, linguistic abilities, and symbolic propensities. As real-life, embodied persons of flesh and blood we humans are also affected by hostility, arrogance, ruthlessness, and cunning, and therefore are inescapably caught between what we have come to call 'good and evil'. This experience of good and evil, and theological distinctions between evil, moral failure, sin, tragedy, and redemption, lie beyond the empirical scope of the fossil record, and therefore beyond the scope of science. It certainly is our evolutionarily developed bodies that are the bearers of human uniqueness, and it is precisely this embodied existence that confronts us with the realities of vulnerability, tragedy, and affliction. For the scientist drawn to the more comprehensive, complementary picture of the dimension of meaning in which *Homo sapiens* has existed since its very beginning, theology may provide a key to understanding the profound tragic dimensions of human existence, but also why religious belief has provided our distant ancestors, and us, with dimensions of hope, redemption, and grace.

## NOTES

[1] The first, and most important biblical reference to the *imago Dei*, is found in Gen. 1: 26–28, set within the so-called Priestly creation narrative of Gen. 1: 1–2: 4a:

26 God said, "Let us make humanity in our image, according to our likeness; and let them rule over the fish of the sea, and over the birds of the skies, and over the cattle, and over all the earth, and over every creeping thing that creeps upon the earth."
  27 So God created humanity in his image:
  in the image of God he created him;
  male and female he created them.
  28 God blessed them, and God said to them, "Be fruitful and multiply and fill the earth and subdue it. Rule over the fish of the sea and over the birds of the skies and over every living thing that creeps upon the earth."

[2] Tattersall also argues that, ironically, it is precisely in our notions of God that we see our human condition most compactly reflected. Human beings, despite their unique associative mental abilities, are incapable of envisioning entities that lie outside their own experience, or that cannot be construed from what they know of the material world. For Tattersall the notion of God is just such an entity. And even with our dramatic increase in knowledge about the unimaginably vast expanse of our universe, our concepts of God – even when expanded commensurately – remain resolutely anthropomorphic (cf. 1998: 202). We continue to imagine God in our own image simply because, no matter how much we may pride ourselves on our capacity for abstract thought, we are unable to do otherwise.

Importantly, from a theological point of view, however, this does not imply the illusory character or the non-existence of God, but in fact might actually reveal the only intellectually satisfying way of believing in the kind of God with whom we might have a humanly comprehensible personal relationship at all.

## BIBLIOGRAPHY

Brown, D. 1994. *Boundaries of Our Habitations: Tradition and Theological Construction*. New York: SUNY Press.

Callender Jr., D.E., 2000. *Adam in Myth and History: Ancient Israelite Perspectives on the Primal Human*. Winona Lake, IN: Eisenbrauns.

Clottes, J., 1997. Art of the light and art of the depths, in *Beyond Art: Pleistocene Image and Symbol*, eds. M.W. Conkey, O. Soffer, D. Stratmann & N. Jablonski. San Francisco: Memoirs of the California Academy of Sciences.

Clottes, J., & J.D. Lewis-Williams, 1998. *The Shamans of Prehistory: Trance and Magic in the Painted Caves*. New York: Harry N. Abrams.

Conkey, M.W., 1997. Beyond art and between the caves: thinking about context in the interpretive process, in *Beyond Art: Pleistocene Image and Symbol*, eds. M.W. Conkey, O. Soffer, D. Stratmann & N. Jablonski. San Francisco: Memoirs of the California Academy of Sciences.

Damasio, A., 2003. *Looking for Spinoza: Joy, Sorrow, and the Feeling Brain*. Orlando, FL: Harcourt.

Davidson, I., 1997. The power of pictures, in *Beyond Art: Pleistocene Image and Symbol*, eds. M.W. Conkey, O. Soffer, D. Stratmann & N. Jablonski. San Francisco: Memoirs of the California Academy of Sciences.

Deacon, T., 1997. *The Symbolic Species: The Co-Evolution of Language and Brain*. New York: Norton.

Deacon, T. 2003. Language, in *The Encyclopedia of Science and Religion*, eds. W. van Huyssteen, N.H. Gregersen, N.R. Howell & W.J. Wildman. New York: Macmillan, 504.

Diamond, J., 1998. *Guns, Germs and Steel*. London: Vintage/Random House.

Donald, M., 1993. *Origins of the Modern Mind: Three Stages in the Evolution of Culture and Cognition*. Cambridge (MA): Harvard University Press.

Donald, M. 2002. *A Mind So Rare: The Evolution of Human Consciousness*. New York: Norton.

García-Rivera, A.R., 2003. *A Wounded Innocence: Sketches for a Theology of Art*. Collegeville, MN: The Liturgical Press.

Gregersen, N., 2003. The naturalness of religious imagination and the idea of revelation. *Ars Disputandi: The Online Journal for Philosophy of Religion* **3**, http://www.arsdisputandi.org/

Hefner, P., 1998. Biocultural evolution and the created co-creator. *Science and Theology: The New Consonance*, ed. T. Peters. Boulder, CO: Westview Press, 211–233.

Henshilwood, C.S., F. d'Errico, M. Vanhaeren, K. Van Niekerk & Z. Jacobs, 2004. Middle Stone Age shell beads from South Africa. *Science* **304**, 404.

Lewin, R., 1998. *The Origin of Modern Humans*. New York: Scientific American Library.

Lewis-Williams, D., 1997. Harnessing the brain: vision and shamanism in Upper Paleolithic Western Europe, in *Beyond Art: Pleistocene Image and Symbol*, eds. M.W. Conkey, O. Soffer, D. Stratmann & N. Jablonski. San Francisco: Memoirs of the California Academy of Sciences.

Lewis-Williams, J.D., 2002. *The Mind in the Cave: Consciousness and the Origins of Art*. London: Thames & Hudson.

Mellars, P., 1990. *The Emergence of Modern Humans*. Edinburgh: Edinburgh University Press.

Mithen, S., 1996. *The Prehistory of the Mind: The Cognitive Origins of Art, Religion and Science*. London: Thames & Hudson.

Noble, W. & I. Davidson, 1996. *Human Evolution, Language and Mind: A Psychological and Archaeological Inquiry*. Cambridge: Cambridge University Press.

Proctor, R.N., 2003. Three roots of human recency: molecular anthropology, the refigured Acheulean, and the UNESCO response to Auschwitz. *Current Anthropology* **44**, 213–39.

Rappaport, R.A., 1971. The sacred in human evolution. *Annual Review of Ecology and Systematics* **2**: 23–44.

Schrag, C., 1992. *The Resources of Rationality*. Bloomington: Indiana University Press.

Simek, J.F., 1998. Steps to an evolution of mind: A review of 'Human Evolution, Language and Mind: A Psychological and Archaeological Inquiry' by W. Noble & I. Davidson. *Antiquity* 72, 444–7.

Soffer, O. & M.W. Conkey, 1997. Studying ancient visual cultures, in *Beyond Art: Pleistocene Image and Symbol*, eds. M.W. Conkey, O. Soffer, D. Stratmann & N. Jablonski. San Francisco: Memoirs of the California Academy of Sciences.

Tattersall, I., 1998. *Becoming Human: Evolution and Human Uniqueness*. New York: Harcourt Brace.

Towner, W.S., 2001. Genesis, in *Westminster Bible Companion*, eds. P.D. Miller, D.L. Bartlett. Louisville, KY: Westminster John Knox Press.

van Huyssteen, J.W., 1999. *The Shaping of Rationality: Toward Interdisciplinarity in Theology and Science*. Grand Rapids, MI: Eerdmans.

van Huyssteen, J.W., 2003. Fallen angels or rising beasts? Theological perspectives on human uniqueness. *Theology and Science* 1, 161–78.

van Huyssteen, J.W., 2006. *Alone in the World? Human Uniqueness in Science and Theology*. Grand Rapids, MI: Wm. Eerdmans.

Welsch, W., 1996. *Vernunft: Die zeitgenössische Vernunftkritik and das Konzept der transversalen Vernunft*. Frankfurt am Main: Suhrkamp.

Wuketits, F.M., 1990. *Evolutionary Epistemology and Its Implications for Humankind*. New York: State University of New York Press.

# 16

# Innovation in material and spiritual culture:
## exploring conjectured relationships

*Keith Ward*

### Religion: the search for origins

This chapter derives from my field of study, the history of religions. Scholars of the history of religions have always been fascinated by the question of the origins of religion. The philosopher David Hume, in his *Natural History of Religion*, depicted religion as 'sick men's dreams', originating in an anxious fear of future events (Hume 1757/1993: 184). Sir James Frazer developed this view with an abundance of anthropological observations, real and imagined. For him, religion was a development from magic, the attempt to influence the powers of nature by causally irrelevant rituals. Realising this did not work, religion posited gods and spirits whom one might seek to propitiate in order to get what one wants. But this did not work either. The successor of religion is science, which at last provides the only reliable way of controlling nature (Frazer 1890).

These early writers were distinctly unfriendly to religion, which they saw as both intellectually and morally misguided. Probably no one would take their conjectures seriously today, but their general attempt to see religion as a primitive and obsolete way of explaining and controlling nature still has its supporters. Attempts to explain religion in social terms – the best known being Durkheim's postulation of a 'group mind' which furthered social solidarity and moral enthusiasm, and Marx's view of religion as an instrument of the ruling class to keep the masses subdued – were similarly unfriendly to religion. More sophisticated attempts to ground religious belief and practice in social mechanisms and distinctions still flourish, though most of them founder on the sheer variety and complexity of religious life, which resists any one-level explanation.

Psychological or psycho-analytic explanations of religion have also been attempted. Freud's infamous fable of the primal horde, the slaying of the father and the institution of taboos on incest, has been laid to rest, but Jung's alleged explorations into the human psyche as the source of religious beliefs seem still to be alive.

All these attempts concerned themselves with the origin of religion, in the strange belief that to find the origin of something is to discover its true essence. Reference to alchemy as the origin of chemistry should be enough to demolish that belief. But in any case, as Evans-Pritchard has put it, none of these writers had any reliable knowledge of the origins of religion (Evans-Pritchard 1965). They assumed that 'primitive' tribes – often Australian Aborigines – were like the first humans. They also assumed that the first forms of religion were more brutish, violent and fantastic than anything we know today.

Nevertheless, they did establish two valuable methodological principles. First, all present religions have developed from simpler beginnings, since humans have evolved from less intelligent species. Second, it is useful to see religion as a global phenomenon, rather than take our nearest religious tradition as normative, and the others as degraded or inferior forms of it. Evolutionary biologists currently think that all members of the species *Homo sapiens* derive from just a few, perhaps even two, individuals who lived on the African savannah. If religious belief and practice in some form existed at that primal stage of human prehistory, it would predate and form the common origin of all present religions. While this would not give us the essence of religion, it might provide insight into how the many present forms of religion have developed in diverse ways from a common source.

But establishing origins is so difficult that Evans-Pritchard castigated any attempt to discover them as little more than guesswork. To reapply a well-known remark of the theologian Harnack, when we look back into the darkness of prehistory, it can be like looking into a deep well and seeing at the bottom, dimly yet inescapably, only our own reflection.

Yet perhaps we need not be too pessimistic. Over the last decade or so a great deal of new research has gone into the study of the earliest human artefacts that we know. Among these are tools, small female statues, tombs and the remarkable cave paintings of Southern Europe. David Lewis-Williams' work (2002, this volume) provides a very helpful exposition and analysis of recent research on these paintings. It seems clear that, while the artistic standard of many paintings is very high, they are not meant to be art for public display. The images are too often in narrow and almost inaccessible passages, too dimly lit, and too often superimposed on one another and overmarked with lines for that.

It seems to me that Professor Lewis-Williams is entirely right in seeing these works as connected with attempts to relate to a spirit world. The journey into the recesses of the cave is reminiscent of the path to the inner shrine of a temple. Surrounded by images that express and convey supernatural powers, by the marks left by priestly or shamanistic rituals to communicate with those powers, and by possible suggestions of sacrifice and the dead (the deposited skulls or teeth of animal offerings), it is hard to escape the conclusion that here indeed are our earliest evidences of proto-religion.

I shall not seek to explain such activities as primitive science, social engineering, ways of coming to terms with unconscious drives and desires, or attempts to overcome simple terror. Instead I shall try to show how primal religious impulses are naturally rooted in the evolution of a form of mentality that was, for the first time, capable of constructing material and spiritual culture. This is, I think, what Steven Mithen calls the development of 'cognitive fluidity' (Mithen, 1996, this volume). Like him, I suggest that the origin of religion is likely to lie in the development of a new mental structure that made possible the rise of culture in both material and spiritual forms. So I will first suggest how 'culture' goes beyond the provision of basic needs to an interest in distinctively mental skills expressed in the creation and appreciation of artefacts. This lays the basis for what will become religious sensibility.

## Material culture

When we speak of culture we are speaking of that which is primarily concerned with the cultivation, the development or improvement by education or training of artistic or intellectual capacities in a specific social context. Most animals manifest behavioural routines that are instinctive or natural to their species. Some learn new behaviour by imitation, and may increase its efficiency by repetition. It is not absurd to speak of the cultural life of chimpanzees – their forms of social relationship, patterns of learning new skills and ways of passing on learned behaviour to others. But most animals do not construct enduring material signs of their cultural lives. Only the human species reshapes parts of its environment so that it expresses, and is intended to express, creative skills that have been learned and developed within specific social groups.

Like other animal species, humans have basic material needs that are necessary to survival – the provision of food, shelter and clothing, together with some way of ensuring the care of offspring, are the most obvious. But humans typically elaborate on the provision of these items in ways that seem to go well beyond what is necessary for survival.

The provision of food is developed into the arts of agriculture and cookery, which in turn develop into more sophisticated arts of landscape gardening and haute cuisine, that seem to have escaped the boundaries of what is conducive to survival altogether.

Building efficient shelters against the weather develops into the art of architecture, and into the building of great temples and cathedrals. From the provision of warm clothing humans move into the world of high fashion. And the efficient rearing of children is transmuted into the construction of educational programmes that may train young people into particular styles of etiquette or competence in dead languages, whether or not they equip them for more efficient survival.

Evolutionary psychologists may discover ways in which such developments are, despite appearances, related to the adaptive constraints of natural selection, but any such relationship will have to be very indirect. Humans as a species do seem to enjoy cultivating forms of training and activity that have little relevance to the provision of basic human needs from which those activities undoubtedly began. Persons of high culture may even be offended at the thought that their highly refined activities have any practical use whatsoever.

Culture may be seen as a form of play, developing skills conducive to the fulfilment of basic needs in ways that have no purpose at all – or, to put it in another way, whose purpose is simply the free and creative expression of those skills, released from the constraints of necessity.

The creation of appropriate clothing requires skills of weaving, sewing and design. Those skills can be developed by education and training into displays of conspicuous ingenuity. In a given society, traditions of design can grow, which can be extended, modified and redirected by people of exceptional creative talent. These traditions come to have their own internal criteria of excellence, and connoisseurs of taste decree which fashions are acceptable and which are undesirable in their culture.

Fashion becomes an end in itself, having no further purpose than to excel in the approved style, or to replace it with another.

The point of culture is not so much the objects it produces as the creative deployment of skills it makes possible. So in matters of fine food and wine, architecture, fashion and education, a premium is placed on creative skill and on the cultivation of refined taste that can appreciate such skill. When we look at material culture, we are looking at the objects produced by a society freed from the constraints of sheer survival. But we are looking at them in a special way – as products of exceptional skill, requiring refinement of taste to appreciate them properly. If the same objects were produced by machines or by forces of nature, we would not have the same interest in them.

What we are really interested in is certain qualities of mind relevant to their production and reception. We admire creative ingenuity, originality and technical competence. We admire the cultivated sensibility that can discern such originality and skill. In other words, we take the material (mostly aural or visual) objects to signify something beyond themselves – an ability that produced them or that is needed to appreciate them.

So we might say that fashion expresses the mind, the creative vision, of the designer, and to see what that is we need to acquire the sensibility that can read from a material object the skills and interests and goals that underlie its creation and preservation in a specific social context.

That may be very difficult – as when the average European comes across Indian music, or when a twenty first century human looks at Palaeolithic cave paintings. Such people realise that these are objects of symbolic material culture, human artefacts intentionally produced as an expression of some creative skill. What they do not know is what that skill is, why it is or was prized, and what makes it admirable – what it means to those who produce, preserve and value it.

This does not yet take us to spiritual culture. But it does establish the link between material culture and meaning. In brief, you cannot have a symbolic material culture unless you have the capacity to see objects as signifying something beyond themselves, and as being valued because of what they signify. By 'signify', I do not mean 'represent' in a picturing way. I mean that an object is valued not just because of what it is, materially, but because of the creative skill it expresses and the sensibility required to appreciate it.

This is not always just a matter of creativity and sensibility. A particular, and very common, approach to the arts is that they carry cognitive content, though of a peculiarly personalistic sort. This is not necessarily a religious view, in any sense, but it lays the basis for thinking that there may be a specific religious 'way of knowing', that would be more individual and self-involving than publicly observable and dispassionate.

## Culture and cognitive content

I have spoken of culture as play. That might be taken as demeaning by artists who devote their lives to creating cultural artefacts, and by those who find the meaning of their lives enriched by learning to appreciate such artefacts. It is perhaps at this point that a divide opens up between those who have no problem with seeing culture as play and others who see it at its highest level as leading to higher forms of apprehension or knowledge.

People belonging to the former group have as their patron saint Jeremy Bentham, who thought that all rational activity aims at pleasure, and that no pleasures are in principle higher than any others. We play for pleasure, and we create cultural artefacts for pleasure, and we should not try to mystify this process by bringing in talk of 'higher pleasures' or 'deeper experiences'.

For others this seems a desperate trivialisation of cultural activity. For them, cultural artefacts signify more than the exceptional skills of their creators. But what could they signify? Poetry or story-telling provides the most accessible key. An epic poem like Gilgamesh, one of the oldest written works that we have, is certainly a product of human imagination and dexterity in language competence. We admire it because it is skilfully constructed. It diverts us and gives us pleasure. But it also tells a story, of what human beings do and what their place is in the universe. That story is, of course, fiction. Yet it may be thought to be 'inspired', revealing truths inaccessible to ordinary consciousness, and only discernible by those who read it in a similarly 'inspired' way.

For such a view, artistic activity is, or can be, inspired, and can disclose normally hidden, unrealised or unappreciated truths. It is play with a serious purpose, a construct of the human imagination that unlocks hidden aspects of the veiled reality of being. In a similar way, pictorial art is sometimes said to disclose the true character of people it portrays, to disclose something significant about a place or landscape, or to enable us to see something about the human condition that we have not previously noticed. But all this is only if we learn to see it in the right way, in a way that unlocks the symbolism, the mood and the meaning of the visual object set before us.

It is not hard to extend this view to music, which evokes moods and feelings that can seem filled with verbally inexpressible profundity. Blues singing can set before us the melancholy hardship and poignant hope of the society it comes from, and let us understand what it is like to be a member of that society in a more profound manner. With haute cuisine and high fashion it is not so easy. Yet what and how we eat and how we dress carry symbolic meanings of which we may not be aware. They carry messages, perhaps of human greed and ostentation, or perhaps of distinctions we make between 'pure' and 'impure', acceptable and unacceptable, or of the social groups with which we associate.

Few human activities are without trains of symbolic meanings, recognised and unrecognised, and the play of cultural productivity uses such symbols to evoke new perspectives on these meanings, which are as ambiguous, as superficial or as deep, as human life itself.

It is clear that many cultural activities are primarily cognitive. The intellectual disciplines of the natural sciences, the meditations of philosophers, the topical essays of journalists, all require imaginative skills of a high order, but their aim is to disclose truth, more than it is to excite the admiration of others. Indeed, if they were not believed to disclose truth, they would rarely be admired.

So there is nothing odd about mental skills being both cultivated for their own sake (for the pleasure they give), and also for their cognitive content, real or alleged. The cognitive content of music and painting does not lie in the provision of dispassionate factual information about the world. Because of this, Benthamites tend to deny that they have any cognitive content. What music and painting express, however, is the personal vision of their creators, in such a way that it is possible to gain direct affective knowledge of what it is like to be in the world as they are, and to see and feel as they do. The cognitive content of art and music is affective knowledge of the subjectivity of others. I do not mean that we gain a magical entry into some purely introspective experience. I mean that we can learn to apprehend and feel the world as they do, to experience in ourselves the unique perspective on the world that their skills enable them to express, sometimes well and sometimes badly. Through training and experience, we can come to feel what it is like to experience the world as they do, though we always do so from our own perspective, which adds another layer of meaning, making this form of knowledge intensely personal and only indirectly communicable, and in that respect quite different from scientific knowledge.

Artists select from the sensory and intellectual stimuli in their environment, in accordance with their own tastes and discriminations. They assimilate these stimuli through *feeling*, the subjective mode in which stimuli are assimilated and evaluated, appreciated or discarded. Then by an imaginative process of integrating these stimuli and feelings in new ways, they try to communicate their apprehension and feeling-response in external visual forms.

Each artist belongs to a tradition that develops such visual forms in a particular way, and each artist continues that development by adding new creative elements that, if successful, express a personal vision and affective apprehension that will change human perceptions of and responses to the world. That is how art and music add to human knowledge. They do not give additional information about the environment. They give knowledge of how the environment, in its widest sense, may be perceived and responded to, of possible ways of being in the world, and of what it is like to exist as a human being.

Such knowledge must itself be received in an involved, affective, discriminating and imaginative way. So learning to appreciate the arts involves a training in discernment, empathy and imagination. It requires participation in a social life in which knowledge is imparted and shared, and creative projects are fashioned in cooperation with others. That is why some find that culture is more than play, in the sense of enjoyment. For them, culture enables a development of what is most truly personal, of forms of knowing that are otherwise unobtainable, and of forms of social life that are of intrinsic worth.

## Material and spiritual culture

This is where the link between material and spiritual culture becomes apparent. The word 'spiritual' may be understood in two main senses (there are, of course, many other senses, but they are not so relevant in this context). It may refer to qualities of mind or intellect, as opposed to the cultivation of physical attributes or the accumulation of property. Or it may refer to some non-material reality that is other and in some sense of greater value than the physical universe. That 'spiritual reality' may not be God, though God is one way in which it can be construed.

A Benthamite sense of culture would not properly be termed 'spiritual', and I will exclude it from further discussion here, though it is quite widely accepted. It sees culture as rooted in human capacities that have escaped their adaptive function, and operate as optional activities that are to be rationally assessed in terms of their production of pleasure. It is natural for such views to seek explanations of cultural activity in terms of the power or status they confer, or of the social discriminations they reinforce. Such cynical explanations have proved very useful in exposing some of the pretensions of cultured elites, who regard all who do not share their forms of life as barbarians. But it is clear that they would be rejected as adequate explanations by those who see cultural activity as more than play.

Of the two senses of the word 'spiritual' that I shall consider, the first may be termed a humanist sense. For it, cultural artefacts (material culture) are seen as manifestations of distinctively human excellences, capacities of discernment, evaluation and imagination that set humans apart as beings of value in themselves. Both the production and appreciation of cultural objects require training in such skills of creativity and knowledge, and a prioritising of the spiritual (mental) world of personal experience and responsible creativity over material pursuits of bodily health, power and wealth.

It was in the European Enlightenment of the eighteenth century that these core values of humanism were most fully articulated. Stress was laid on creative individuality, the fullest use of all distinctively human capacities, on the importance of the emotionally charged insights of personal experience, and on the formation of a society in which such capacities and insights could be shared as fully as possible.

The importance of creativity, of affectively charged personal experience, and of their development by free participation in a complex social culture, are the hallmarks of humanism, of that concern for human development and self-realisation that marked the Enlightenment and its transition to Romanticism. But those features can be found in different ways in Confucianism, in Stoicism, and in mediaeval Catholicism, too. They were not newly invented in post-Reformation Europe, although they took new forms and definitions then.

Humanism asserts the primacy of the personal. But the second main sense of the word 'spiritual' goes much further and asserts that the fundamental nature of reality, deeper and more important than the physical, is personal. It has characteristics of awareness and intentional agency, and possibly of social relationship, too. Within such a worldview, cultural artefacts do not only provide information about human perspectives, visions, ideals and goals. They provide information about the world of Spirit, a supraphysical realm whose basic nature is more like awareness and intentionality than it is like insensate matter or the blind interplay of chance and necessity.

Spiritual culture now becomes the exploration of the realm of Spirit, and the expression of particular ways in which humans interact with and imaginatively conceive of that realm. Many, but not all, creative artists think of their artistic productivity in this way. Just as some mathematicians see themselves as discovering facts about an intelligible and purely conceptual realm, so some artists think of themselves as bringing to expression features of spiritual reality that cannot be dispassionately or objectively described, but can be disclosed by creative imagination and insight, as they are able to discover and articulate new and surprising features of the spiritual realm.

For such a view, the artefacts of material culture become more than expressions of human imagination and creativity – though they are that. They are also expressions of spiritual culture, symbols of spiritual reality. They can, and at their best they do, communicate something of that reality to those with eyes to discern what they express.

## Spiritual culture and religion

For this second sense of spirituality, there is a close connection between the arts and religion. There is much debate about how one might define 'religion', and indeed about whether it is possible to define it at all. But I think that one can pick out human beliefs and practices, varying enormously in their specific character, that are concerned to alleviate human anxiety or obtain human goods and avoid personal harms by conscious relation to a supernatural reality, conceived by means of symbols drawn from the culture and experience of each society, and probably mediated by a small group of expert practitioners. I think it is useful to have a term to mark off those beliefs and practices. 'Religion' seems to be very suitable for that purpose.

It is not useful, however, to think that one can, in every case, mark out a clear boundary between what is religious and what is not. An artist may feel that her work is somehow communicating spiritual power and meaning that is more than merely human, without being a member of any religious organisation and without undertaking any personal discipline of prayer or practice of ritual worship. Her work may stand about midway on a continuum between seeing art as play and seeing it as helping to express the beliefs and practices of a formalised religious institution.

When poets like Blake speak of holding 'infinity in the palm of your hand, and eternity in an hour' (Blake 1956: 2443), they are speaking of a sense of an underlying transcendent spiritual reality, that art or poetry may evoke. But they are not necessarily supporting any official religious formulation of belief. They may even reject all such formulations as unduly restrictive. So, while their work conveys depth that may be called religious (in Schleiermacher's early definition of religion as 'the sensibility and taste for the infinite') (Schleiermacher 1799/1988: 103), they may be opposed to all systems of formalised religion they know. It was indeed part of Schleiermacher's strategy to convince the antireligious Romantic poets of Berlin that they were really religious, though they did not realise it.

It might be helpful to distinguish between an awareness of a personal depth to reality (which I will call, after Rudolf Otto but without following his specific definition of the term, a numinous sense) (Otto 1917/1959), and a set of defined beliefs or practices that specify a normative way of relation to Spirit (a canonical sense). Such a distinction would be rather like Whitehouse's distinction between 'imagistic' and 'doctrinal' modes of religion to which Steven Mithen refers in his paper (Whitehouse 2004; Mithen this volume).

The boundary between these modes is not sharply defined. Schleiermacher wanted to persuade those with a numinous sense that they could without hypocrisy ally themselves to a particular canonical form of religion (in his case, what became known as liberal Protestantism). There are many who would agree with him in thinking that some forms of canonical religion are very hospitable to, and overlap with, many varieties of numinous religion.

In the developed world, there are many 'New Age' practitioners who claim to evoke awareness of transcendent Spirit and mediate spiritual powers for human good, without thinking that there is one 'correct' and universal way of doing so. There are also many, particularly in modern developed societies, who wish to say that they are 'spiritual' without being 'religious'. One way of capturing this vague distinction is by contrasting numinous (not intellectually defined or limited to a specific set of revealed beliefs) and canonical (guided by orthodox definitions and practices) religiousness.

Canonical traditions typically have a 'revealed' definition of what the spiritual world is, and recommend a mental discipline to achieve conscious relationship to it. Within such traditions, the word 'spirituality' has the well-established sense of referring to disciplines of prayer, especially disciplines conducive to 'mystical' or personal experiences of the divine. Numinous forms of spirituality often also stress the importance of personal experience of spiritual reality, but the extent to which there are thought to be normative beliefs or disciplines of prayer and meditation varies considerably.

### Humanist, numinous and canonical spiritual culture

So I have distinguished three main types of spirituality, which correlate with three kinds of spiritual culture.

First are those, broadly speaking humanists, who would see the development of the distinctive mental capacities of humans as of intrinsic worth. Spiritual culture is what enables material artefacts to be valued as products of outstanding personal vision and creative excellence, and what gives a sense of value, purpose and significance to human life. This sense might be thought to be nonreligious, and sometimes it claims to be. But it is hard to have a sense of the moral priority of the personal without having some sort of worldview that gives spiritual (personal) properties ontological priority.

Thus Confucianism is usually considered to be a religion, even though it concentrates almost entirely on the way of being properly human. To think that there is a way in which it is proper to be human, that this is somehow an objective truth about the world, and that the world is such as to make the ideal human life realisable, is to ground moral principles in a view of human nature, in an ontology, that subordinates the material to the spiritual. God or the gods are not very important for Confucianism. But there are temples, rites of venerating the ancestors and spiritual presences, and beliefs that the social order should mirror the 'Way of Heaven', and thus realise on earth a cosmic order and harmony.

Here the boundaries between religion and moral practice are diaphanous. Confucians do want to utilise spirit powers for good, and those spirit powers are more than individual human activities. Spirit is not conceived as a personal God, or even as individuated in obviously personal spirits. It is more like a cosmic moral order, a tendency towards the Good, which individual humans ought to accept and promote. The Confucian moral code is rooted in a specific way of seeing authentic human existence, and a specific way of being human. This is a monistic conception of spirit, for which the supernatural is not something other than the natural, but an important aspect of the natural rightly seen. But humanism is only ambiguously religious. I would not wish to call it a form of religious life as such, and a decision about whether there can be a humanist form of religion will probably depend upon whether or not specific humanists are prepared to talk about a 'supernatural' reality at all, monist or not.

The second and third types of spirituality can less ambiguously be called religious. The second type is what I have called numinous religion. Its adherents see the spiritual as an existent level of reality, probably more fundamental and of greater value than the physical. For them, spiritual culture enables humans to discern and consciously relate to the spiritual, though without gaining any precise theoretical knowledge of it. The spiritual is expressed by symbols taken from significant features of the environment, that reflect the interest and history of specific social groups. The spiritual is thus essentially vague, polysemic and accessed by personal imaginative vision, but such access provides human life with its most profound forms of happiness and fulfilment. As I have pointed out, thinkers like Schleiermacher try to assimilate this sense of the numinous very closely with canonical (orthodox) religion, and again a decision about whether or not to accept this assimilation will depend upon the extent to which individuals link the arts with a discipline aiming to discern a supreme objective Good, as described in a cumulative ritual and symbolic tradition.

The third type of spirituality is comprised of adherents of canonical traditions (traditions with an authoritatively defined canon of revealed text or beliefs) who think that material culture should be put at the service of systems of belief and practice, so that it can be a reliable medium of expressing and achieving a beneficial relationship to the spiritual (which may be construed as God or the gods, or in other ways).

Canonical spirituality is the aspect of formalised religious life that concentrates on mental disciplines believed to be conducive to personal experience of the religious object.

For those who hold such a view, some forms of material culture may be misleading or even demonic (accessing harmful or destructive aspects of the spiritual). Most religious institutions will place constraints on the sorts of art that properly express a spiritual sense – which is perhaps why creative artists sometimes rebel against organised religion. Orthodox Judaism and Islam forbid the making of representational images. But they encourage the creation of beautiful songs or chants, and revere the highly metaphorical and symbolic language of their holy texts. For centuries, Christians insisted on authorised forms of iconic representation, and church authorities disapproved of sacred music if it got too emotionally powerful or grandiose. It may even be said by some that material and spiritual cultures are opposed to one another, though it should be apparent that this is usually not quite true, since some aspects of material culture are almost always valued as means to access the spiritual – even the Jains, adherents of the most ascetic of faiths, have beautiful temples and elegant images of their Tirthankaras, or liberated souls. Even at its most aniconic, canonical spirituality almost always uses artefacts of material culture to give expression to its conceptions of Spirit.

## Religion and culture

Material and spiritual culture are closely related, and religion, in various senses, is a natural expression of their origin in human animals. So there is reason to think that some form of religiosity is hard-wired into the human brain, and is closely associated with the rise of cultural activity, and the emergence of cognitive fluidity among hominids. This in turn is connected with the origin of distinctive mental capacities and opportunities in human evolution.

There could not be culture without freedom from the constraints of directly adaptive behaviour, without the mental skills to remember, imagine, plan and create, and without a desire to produce artefacts that will express and record for future societies something of the inwardness of personal experience, the self-conscious recollection of affective response and the striving for excellence that characterises personal existence. It seems certain that culture arises with the development of a sense of reflexive personal identity, and thus with a decisive saltation in the development of the human brain.

It is natural for a sense of the significance of the personal to arise with such a development. And it is natural for that sense to be extended, at least by some, to embrace the whole of the humanly experienced world. So one can see how religion arises as a natural but not universal corollary of cultural activity. It has its own proper sphere in the attempt to achieve conscious relationship with transcendent personal powers (spirits) in order to gain good and avert evil. It is closely related to humanist and numinous forms of cultural life, and it develops by various paths to the more moralised and rationalised forms of religion that exist in the world today.

It seems that its simplest common origin can be found expressed in not wholly inaccessible ways in the caves and tombs of Southern Europe. Canonical (revealed) traditions did not then exist, though there could have been imagistic religion, or forms of 'inspired' teaching from elite experients of the spiritual (something analogous to shamans, perhaps), that came to form local traditions. A question of great interest to the historian of religion is whether the cave images suggest some form of humanist celebration of human creativity (so-called 'cave art'), or whether they point to a numinous awareness of a spiritual realm, and are aids to seeking knowledge of such a realm. It is also of great interest to know how such a realm was conceived, and what sort of relationships humans could have with it. We are probably confined to hints and guesses when dealing with such remote and unchronicled times, but some guesses can be much more educated than others. At that point, the conceptual theorist can gratefully turn to detailed empirical studies of these early forms of human life and culture, to see what more can be learned about the origins and early forms of religious life.

**REFERENCES**

Blake, W., 1956. Auguries of Innocence, in *The Penguin Book of English Verse*, ed. J. Hayward. Harmondsworth: Penguin, 2443.

Evans-Pritchard, E., 1965. *Theories of Primitive Religion*. Oxford: Clarendon Press.

Frazer, J., 1890/1996. *The Golden Bough*. Harmondsworth: Penguin.

Hume, D., 1757/1993. *Natural History of Religion*, ed. J.C.A. Gaskin. Oxford: Oxford University Press.

Lewis-Williams, J. D., 2002. *The Mind in the Cave: Consciousness and the Origins of Art*. London: Thames & Hudson.

Mithen, S. J., 1996. *The Prehistory of the Mind: A Search for the Origins of Art, Religion and Science*. London: Thames & Hudson.

Otto, R., 1799/1959. *The Idea of the Holy*, trans. J. Harvey. Harmondsworth: Penguin.

Schleiermacher, F., 1799/1988. *On Religion*, trans. R. Crouter. Cambridge: Cambridge University Press.

Whitehouse, H., 2004. *Modes of Religiosity*. Walnut Creek, CA: Altamira Press.

# Index